AMERICA'S FINANCIAL APOCALYPSE

HOW TO PROFIT FROM THE NEXT *GREAT DEPRESSION*

D1122742

AMERICA'S FINANCIAL APOCALYPSE

HOW TO PROFIT FROM THE NEXT *GREAT DEPRESSION*

CONDENSED EDITION

STATHIS

ISBN-10: 0-9755776-7-0
ISBN-13: 978-0-9755776-7-7

DISCLAIMER

This book was written to provide certain risk and investment perspectives, but was not meant to substitute for professional financial advice. It was intended to be used as one of many sources of information any prospective investor might consider. The primary intent of this book is for educational purposes only. It provides educational information and opinions about investing, and observations on markets and their prospective financial future. It is not professional financial advice, nor should not be treated as such. By reading this book, the reader understands and agrees that they are not guaranteed any income, assured any profits, prevention of loss, or success by following any of the recommendations or analysis herein. By accessing the material in this book, the reader hereby releases any claims of any form against the author and publisher.

All opinions regarding economic and financial scenarios and investment ideas are speculative and based on a variety of outcomes that are outside the control of the author and publisher of this book. All data and information presented in this book has been taken from sources the author and publisher believe to be accurate and reliable. However, the author and publisher have not independently verified or otherwise investigated all such information. The analysis within this book is subject to change with time, altering economic and market conditions, and other factors. While historical information may be used as a tool to assist in examination of the risk and merit of investments, past performance should not be considered representative of future performance.

As with any investment decision, the reader of this book understands that he or she is responsible for making their own investment decisions. Each investor has a different investment suitability based in part on their level of professionally determined investment risk tolerance, investment objectives, income needs, liquidity needs, and investment time horizons. Therefore, prior to any purchase or sale of securities or any other investment strategy, it is strongly recommended that each investor consult his or her financial advisor, stock broker, or other professionally registered financial representative who is familiar with their financial profile to ensure that any of the strategies or recommendations presented or implied in this book are consistent with their investment objectives, risk tolerance, liquidity and capital requirements.

By continuing to read the book, the reader agrees to accept these terms and conditions, and accepts they are both clear to him or her, and fully understood. Any confusion in the interpretation of this disclaimer should be clarified by the reader's attorney.

About this Book

This book is an abbreviated version of the original publication, first released in 2006. This condensed edition was intended to provide a more easily readable rendition of the author's insights. Some of the material has been updated to reflect events since 2006. Readers wishing for a much more detailed presentation of this material should refer to the original edition. A second edition with comprehensive updates and expanded material is expected for release in early 2009.

Contents

Introduction

For more than two decades, numerous experts have predicted a major depression in America. Many of these forecasts were written in the early '90s as an aftershock of the '87 Crash. While most ignored these warnings, cautious investors withdrew from the capital markets. But the expected turmoil never appeared, at least not for over a decade. In fact, the U.S. economy mounted what appeared to be a tremendous rebound, experiencing what most have labeled as its strongest decade of growth since the post-World War II era.

In the mid-90s, the Internet was released. Soon, hundreds of companies sought to harness this new technology. By 1999, the Internet stock bubble had swollen beyond belief, and everyone wanted a piece of the action. Television ads by online brokerage firms convinced everyday Americans that it was easy to make money in the stock market; and many did.

Over the course of its 13-year stretch, the market appreciated by over 600 percent, with average annual returns in excess of 18 percent. Mutual fund managers were thought of as geniuses and treated like rock stars. Even soccer moms were giving stock tips and investment advice. Inspired by astounding investment gains and tacky commercials, much of America's youth made plans to retire by age 40. Of course these are some of the clear signs of the greed, mania and delusions that occur towards the end of an asset bubble. And we all remember what happened at the start of the new millennium.

Even after the deflation of the Internet bubble, timid investors who pulled out of the market a decade earlier missed out on spectacular market gains. In fact, most who remained invested since the early '90s are still much better off today. On the other hand, those who entered the bubble near its peak suffered devastating losses. While this correction revealed the most recent illusions embedded within the economy, it's only a prelude of what to expect in the coming years. Regardless, the timing of the impending catastrophe is critical because a mistiming could lead to results that might be equally devastating.

Despite the avalanche of recent scandals from within corporate America and Wall Street, some investors fail to recognize that the post-bubble period is quite different from the bull run of the '90s. In fact, many are still clinging to the former "darlings of Wall Street" that performed so well during the Internet bubble. Today, the capital markets have been realigned with authenticity. And now, economics control the investment cycle rather than hype generated by Wall Street. Accordingly, Washington can only hide the realities of America's decline for so long before the truth is revealed.

Since the deflation of the Internet bubble, we have already witnessed a portion of this transition. Subsequently, many of the spectacular investments of the previous bull market have performed poorly. But this offers incentives to realign one's investment strategy. Currently, we are in the middle stages of a secular bear market that began in 2001. Upon examination of the Dow Jones Industrial Average since 1900, it's clear that the stock market must correct downward, or else encounter a period of modest returns through 2012. But still, muted gains will only partly compensate for the spectacular appreciation of the '90s; a period fueled by excess consumption.

In order to fully appreciate the risks ahead, we need to consider a longer period in history. During the post-war boom, America celebrated its much improved economic position by increasing the size of the average family. As a result, birthrates soared for two decades leading to the baby boomer generation. This birthing boom was also marked by the emergence of the United States as the world's manufacturing powerhouse. For over two decades after World War II, the world relied on America to supply a wide variety of consumer goods. As more money flowed into the nation than out, America became the world's largest creditor.

When the post-war boom began to lose steam in the '60s, consumption started to exceed productivity. But Americans refused to concede a decline in living standards. They continued to consume as they had in the past despite declining net productivity. Up until the '70s, America fueled this consumption-production disparity using surplus wealth generated during the post-war boom. During the '80s, growing consumption was compounded by massive government spending and a devastating oil crisis. This was the period when its debt problems began. Shortly thereafter, the consumer credit industry grew to meet the demands of a nation in decline.

Advances in telecommunications and e-commerce have now transformed the developing world into a global marketplace. Today we see that competitive forces from abroad are much more influential than in the past. In the mid-1990s, President Clinton signed off on NAFTA and the World Trade Organization, promising free trade would deliver better jobs and higher wages for all. But for the majority of Americans, the opposite has occurred. While corporate profits and GDP have been strong, the resulting income and wealth distribution have been skewed towards America's wealthiest citizens.

America entered the free trade paradigm as a losing participant from the start since all other nations place the burden of healthcare and pension costs with the government. While it still remains as the centerpiece for the global economy, America now relies on record debt to maintain its status as the world's strongest consumer marketplace.

For over three decades, more money has been leaving America than coming in. As a result, the U.S. is now the world's largest debtor nation. Rather than increases in net wealth, America's "growth" has been fueled by credit spending. This has created the illusion of impressive productivity, while serving to mask declining living standards for the majority. As corporate America continues to achieve record profitability, these gains have come at the expense of its core citizens; the middle class. This was the group that made America so great, but now threatens extinction. As well, poverty continues to grow while the wealthiest quintile increases its wealth. These trends have been masked by record levels of credit-based spending and manipulation of economic data.

As a result of these trends, the United States is now more dependent upon foreign nations than anytime in its history. Declining oil reserves and a foreign-funded credit bubble have positioned its fate in the hands of the world. And its vulnerable role in the New Economy threatens to erode its empire status. Already, the effects of America's decline have registered. Declining competitiveness and reliance on foreign debt can be seen by noting the weakness of the dollar. As foreign nations lose interest in financing Washington's deficits, interest rates will soar.

Soon, America will face the economic burden of 76 million aging boomers. Beginning in 2011, expenditures for Medicare, Medicaid and Social Security will start to grow rapidly. And by 2025, these expenses will have swelled to unthinkable levels. During this same period it is likely that peak oil will have been reached; this alone promises to cause worldwide devastation, perhaps leading to the next world war.

There's no way America can pull through this mess using debt as it has in the past. Even if it were able to avoid this corrective period in some miraculous way, historical data implies that the post-bubble correction alone will last until at least 2012, yielding average annual returns of 3 percent. Thus far, these predictions have held. But I expect economic conditions to get much worse beyond this period.

In summary, I have presented what I feel to be a strong case for America's declining economic position and weakened competitive landscape by addressing the major issues at hand—the trade imbalance and federal debt, free trade, healthcare, Social Security, pensions, the real estate bubble, the war in Iraq, tensions in the Middle East, the global oil shortage, and the effect baby boomers will have as they enter what they expect to be their Golden Years.

I have also included some alternative investment strategies expected to shield investors or allow them to profit from the consequences of America's inevitable correction. In the final two chapters I summarize relevant macroeconomic trends and discuss those asset classes and industries expected to deliver the best risk-adjusted performance over the next ten to twenty-year period. Finally, I illustrate how investors should approach risk.

I cannot tell you with any level of confidence *which* of the issues detailed in this book will be the triggering event for America's socioeconomic correction. As well, I am not able to tell you with absolute certainty *when* America will slip into economic darkness. It might happen by 2016 or as late as 2025. What I can tell you with confidence is that a corrective period of enormous magnitude and variable duration is going to occur; most likely within the next two decades. The law of supply and demand dictates that it must. It's simply a rebalancing act required to correct extremes that have built up for over two decades.

If all of this sounds uninformative, I should remind you that attempting to pinpoint the sequence, timing, and duration of complex events of this magnitude would only result in a misleading level of comfort. One doesn't need to know precisely when or exactly how a catastrophe will occur in order to profit. Those who are aware of the risks will be positioned to recognize the early warning signs and react accordingly. Therefore, the real value of this book is to provide the reader with an understanding of the problems and related risks faced by America. This insight can be used as both a risk management tool and as a method to identify lucrative investments. In addition, my hope is that this book will introduce voters to the real issues facing this nation.

As you might appreciate, the more comprehensive and detailed a book is, the larger opportunity for potential disagreement among readers, due to the number of topics discussed. I have chosen to take the risk of potential criticism because any predictions of a depression mandate a comprehensive treatment, with extensive data, analysis and occasionally even bold assertions. To fall short of this would not do justice to the topic.

Regardless what may or may not turn out to be America's darkest period in at least 70 years, I am not predicting an end of this nation's dominance. If managed appropriately, this correction period will only represent an oscillation of its socioeconomic cycle. Wealth and income gaps will close and the exploitation of consumers by corporations will cease. Finally, Washington will create new opportunities for entrepreneurs. Together, the American people will reclaim their nation from corporate America and the wealthy elite. Only then will they benefit from the prosperity enjoyed by past generations.

Focused readers may notice repetition of certain concepts throughout the book. For instance, I often conclude that many of America's problems are ultimately due to free trade, declining living standards, and its poorly run and costly healthcare system. The effects of the baby boomers and peak oil are also tied into these themes. The reason for such repetition is to demonstrate the dependent nature of the nation's core problems.

The reader may choose to read those chapters of most interest first and refer to others as desired. Whether you are an investor or a concerned voter, I hope you will view this book as a valuable resource. And I hope it helps you in some way.

PART I

AMERICA'S PAST, PRESENT & FUTURE

A Brief History of
America

Although the duration of America's socioeconomic evolution is relatively brief, its existence has been riddled by a flurry of landmark events since its partition from England some two hundred years ago. The *Prima Facie* indicators of America's dominant presence can be attributed its climatic period of inception, as well as its unique alliances with England and Europe.

To recapitulate American history post-rebellion from British rule, in 1776 the British Colonies won independence from Great Britain in the Revolutionary War. Thereafter, they became recognized as the United States of America following the Treaty of Paris in 1783. This landmark defeat signaled what would be the onset of England's gradual decline and the rise of America as the next world power; a transfer that would materialize over the next 150 years.

Even before their break from the mother country, the colonies were experimenting with the use of currency notes in-lue of gold and silver coinage. The first paper money appeared in colonial America in 1690, as payment for soldiers going to battle in Canada. Nearly one hundred years later, it was decided that no currency of the newly formed America would be substituted with any payment other than gold and silver. According to Article 1, § 10, clause 1 of the U.S. Constitution,

"No state shall coin Money; Emit Bills of Credit; make any Thing but gold and silver Coin a Tender in Payment of Debts."

Bitter Sweet Transition

After gaining independence from England, European immigrants flocked to America to take part in the opportunities promised by this fertile land. In order to develop the Midwestern plains, colonists were offered several acres of land at little or no cost as an incentive to settle this unchartered territory.

This period up to the 1840s would be known as the first industrial revolution. At this time, the primary focus was on farming and textile production. This created an even greater demand for further industrialization. The nation's rapid growth prompted the southern region to bring in slaves from Africa purchased at auctions held by powerful African nationals.

By the early 1800s, America was well on its way to gaining the envy of the world. While most of the nation was still uninhabited, vast railroad lines were being constructed to connect the north and south and the east with the west. The northeastern states enjoyed a vigorous period of manufacturing and political innovation, which served to strengthen the foundation of this new nation. Meanwhile, southern states benefited from the inhumane slave labor provided by African captives, who helped build America's agricultural powerhouse.

In 1848, gold was discovered by James Marshall at Sutter's Mill. Soon, thousands flocked to the California bay area from all over North America and several other nations—from Chile to China—all seeking wealth. This period became known as the California Gold Rush and was responsible for the rapid settlement of this state.

A decade later, as America was emerging as a world leader in commerce, an internal bloody war began in 1861, matching the north against the south. As it was not yet financially stable, the U.S. government made use of currency notes in-lue of gold and silver coinage during this war. The outcome of the Civil War would determine the next direction America would take as a unified nation. Within two years after the war ended, slavery was officially abolished. But it would take several decades before African Americans would be able to completely sever the lasting affects of their slavery legacy.

The second industrial revolution began in the late 1800s marked by the birth of the steel industry. This period would be remembered for catalyzing the formation of large corporations, while delivering some of the most creative innovations in U.S. history. Most notable were the inventions of Thomas Edison (light bulb) and Alexander Graham Bell (telephone). Finally, electricity discovered by Benjamin Franklin over 100 years earlier would be used for much more than the telegraph.

Monetary Reform

America entered the twentieth century as a young adult, as evidenced by its transition into a unified and productive nation. Yet, its banking system was new, and thus subject to periods of vulnerability. One of the early indicators of monetary weakness occurred when international gold shipments were delayed in 1907. This exhausted bank reserves and created a "money panic," prompting outcries for monetary reform.

This led to the mysteriously rapid passage of the Federal Reserve Act on December 23, 1913. It created 12 privately owned Federal Reserve Banks, whose stock would be owned by member banks that were themselves to be privately owned. This monetary system was to be controlled by a twelve-man Board of Governors, seven to be appointed by the President of the United States. The currency issued by the Federal Reserve was known as Federal Reserve Notes. They were to be "redeemed in lawful money," defined as gold and silver coinage according to the U.S. Constitution.

Despite the original mandates of the Constitution, the Federal Reserve Banking System was also afforded the power to borrow money and expand or contract the number and amount of outstanding bills of credit. This drastic change in monetary policy would influence America's economic future for better and for worse.

WWI and the Roaring '20s

During this same time period, England was still viewed as the world power, and rightly so. One of the first signs of a shift in power would be demonstrated when the Federal Reserve Banking System used its monetary authority to borrow lines of credit during World War I. This proved to be a successful tactic in financial warfare, and was largely responsible for victory by the Allies.

Continued expansion and utilization of government credit led to a decade-long period of impressive post-war expansion. By the early 1920s, America's capital markets were showing signs of maturity, as the first great bull market had commenced. America had finally arrived and was now challenging England as the new economic powerhouse. Throughout this period, the Federal Reserve Banks continued to exert monetary control by expanding and contracting the currency supply for the purposes of controlling the economy.

Subsequently, it was the Federal Reserve's inflationary policy during the 1920s that ultimately led to what became known as the Roaring '20s; a period remembered as the first unified celebration of wealth, happiness, freedom, and hope for America's future. By the mid-1920s everyone seemed to be invested in the stock market. Widespread speculation soon led to a stock market bubble.

Like all bubbles, this one would burst without warning. The consequences would unmask the political and economic disparities that had accumulated since the post-war period. On October 29, 1929 (known as "Black Tuesday") the stock market began its long and painful correction with an initial market crash. This sell-off would be the first of many more to come, and would ignite a series of catastrophic events unlike anything ever witnessed in America.

The Great Depression

The Great Depression remains in history books as the most challenging socioeconomic period faced by America. While many wealthy Americans suffered, it had an especially devastating affect on the lower class. In total, this decade-long correction witnessed two recessions, with an unemployment rate over 25 percent at its peak. Low morale spread throughout the nation, causing many to regard suicide as the only way out.

President Franklin Delano Roosevelt entered office on March 4, 1933 in the midst of America's darkest period. In an attempt to calm widespread panic, he immediately declared a banking holiday. Unfortunately thousands of banks would never reopen, taking with them the savings of millions of Americans. A few months later, the 1933 Emergency Banking Act was rushed through Congress without proper review by the House. This law allowed the U.S. Treasury Department to acquire possession of all gold in the United States.

This would be the first step leading to the eventual detachment of the U.S. dollar from the gold standard. There would be several additional laws (The Gold Reserve Act of 1934) and Executive Orders passed by FDR that would further relieve the government's obligation to settle U.S. currency in gold and silver payments. Despite these changes, foreign central banks still retained dollar-gold exchange privileges. Thereafter, FDR created several government agencies and laws collectively known as the New Deal, in order to refortify and preserve the financial stability and future security of Americans.

Only from the impact of this crisis were politicians able to muster sufficient courage and wisdom to implement change. As a result, the inequities of wealth and power, greed and excess, exploitation and corruption—all of which had formed for over two decades—had now been greatly diminished. By the late '30s, the economy was showing signs of stability.

World War II

In the mid-1930s during the apex of the depression, Germany began a series of hostile military campaigns in Eastern Europe. Soon, more nations became involved, signaling what would be later known as World War II. In the early stages of this war, America chose to remain neutral and felt that isolationism was the best way to solve its problems.

By 1940, America's economy and morale appeared to be stabilizing. Industrial production created secure well-paying jobs, while unemployment declined. Oil was now of great importance and was largely responsible for America's rapid industrial advancement. Soon, the U.S. emerged as the world leader in oil production due to the availability of investment capital required for exploration. But this leadership in oil would turn into a double-edged sword. When the U.S. refused to sell Japan badly needed oil, they attacked Pearl Harbor on December 15, 1941. Only a few days later, FDR asked for a declaration of war for which Americans were too anxious to enter.

Just as war proved to be the defining event in its previous two centuries, World War II was the defining period for twentieth century America. A unique sense of urgency and patriotism sparked new innovations that led to a unified war effort. Notably, America's war contributions were aided by its immigrant population. In fact, despite intense racism and discrimination against Italian-Americans, it was this ethnic group that provided the majority of soldiers for the U.S. military. Also noteworthy was the courageous participation of several African-American soldiers as segregated units within the military.

The wartime period also brought many brilliant minds to America to escape the repression of Nazi occupation in Europe. Although Albert Einstein did not work directly on America's secret nuclear program (the Manhattan Project), it was he who encouraged FDR to start a nuclear fission program for fear that Germany would develop an atomic bomb. It was this unique combination of freedom, patriotism, and innovation that, together with British forces, helped liberate the world from the repression and brutality of Nazi Germany and its allies.

Post-war Recovery

Due to the devastating effects of WWII on much of the developed world, America emerged as the global leader in manufacturing and production. As a result, post-war America became the world's factory for consumer goods and agricultural products. This period was really America's second industrial revolution, providing Americans with modern machinery and automobiles fueled by the abundance of oil.

It was during the early post-war period that free trade policies would be enacted to help European and Asian nations rebuild what they had lost. The General Agreement on Tariffs and Trade (GATT) was established in 1947 as a part of a United Nations campaign to promote rebuilding operations in war torn nations. Similar to many of the free trade agreements today, GATT eliminated tariffs and enacted other laws that were meant to open trade. Unlike today, America did not suffer any adverse consequences of free trade during the post-war period. Most of the economic infrastructure of the developed world had been demolished, and therefore offered very little competition.

Consequently, America's newly found prosperity, patriotism, and overall "good feelings" during the post-war period fueled a large rise in birth rates from 1946 to 1964. And the 85 million Americans born during that period were labeled baby boomers.

It was also during the post-war period that U.S. oil production surged and soon surpassed coal use. At that time, America had vast oil reserves with seemingly no end in sight. But there was one geologist who felt otherwise. In 1956 during a national oil conference, Marion King Hubbert made what seemed then as an absurd prediction. His research indicated that the U.S. would encounter a permanent decline in daily oil production within the next fifteen years. He referred to this theory as Peak Oil.

War on Communism

With its unprecedented economic expansion well under way, America abandoned isolationist policies and began to "protect" other nations from communist takeover, namely South Korea in the 1950s and Vietnam in the '60s and '70s. In the late '70s, shortly after an OPEC oil embargo, inflation took off. Even after the Iranian embargo was lifted, OPEC raised prices, resulting in another oil crisis with further inflation. Throughout this period, prices for gold and silver soared to unimaginable levels aided by market manipulation.

By the early '80s, the oil crisis had pushed inflation into double-digits, causing severe economic problems. But Fed Chairman Paul Volcker was able to restore the buying power of the dollar using a series of bold interest-rate hikes. By the time he was finished, interest rates reached 19 percent. On the heels of the inflation crisis and through the use of unfair trade practices, Japan was gaining significant traction into the U.S. economy, resulting in the destruction of millions of manufacturing jobs.

During this same period, America had entered a Cold War standoff with the Soviet Union. Ultimately, the threat of a Soviet invasion was remedied by President Reagan, but at the expense of mounting national debt. Yet, low oil prices and continued foreign and domestic investment catalyzed another impressive bull market that began just as Reagan departed from office.

By 1991, the Soviet Union had finally collapsed due to several years of corrupt political and economic policies which left very little for its citizens. The world was beginning to look more peaceful. For America, things seemed particularly promising. In fact, it appeared as if the '90s would catapult the U.S. into the next millennium with further prosperity.

The accomplishments of President Reagan might only be surpassed by his widespread appeal. By the time Reagan finished his second term, he had extinguished the Cold War, demonstrated America's dominance in space exploration, strengthened intellectual property laws, and positioned the economy for the greatest bull market in U.S. history. But these triumphs came at the expense of huge levels of debt. Still, things seemed a lot better now that the economy was back on track and the Soviet Union no longer posed a threat. After a 22 percent stock market crash in October 1987 ("Black Monday"), the U.S. economy would rebound stronger than ever, ushering in the Great Bull Market.

The Roaring '90s

The Clinton years were marked by a celebration of world freedom coupled with America's tremendous economic expansion. This growth was fueled in large part by millions of baby boomers who were now in their peak income years. As President Clinton approached the end of his first term, America's economy seemed unstoppable. And many industries swelled to meet the needs of the boomer generation. Meanwhile the Internet had just been launched.

The U.S. economy was very strong by every traditional indicator. Many became wealthy in a short period due to the tremendous appreciation of the stock market. But this too was ultimately fueled by the boomers. While many thrived, economic data suggests that the vast majority of Americans did not extract much benefit during this period.

Despite the perception of world peace, a new enemy had been gradually organizing. This enemy was even more complex and dangerous than Communist forces because it involved religion, culture, and an unimaginable dedication towards the pursuit of its mission. Now, America and the rest of the free world continue to face the threat of terrorist activities by these groups, with which OPEC nations have direct ties. Unfortunately, these nations also control America's lifeblood—oil.

Oil and the U.S. Economy

Perhaps more so than any single factor, the commercial oil industry gave rise to the economic stability of America's middle-class, enabling most to achieve the American Dream. Access to inexpensive oil was largely responsible for creating America's industrial machine, which churned out products for consumers worldwide.

The global dominance of its economic engine led to well-paying and secure manufacturing jobs. As America's industrial complex matured, companies provided employees with pension plans, hoping to encourage career loyalty in exchange for guaranteed retirement benefits. This was the beginning of a new route towards financial stability for American workers.

After the oil crisis of the early '80s, America enjoyed a decade-long period of tremendous economic expansion, symbolized by the greatest bull market in history. To a large extent, it was the availability of inexpensive oil that was responsible for this booming period. Fortunately, President Nixon secured agreements with Saudi Arabia only a few years earlier that would secure America's strength in the global economy. Shortly after Saudi Arabia began accepting the dollar as the only payment for its oil, OPEC followed suit. Ever since that time *the dollar, once backed by gold, has been backed by oil.*

This unique arrangement has accounted for the mysterious "good relations" between America and Saudi Arabia. As long as the U.S. protects the Royal Family from uprisings, the dollar will remain the only legal tender for the world's most valuable natural resource, ensuring its position as the global currency. This is the only force keeping the dollar from a complete collapse.

From Manufacturing to Technology

When America's second industrial revolution began, the world was soon convinced of its position as the new leader in manufacturing. Shortly after WWII, U.S. industries dominated the world churning out autos, televisions sets, vacuum cleaners, telephones, toasters and other consumer goods. America's massive manufacturing base enabled it to supply citizens with automobiles and telephones, helping to mobilize commerce and facilitate its booming economy. By the 1950s, no less than twenty-seven U.S. television companies led the world in technology and production. Its manufacturing dominance was similar for autos, airplanes, electronics, and many other goods. Back then, seeing "Made in America" was as common as seeing "Made in China" today.

For two decades after the war, America's economic engine seemed unstoppable. Unlike today, its manufacturing dominance drove productivity, while intellectual property was viewed as a weapon of economic destruction. In fact, during the 1970s, the chances of a patent being deemed valid by U.S. courts were very slim. The prevailing opinion of the U.S. Department of Justice held that patents damaged the economy by establishing anticompetitive monopolies. Therefore, rather than paying royalties to patent holders, many companies chose to risk infringement knowing that their chances of being found guilty were quite low.

However, between 1982 and 1985 several government agencies enacted a variety of laws, signaling a paradigm shift in U.S. economic policy. In 1982, a federal court of appeals (the USPTO) was established for the sole purpose of hearing intellectual property cases. As a result of this change in policy, today the chances of being found guilty of infringement are quite high. As a result, most companies prefer to pay royalties rather than risk infringement litigation.

It turns out that U.S. courts began to protect intellectual property just as Asia began to threaten America's manufacturing dominance. Ever since that period, the U.S. has placed more emphasis on innovation than production. This shift in economic policy has accentuated the decline of its manufacturing industries.

In the '80s, as millions of manufacturing jobs were lost, many workers were forced to accept lower wage service jobs. As a result, U.S. tax revenues declined. Meanwhile, the national debt continued to soar due to the Cold War. Although patent laws were now recognized, America's inflation crisis inhibited the risk-taking activities needed to fuel new innovations. In response, Washington loosened credit to encourage new ventures. Unfortunately, this led to numerous fraudulent activities, ultimately leading to the Savings & Loan Crisis. Since that period, innovation has led to tremendous economic growth, and has become America's new economic engine. But its lead in technology innovation is now being challenged from abroad.

Clinton's Free Trade Disaster

When President Clinton convinced Congress to pass the North American Free Trade Agreement (NAFTA) in 1994, this signaled the final disappearance of U.S. manufacturing. NAFTA removed all barriers of trade between the U.S. and its North American neighbors, ensuring further sabotage of U.S.-based manufacturing. The following year, Clinton entered the U.S. into the WTO, adding further strain to manufacturing. The consequences of these decisions have effectively removed all protection from unfair trade and labor practices from foreign nations.

As his final act in promoting the free trade "engine of destruction," President Clinton provided Permanent Normalized Trade Relations (PNTR) status to China in the year 2000. Interestingly, *after being granted favorable trading status, China strengthened its currency peg to the dollar, ensuring its position as the top exporter of goods into America.* Consequently, the collapse of U.S. manufacturing has been particularly brisk since 2000.

President Bush continued to expand free trade by signing the Central American Free Trade Agreement (CAFTA) in 2004. This law extends the free trade policies of NAFTA to the Central American nations of El Salvador, Honduras, Nicaragua, Guatemala, Costa Rica, and the Dominican Republic. Similar to its NAFTA counterpart, CAFTA facilitates the relocation of U.S. manufacturing plants to Central America, thereby decreasing the cost structure of American goods at the expense of the U.S. labor market.

As with NAFTA, the officially stated goal of CAFTA is to increase the living standards of all member nations. However, even before the passage of CAFTA, these nations were already afforded duty-free exemptions for about 80 percent of their exports. Therefore, it appears as if corporate America stands to gain much more than consumers. While they might benefit from short-term gains, low-income and middle-class Americans will suffer from the longer-term effects of overseas expansion, which all but guarantee the continued exportation of U.S. jobs.

America's Future

Today, the United States is approaching the nadir of its socioeconomic cycle much like it did eighty years ago before the Great Depression. If in fact the coming correction will only represent a rebalancing act, no doubt, at some point in the future the American empire will fall similar to others before it. When this happens, it will be placed on a boom-bust cycle of longer duration, requiring many centuries to regain its empire status. Thus, the nation's leaders must be highly sensitive and responsive to the coming correction, since its mishandling could result in the nation's permanent demise.

2

RECENT HISTORY OF THE STOCK MARKET

During the early 1990s, a stock market bubble began due to Alan Greenspan's overly generous monetary policy. With open access to credit, the baby boomers fueled a credit bubble that added to the bull market. And after the Internet was released to the public, the stock market began its bubble expansion. Economists and analysts were now proclaiming the beginning of the Information Age.

Seemingly overnight, thousands of entrepreneurs created dotcom companies to harness the economic power of the Internet. And investors lined up to claim a stake in high-tech companies poised to change the world. Investment capital poured in from around the globe. With the early success of Yahoo!, AOL, eBay and Amazon.com, venture capital flooded dotcom companies and any other company linked to the Internet. Incidentally, much of this money came from public and private pension plans.

Perhaps you remember Grocery.com, Pets.com and WebMD—just a few of hundreds of dotcoms that promised to revolutionize every business under the sun. Often, all one needed was a slick idea jotted on a napkin and they got funded by venture firms. Although creative ideas and new ventures seemed endless, too much money was chasing too many bad business ideas.

But things seemed to be going well for America. Most high-tech companies had more money than they knew what to do with, while business prospects seemed endless. Entry-level employees were granted lucrative stock option packages that promised to make them millionaires. Many investors were getting wealthy, often effortlessly, while the concept of risk never entered the picture. Wall Street helped swell the bubble by proclaiming that all brick-and-mortar businesses would be replaced by online companies due to the power of the Internet. Many of America's greatest companies were labeled "dinosaurs" if they hadn't formed an Internet strategy.

But this was only the beginning, as the telecom and computer networking revolutions would also be seen as key players in the Internet craze. By late 1999, Amazon.com had a price target of over $400, Qualcomm $800, while many Internet other high-tech IPOs were closing their first day of trading at over $100 per share. Investors simply couldn't get enough of these stocks. Meanwhile, aggressive advertising campaigns by online brokers helped spread these delusions of grandeur, leading to speculative behaviors by investors looking to claim a piece of this "pie in the sky."

Ultimately, SEC negligence helped transform the world's largest and most reputable stock market into an online casino. Online trading firms sprung up to meet the demands of the bubble's illusion. Now, anyone with a computer could buy and sell stocks. And low commissions led many to believe that they too could become successful traders. Unprecedented access to the stock market favored Wall Street and corporate America, which now had an unhindered entrée to the money of greed-stricken, unsophisticated and unwary investors. Sadly, despite the scandals surrounding this recent period, the stock market continues to be used as an online casino, less than five years after these catastrophes surfaced.

The NASDAQ was seen as the superstar exchange for high-tech companies. Most believed that companies listed on this exchange would serve as the engines of commerce for the New Economy. And for many of the early investors, these companies delivered astounding new wealth, often overnight. By 1999, Wall Street's propaganda campaign worked. Almost everyone thought the rules of business and investing had changed. The Internet-driven technology revolution was envisioned as the sole tool that would create drastic and immediate improvements in living standards. In reality, it was the monetary policy of Alan Greenspan that was responsible for this illusion.

Prior to the first correction in the NASDAQ, Greenspan saw the bubble swelling, but did nothing to stop it. Instead, he watched in comfort after delivering his "irrational exuberance" speech a few years earlier. Rather than raise interest rates to decrease the money supply and tighten credit lines, he let asset values swell like never before. Meanwhile, the smart money gradually and quietly made its exit at the top, shifting assets into real estate, basic materials, cash, and other assets that had been beaten down throughout the bubble frenzy.

The Internet bubble of the late-1990s was arguably the largest asset bubble in U.S. history. At its peak, the NASDAQ and S&P 500 were trading at over 240 and 35 times earnings respectively. Yet, this surge in valuations seemed reasonable at the time. After all, "hot-shot" analysts and economists were claiming the Internet had created a new business paradigm. And most investors believed this fantasy, as they always do when caught up by the greed surrounding a bubble. Unfortunately, greed is a powerful instinct that often masks rational thinking. In the end, the majority gets hurt, while the handful of insiders profit. This bubble was certainly no exception.

The Bubble Bursts

As with all bubbles, this one came to a halt, resulting in financial and emotional devastation for millions. By mid-March 2000, the NASDAQ began a series of sell-offs that spread to the Dow over a three-year period, leaving investors holding the bag when it emptied. Even when the bubble was well into its deflation, most were still unaware of the disasters ahead.

Wall Street refused to tell the truth about the economy. But the warning signs were clear for those who paid attention. Inventories were high and rising. Internet ad revenues were dropping off. Soon, virtually every business connected with the Internet began a painful downward spiral. The NASDAQ deflated from its high of over 5000 down to a low of about 1200 over the next two years; a 78 percent decline. And unfortunately, many investors rode the market down, not knowing what to do; waiting and hoping for a rebound.

It wasn't all bad in 2000, as the Dow and S&P 500 continued to remain strong. But the uncertainty of the controversial presidential election caused these markets eventually to drift downward. Still, most were in a state of denial and felt the markets would recover once a clear winner was named. But experienced investors could smell the stench that promised to only get worse. Consequently, the market continued its weakness in 2001. And when the tragic events of 9/11 occurred, the stock market crashed. But the worst had not yet occurred. The market wouldn't make its deepest decent for another two years, as the economy slipped into a deep sleep.

Despite a reasonable rebound a few weeks after 9/11, economic data continued to get worse. Then came an avalanche of corporate accounting scandals—Enron, WorldCom, Tyco, Halliburton, Global Crossing, America Online, and a host of other Internet and telecommunication companies once praised by top analysts. Wall Street was now filled with the blood from the Internet bubble.

All of these events caused Federal Reserve Chairman Greenspan to issue a series of rate cuts beginning in late 2001, sinking short-term rates to 43-year lows over the next two years. And soon, long-term rates followed. But even Greenspan's currency printing presses couldn't prevent the largest corporate bankruptcies in history, as well as record earnings restatements, write-downs and write-offs for many that survived. It was only in late 2002, when many stocks were at multi-year lows did Wall Street start issuing sell signals—long after 9/11, the collapse of Enron, WorldCom and dozens of other companies. By then, many of the former "darlings of Wall Street" were penny stocks, while many Internet companies went bankrupt.

By October 2003, investors finally had it. The market plummeted to new lows, as economic numbers continued to weaken with no end in site. Within two years of the stock market correction, much of the wealth Americans had gained over the past decade had vaporized. In total, approximately $7 trillion of paper wealth was lost due to the pernicious events that would cause investors to lose all confidence in the stock market. But not everyone lost money. It's safe to say that $7 trillion was transferred from the hands of individual investors and pensions into those of corporate executives, Wall Street bankers, venture capitalists, and big time Wall Street traders.

Greenspan's Illusion

After the market lows in October '03, the economy appeared to show signs of improvement, with strong consumer spending and robust GDP growth in 2004—all according to Washington. In reality, these "improvements" were fueled by record levels of federal and consumer debt. The Fed was working the U.S. Treasury printing presses in overdrive in a desperate attempt to stimulate the economy. Since then, low mortgage rates have been feeding a real estate boom. Meanwhile, home equity loans continue to be as much in vogue as the iPod.

Throughout this time, Washington and the Fed have applauded the "recovery," as if they were blind to what was really going on. All throughout the post-Internet bubble period, consumers have been "growing" the economy by increasing their debt—using their credit cards and homes as ATMs and speculating in the real estate market. Sadly, much of this credit-spending was used to purchase non-essential goods from Asia. This has led to more job exportation, while increasing America's dependence on foreign debt.

America's auto, steel and other manufacturing industries have all but died due to the inability to compete with the cheap labor, currency pegs, and unfair pricing practices from Asia. As more nations continue to finance its reckless spending habits, America has strengthened its position as the world's largest debtor nation, owned in large part by Europe and Asia. Despite the transfer of wealth from the U.S. to nations abroad, this dangerous pattern of excess consumption continues to delay a much needed correction to the U.S. economy.

Greenspan dampened the impact of Internet bubble correction by decimating short-term interest rates. As a consequence, the stock market bubble has been transferred into the real estate market which is now poised to collapse. The only way out of this mess is for a significantly improved economy, leading to improved living standards, healthy savings rates, and elevated job and retirement benefits. As you shall see throughout the remainder of this book, these changes are not going to materialize for several years at best, and not without harsh consequences. Payback time is coming for America. And the effects are going to be devastating for most.

Bubble Maestro

At some point in the future, if history books document an accurate portrayal of Alan Greenspan's leadership of the Federal Reserve banking system, historians will nickname him the "Great Bubble Maestro" as I have. Thus far, the media has labeled him a genius, crediting him for the bull market period of the '90s. They bask in envy how America "only experienced three small recessions" during his tenure of nearly two decades.

What they fail to mention is that Greenspan avoided recessions and delayed the inevitable economic meltdown by flooding the banking system with dollars. But where is Greenspan now that America needs a way out of this mess? Alas, he has made a timely exit, having passed the reigns of monetary leadership onto a new Federal Reserve chairman. And now, Ben Bernanke will assume the responsibility of navigating America through the huge mess Greenspan made.

As hard as he tries, Federal Reserve Chairman Bernanke won't be able to fix the problems created by his predecessor. If America slips into a depression while Bernanke is in office, he alone will be blamed. But it will be Alan Greenspan and several years of mismanagement by Washington who will share the dual responsibility. Until another Fed Chairman matches Greenspan's performance of forming three asset bubbles in just under two decades, Alan Greenspan will continue to be known as the "Great Bubble Maestro," at least in my mind.

3

IMMIGRATION

As reviewed in the first chapter, America won its independence from British rule in 1776. Thereafter, word spread of this nation formed on a foundation of democracy and capitalism, promising to protect freedom of individual choice; a nation where hard work was rewarded; a nation open to all possibilities. Over the next 150 years, several waves of immigration would empower America's greatness.

For over two centuries, the American Dream has brought millions to the U.S. from around the globe, by both legal and illegal means. Many who have entered illegally have risked their lives for the economic mobility, freedom, and prosperity promised by America. But today, several factors have positioned recent immigrants to destroy the nation that has always been so dependent upon the power of diversity.

Clearly without immigrants, America's success would never be. The uniqueness of each ethnic and racial group added to the ill-defined, yet resilient American culture. The first major immigrant movement was from England, followed by the Irish and Germans in the early 19th century. Next, a large number of Chinese migrated to California during the gold rush. In the early part of the 20th century, many other Europeans immigrated to the U.S. Finally, throughout U.S. history, a steady flow of immigrants from Mexico have entered U.S. borders.

Throughout America's brief history, each immigrant wave brought with it several barriers and sacrifices for every ethnic group. But they endured and added to America's greatness. Most did not have money and were not educated, while others did not know English. Some had all three deficiencies. But they did not complain, nor did they demand help. Instead they helped themselves. They worked hard to overcome these barriers and they were rewarded with the American Dream. This was the philosophy that instilled a strong work ethic for their children to live by because it offered them hope for their future, as well as the promise of the American Dream.

Unfortunately, a large percentage of immigrants from the past three decades have been transformed into slave labor by the economic policies of the U.S. government. Compounding these trends have been the effects of recent illegal immigration from Mexico and South America. Unlike several decades ago, many of America's most recent immigrants have lived by a day-to-day mentality, due in part to their own choice, but also due to government actions. As a result, *they have not made good use of the resources America has to offer, and have therefore missed out on many of its best opportunities.*

America's early immigrants were in many ways like the immigrants of the present day. However, America's early immigrants responded to challenges in a different manner than immigrants from the past three decades. Up until the Reagan administration, most immigrants worked hard to rise above hurdles. In the process, they embraced the American spirit as they integrated within society.

Since then, demographic changes and open trade have created economic difficulties for the U.S. As a consequence, the pool of migrants entering the U.S. is very different than in the past. Fueled by the demands placed upon the economy by the boomer generation, America's consumption during the 1990s was tremendous. In order to meet these demands, America needed workers to do labor the middle class was too busy for or unwilling to do.

Figure 3-1. Immigration to the United States (1900-2000)

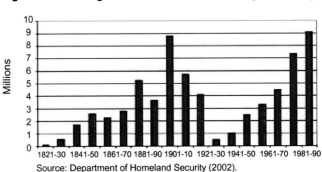

Source: Department of Homeland Security (2002).

As trade barriers were lifted, the global marketplace wanted a shot at America's credit-spending consumers. The only problem was that much of this trade was one-sided, especially with Asia. As a result, U.S. companies found it increasingly difficult to compete with the cheap labor of other nations. Washington's response to intense global competition was NAFTA. Its passage symbolized the beginning of the nation's transformation into a service economy, dependent on credit-spending.

By the end of Reagan's second term, border patrol had become an illusion. Washington looked the other way when illegal aliens entered because they would serve a vital role in providing inexpensive labor to compensate for America's declining living standard. In short, free trade has accelerated illegal migration into the U.S. But the benefits of this inexpensive labor pool have failed to counter the economic impact of job exportation, while adverse socioeconomic consequences have already registered.

What was once a small minority, the Hispanic population now stands as the largest non-white race in the United States. And it's expected to become the nation's most populous racial group within the next fifty years. The problem is that, over the past two decades, too many illegal aliens and immigrants were allowed in too fast. And most have been unprepared or unwilling to assimilate fully into American society. This trend has been especially prominent ever since free trade began. In addition, illegal workers have been exploited by contractors, making it difficult to overcome gaps in language and education.

Corporate America has also played a role in societal disruption by integrating the Spanish language into business commerce. I certainly don't enjoy viewing signs in banks and stores written in Spanish, listening to automated phone calls in Spanish, or having an ATM machine list a chose of languages. English-speaking Americans should not be punished because others chose not to learn English. America is nation of English-speaking people. And citizens who want to emphasize this fact must inform corporations that they must make a choice—to serve English-speaking consumers or those who are too lazy to learn English.

Corporations have essentially snubbed American citizens by engaging in this practice, thinking they can obtain more revenues if they facilitate those who refuse to learn English. The government is also taking part in this practice. Some states now require K-12 teachers to learn Spanish, while others are recruiting bilingual teachers in Mexico. That's right. Your taxpayer dollars are going towards facilitating an environment of illegal aliens and others who refuse to learn English. Needless to say, these behaviors have also helped illegal aliens function in the U.S.

Only by fully assimilating will Hispanics and other migrants benefit from the opportunities America offers. Only then will they begin to feel the strong sense of patriotism Americans have become so famous for. In contrast, the continued inability or unwillingness of this population to integrate is going to increase societal friction.

Because many recent immigrants do not see themselves as truly American, this has had an adverse effect on the unity and patriotism of the United States. It appears as if many of these immigrants treat the U.S. as a nation with no central theme or culture, and chose to retain their own culture without realizing the importance of America's multicultural theme.

American culture is complex and lacks the definition found in most other nations due to both its inherent flexibility and recent formation. While America is a land of many ethnicities, races, and cultures, there are certain things that distinguish Americans from other nations. The American culture is about embracing all others from different backgrounds, races, ideas, religions, and other differences. An implicit tenant of American culture is the acceptance of one's own cultural roots as a secondary identity, while embracing the American spirit as the top priority. This approach fosters solidarity while preserving individuality.

The concept of diversity lies at the core of American culture. Yet, this concept remains undiscovered by many groups in the U.S. They view themselves as Mexican or Asian first, and only American when they need something from the system. This behavioral trend is in stark contrast to the immigrants prior to the Vietnam War. Unless America corrects these trends, it will continue to suffer the effects of declining unity, which could also lead to increased vulnerability to national security. In fact, combined with continued economic disparities and the disappearance of the middle class, a civil war is a possibility at some point if these trends are not reversed.

NAFTA and Illegal Aliens

Addressing the economic burden of some 20 million illegal aliens remains another concern. First, we should consider why so many Mexican nationals have illegally entered the United States. Clearly, America is the world's role model for opportunity and freedom, and claims to provide the highest living standard in the world. While America can no longer claim the highest living standard, it's certainly much higher than in Mexico.

Another reason for the explosion of Mexican illegals over the past decade is due to the effects of NAFTA. With one of the lowest labor costs in the world, Mexican industry stands to gain big from NAFTA. Thus far, NAFTA has only produced benefits for Mexico's wealthy elite, while destroying the livelihood of Mexican laborers. Subsidies for American corn farmers enabled an influx of U.S. corn crops into Mexico at much lower prices, forcing Mexican farmers into bankruptcy. Faced with no other options, millions relocated to the U.S.

By facilitating the entry of illegal workers into America, Washington has created a source of cheap labor for companies, enabling goods and services to be delivered at a lower cost to consumers. Ironically, with most of Mexico's farmers now out of business, the recent use of ethanol in the U.S. has caused corn prices to soar. Sadly, Mexican farmers are no longer in business to take advantage of these trends.

Two-Income Households

For over three decades, Washington has turned its back on border patrol. Our trusted politicians have allowed illegal aliens to enter U.S. borders to hide America's declining living standards. America's decline has also made it a necessity for two-income households.

Most Americans measure living standards in terms of material possessions, while failing to recognize the adverse effects of two-income households. In short, two-income households can create gender identity issues, inadequate parenting, and many other problems that weaken the family unit. But for many, there is no other alternative because they're getting beaten up by the economic effects of free trade. Others find themselves working overtime to pay for things they really don't need. Today, most Americans can be categorized into one of two groups; those in need, and those with excessive greed.

The Real Cost of Cheap Labor

Over time, the costs of education, healthcare, welfare assistance programs, and incarceration of illegal aliens will destroy federal, state and local budgets. Today, America has over 40 million Hispanics, many living in poverty, with some 20 million who are illegal. As a consequence, virtually every government assistance program is backlogged with non-English speaking Mexicans and other Hispanics.

This massive volume of impoverished illegals has created a bottleneck in government-assistence programs. If you pay a visit to virtually any state, local, or federal assistance facility—from the local IRS office to the county health department—you're likely to see a long line of non-English speaking individuals, many of which are illegal aliens. Even the Social Security Administration is prepared to assist these individuals with signs written in Spanish. It's a very big problem that has been a leading cause of state budget shortfalls due to education and healthcare costs alone. Now that the economy is in trouble, the U.S. cannot afford this added liability. But it also cannot afford to lose the economic benefits of cheap labor.

Washington's open border policies are a direct reflection of its inability to reverse the effects of a nation in decline. Allowing illegal aliens to enter the U.S. adds productivity at inexpensive rates. That's precisely why the minimum wage remained unchanged for over a decade. Washington didn't want to raise the minimum wage because it's going to neutralize the positive economic effects of allowing millions illegal aliens to work in America.

Table 3-1. Changes in Cost-of-living and Minimum Wage Since Sept 1997*

Overall inflation	26%
Food	23%
Housing	29%
Medical care	43%
Child care and nursery school	52%
Educational books and supplies	61%
Gasoline, unleaded regular	134%
Minimum wage	0%

Source: CBPP

*Adjusted for inflation, the buying power of minimum wage is lower than it has been since 1955.

A low minimum wage was partly responsible for the cheap labor that fueled the previous economic boom. It served as an experiment by the government to determine if outsourcing (or its domestic equivalent, insourcing via illegals) could help mask the effects of a declining economy. Needless to say, the experiment has been successful, but only for the short-term. Similar to a nation that disregards the effects of pollution in order to maximize productivity, there will be high costs in later years to cleanup the mess created by the lure of cheap labor from illegal aliens.

4

ECONOMICS & EDUCATION

Present-day America is certainly much different than the great post-war period. Shortly after the war, U.S. manufacturing capacity grew to meet the demands of consumers worldwide. Growth of the commercial oil industry expanded the availability of the automobile, leading to the rapid modernization of America's transportation infrastructure. America became the world's leading exporter of goods, including oil. Middle-class America grew to represent the majority due to an abundance of stable, well-paying jobs and pension plans. This was all possible due to America's oil-fueled economic engine, as well as little competition overseas.

This period of prosperity was marked by greatly elevated living standards. Heightened moral and economic success led to a surge in birthrates, otherwise known as the "baby boom." This post-war generation would later contribute to what most have considered another great economic expansion four decades later.

In contrast to America's tremendous post-war expansion, that during the 1990s was fueled by inexpensive oil, overconsumption, and the comfort of national security. Millions of middle-class boomers entered their peak income years, while living the American Dream. But this period of tremendous growth was an illusion fueled by massive credit spending. Regardless, these consumption trends led to the stock market bubble that magnified this illusion of growth.

After the Internet meltdown, Washington spread the word of an economic recovery. However, since 2001 the economy has been kept on life-support by a dangerously loose monetary policy. As real estate prices surged, Americans used their homes as ATM machines while piling up record debt, buying gas-guzzling SUVs and plasma TVs. But all was well for Washington, as long as consumers spent; even if they spent what they didn't have. After all, the U.S. had built the world's biggest credit industry to feed the appetite of Americans in need, as well as those possessed by excessive greed.

Corporate America was also happy in generating its most profitable four-and-one-half year period since 1947, despite the absence of net wage growth. Over the next several years, corporate America will do more than take advantage of the cheap labor overseas. Many of America's largest companies will begin a more aggressive marketing campaign directed at foreign consumers since Americans will not have much money to spend. This will have adverse consequences for most U.S. workers.

America the Bankrupt

As a separate issue, America faces the insurmountable challenge of dealing with its massive boomer population. If drastic policy changes are not made immediately, astronomical sums of money will be needed over the next five decades to fund current liabilities for Social Security, Medicare, and Medicaid. *These liabilities have a total present value of $51 to $72 trillion, or $473,456 to $602,914 per U.S. household.* These numbers do not include total U.S. debt figures which add another $9.0 trillion, the $8.5 trillion borrowed from Social Security and other trust funds by Washington, as well as consumer and mortgage debt, which add another $15 trillion. *In total, these liabilities amount to nearly $1,000,000 per U.S. household.*

What happens when the people of a great nation no longer have affordable access to the essentials of modern life—healthcare, utilities, higher education, and retirement security? That nation, or in America's case, the "empire" reverses towards a devastating decline. Why can't America provide healthcare for all of its citizens and reasonable prices for gasoline and utilities, yet can spend trillions of dollars as the "world's peace keeper?" How long can America remain the world superpower if it cannot provide these basic needs for its citizens? Why is corporate America unable to follow through with its legally-binding guarantee to provide full pension benefits to its employees? How can Washington stand by and watch American jobs disappear as corporations earn record profits?

The American Dream can only exist if America maintains a competitive edge with foreign nations. However, due to the passage of free trade laws, most foreign nations now hold a competitive edge over U.S. trade. As well, many nations in Asia are not playing by fair rules. For many U.S. industries, it's already too late. Unfair trade and pricing practices by China and Japan have already caused the collapse of critical U.S. industries such as steel, chemicals, rubber, furniture, and textiles, along with a permanent exportation of jobs and wealth out of America.

Wealth & Poverty

In August 2004, the U.S. Census Bureau reported a poverty rate of 12.7 percent. This was the rate used by government economists and politicians to determine expenditures for federal, state and local assistance programs. The Census Bureau added that poverty could be as high as 19.4 percent or as low as 8.3 percent, depending on how income and basic living expenses were treated. According to the U.S. Census' conservative formula for poverty, in 2004 there were:

- 37.0 million Americans in poverty (12.7%), up from 35.9 million (12.5%) in 2003.

- 7.9 million American families in poverty (10.2%), up from 7.6 million in 2003.

I for one feel that the real poverty rate is much closer to the 19.4 percent figure (and most likely even higher) due to the unwillingness of Washington to update its criteria for poverty. As defined by the Office of Management and Budget and updated for inflation using the Consumer Price Index (CPI), the average poverty threshold for a family of four in 2004 was an income of $19,307; for a family of three, $15,067; for a family of two, $12,334; and for unrelated individuals, $9,645. Over the next two decades, as the majority of America's estimated 76 million baby boomers are expected to retire in poverty, (as defined by the government's conservative criteria) the real numbers could easily surpass 30 percent.

How is it that record oil prices have not allowed for upward adjustments to poverty criteria? Keep in mind that inflation of basic necessities such as food, energy, and healthcare affects the poor by a much larger factor than wealthier consumers because they have less to spend on other items. Thus, *inflation of basic necessities becomes a tax on low- and middle-income Americans.*

In addition, it seems odd that the poverty level is not adjusted for the living expenses of each city or state since this would account for regions with higher living expenses. As it stands today, the government's formula for poverty is only applicable to states with the lowest cost of living such as West Virginia, Mississippi, Arkansas, and Alabama. Even in these states, poverty levels are quite high according to Washington's conservative criteria. How many Americans living in larger, more costly metropolitan areas are making more than the government's poverty level, yet are not counted in its official numbers?

Based on the government's conservative data, nearly 40 million Americans are literally on the verge of being homeless. But if appropriate adjustments for basic living costs were made, the poverty level could easily be 80 percent higher than reported. Even with all the tricks government agencies use to hide the truth, they cannot dispute that poverty is on the rise. And for many reasons—free trade, rising healthcare and oil prices—it's only going to get worse for many years to come.

Bankruptcy Reform

The recent passage bankruptcy reform was a message by Washington that consumers will have no second chances. Arguably, reform was needed due to two decades of abuse. In many cases, it became commonplace for individuals to file for bankruptcy just to eliminate credit card debt since there were no real consequences. But the consumer credit industry has been permitted to exploit consumers by the use of unfair business practices and deceitful disclosure tactics. Thus, much of the blame must rest with this industry. Yet, this law now provides banks a means to deliver higher earnings predictability since, with rare exception all debts must be paid.

Until America's most critical problems have been solved such as astronomical healthcare costs and job exportation, it seems as if *the timing of this bankruptcy law was extremely poor unless Washington's main priority was to empower the financial industry.* During a period when consumers are struggling more than in the previous six decades, one would expect reforms to address the unfair business practices used by the credit card industry.

Why would President Bush pass a law that punishes consumers for their inability to pay for a ridiculously priced healthcare system, while favoring an industry that addicts them to credit? It simply makes no sense to pass bankruptcy reform after Greenspan handed out money like it was free and after so many jobs have been destroyed, while corporate America has earned record profits. Of course, financial industry lobbyists are quite influential. In fact, MBNA was President Bush's top campaign contributor for his first term.

America's Wealthy

Washington likes to remind critics that Americans enjoy the highest living standard in the world. As evidence of this, government "experts" discuss statistics such as GDP growth, wealth, income, wage growth, and other indicators without defining exactly what they are referring to. But even the government's own data on income and wealth disparity paint a much different picture.

When one examines the data, it is clear that *only America's wealthiest 5 percent have benefited from the credit-driven economic expansion that began over two decades ago.* Shortly after 1980, real incomes of the top 5 percent soared over the next two decades, from 3.5 to 5.5 times the median income (in 2001 dollars). In contrast, real incomes for the bottom 80 percent barely moved, while inflation for basic necessities (such as healthcare, energy, and higher education) soared. These expenses have further reduced the disposable income of most Americans. In contrast, the post-war economic expansion was much more evenly distributed across all wage earners. This balanced expansion continued until the high inflation period of the early '80s.

Even more disturbing, *America's wealth disparity is much greater*, with the top 5 percent having accounted for a much larger percentage of wealth growth from the decade since 1979 than the bottom 95 percent. Ten years later the gap is even larger, with the wealthiest 5 percent having on average 23 times the wealth of the remaining 95 percent.

The problem is that households with a low net worth have very few assets. Thus, they will be affected more by price increases in basic necessities. In addition, they will be less able to weather unexpected difficulties, such as medical emergencies or a job loss. Accordingly, Edward Wolff has estimated that 40 percent of households headed by individuals aged 25 to 54 could exhaust all financial assets (excluding their home) within one week upon losing their income; something very possible given the strong outsourcing and inflation trends seen today.

Educating America

At the root of America's declining competitiveness is the ineffectiveness of its public K-12 educational system, which continues to fail in preparing the nation's youth for the modern economy. When comparing the educational skills and achievement scores of K-12 students to foreign counterparts, Americans consistently score in the lower quintile. But money is not the problem as many seem to believe. When one compares students from China, Korea and other developing nations to their Chinese- and Korean-American counterparts, similar disparities exist. Therefore, it must be the family unit and value system within these nations that are responsible for high achievement levels.

While the U.S. still retains a significant edge over most nations in higher education, the gap is closing fast. Despite superior research facilities afforded to American college students, the U.S. continues to produce fewer scientists and engineers than in the past, while Asia and Europe continue to produce more. The early results of these trends have already materialized, as foreign economies continue to expand daily, narrowing the gap between what was once without question the most powerful nation on earth.

Furthermore, America's most talented students no longer have the resources enjoyed by previous generations. For several years now, a larger portion of expenses have gone towards special education programs due to the Americans with Disabilities Act passed during the Clinton administration. While it has provided a great service to those with disabilities, it has diverted funds from core and accelerated programs, opened the door for frivolous lawsuits, and restricted the authoritative power of teachers. Thus, it has led to more harm than good.

When the global marketplace opens for daily business, consumers do not care whether you have transformed special education students into overachievers. They only care about where they can obtain the best goods and services at the best price.

Certainly, everyone deserves a chance at a good education. Access to education promotes moral unity and economic equity. But if the U.S. intends to preserve its global leadership, it cannot permit schools to overweigh special education programs at the expense of traditional and accelerated programs. This policy is in opposition with the competitive spirit that's made America prosperous.

Rather than punishing the most promising students, there's a much better way to help the less fortunate. Washington must encourage philanthropists and corporations to help finance programs for the disadvantaged. *America's philanthropists need to keep more of their charitable dollars in America to help their own citizens rather than trying to win a Nobel Peace Prize.* America has its own problems to deal with. And without radical solutions, these problems will only get worse.

Teaching in America

Adding to America's education crisis has been the inability of K-12 schools to attract qualified science and math instructors. Even when they're found, bureaucracy, waste and corruption by administrators has overshadowed the efforts of the finest teachers to deliver their best resources to America's youth.

In many cases, it has become difficult to find qualified non-science teachers for inner city schools due to the violence and lack of respect exhibited by many teens, as well as the lack of disciplinary authority schools must cope with. *In fact, the inability of teachers and principals to discipline students in an effective manner has accounted for part of the breakdown in the public education system.* But how can you expect teachers to discipline students when parents are limited in the ways they can legally discipline their own children?

No doubt, the increase in behavioral issues seen in U.S. teens has been an adverse consequence of two-income households, which are almost mandatory today. No longer do parents have the time to become involved with their child's education or social development because they're working all of the time. In short, *many parents have sacrificed parenting responsibilities for better wages, thinking that two incomes will lead to a better life for their family. In reality, America's trend of two-income households has led to a breakdown of the family unit.*

That's not to say that there are no students exiting secondary schools with a solid foundation. But for those who have attained a strong educational background, most enter college to prepare for high-paying, higher status careers, such as medicine, business and law. One can obtain any undergraduate degree and follow it up with an MBA or law degree and be rewarded with many times the salary of a Ph.D. scientist, which requires several more years of rigorous study.

Who Wants to Be a Scientist?

America's population has one of the highest percentages of high school graduates in the world, at around 96 percent, as well as a literacy rate of 97 percent. In addition, it has the world's best university system equipped with the finest research facilities. But when it comes to continuing their education in the "rough" fields of academics like the physical sciences, engineering and math, America's youth no longer makes the grade.

Because Washington has allowed free trade to evaporate the nation's manufacturing base, *one would expect an emphasis on intellectual property to have positioned the nation with an abundant supply of future scientists and engineers.* However, for over two decades, America has been producing a declining number of scientists and engineers relative to its economic growth. With declining rates of new American-born scientists and engineers, one can only fantasize how the U.S. will be able to hold on to its last remaining economic leg.

With such a high dependency on innovation, one might reasonably assume that the average American would have math and science skills comparable to Asian and European counterparts. But this is hardly the case. As you might suspect, the problem for U.S. students begins in grade school, where Asian counterparts perform decisively better.

When literacy and high school graduation rates in India and China are examined, the numbers are quite low. But this is to be expected since most of these populations are located in remote areas with poor access to educational resources. But this is changing. China continues to expand its modern transportation infrastructure that will link urban and rural regions. With 50 percent of its college degrees in science and engineering, China is already producing a much higher percentage of scientists and engineers. In contrast, America's youth continues to show a declining interest in science or math-based careers. The academic rigor is too difficult and the pay is too little. Even though U.S. enrollment in science programs has increased over the past few years, most use this preparation as a stepping stone for higher-paying healthcare fields.

Compensation is not the only problem. The career of a scientist is not viewed with the same level of prestige as in other nations. And it's never portrayed in an attractive or sexy manner by the media, unlike careers in business, law and medicine. The most popular television shows continue to be based on physicians, businessmen and attorneys, with exciting portrayals of sexual escapades and drama. So who can blame America's youth for not wanting to study science and math? Many other career choices offer better wages, less time in school, less effort, and more respect.

In the past two decades, the average annual cost of a four-year public university in the U.S. has increased by over 240 percent, or more than three times the rate of inflation. Today, the average annual cost is over $23,000. As corporations continue to outsource high-technology jobs, why would parents encourage their children to pursue the cost and rigor of a science or engineering degree? It simply makes no sense.

Millions Left Behind

When President Bush signed the No Child Left Behind Act in 2002, he promised it would provide a core education level for all. The act called for all public schools to be proficient in reading and math by 2014. Schools are required to report scores based on race, poverty, migrant status, English proficiency, and special education. According to the guidelines, if a school fails in one category it has failed in all categories. The law requires that all schools receiving federal assistance demonstrate annual improvements for students in all racial categories, or risk penalties such as extension of the school year, changing the curriculum, and firing the administration and/or teachers.

This seemed like a good start for addressing a portion of America's education crisis. But according to a study conducted by the Associated Press, President Bush has allowed millions of students' national test scores to be "left behind" in order to create the perception of academic achievement and success of the program. Due to a loophole in this law, *states are helping schools get around the reporting criteria by allowing administrators to ignore scores of racial groups that they consider "too small to be statistically significant."*

As national test scores continue to disappoint officials, over two dozen states have successfully petitioned Washington to allow schools to discard a larger number of racial groups. Today, most schools are permitted to ignore the test scores of up to 50 students in any one racial group. *The results of the Associated Press study found that in the 2003 to 2004 school year about 1.9 million scores or 1 in 14 were not counted in the final results.*

It turns out that the vast majority of uncounted scores were from minorities such as Hispanics, African-Americans, and Asians. As a consequence, *minorities are seven times more likely to have their scores not counted as whites.* And the rate of uncounted scores among minorities is rising each year. Spread across America in equal distributions, these excluded scores might appear to be reasonable statistical exclusions. But consider that in California, more than 400,000 scores were not counted. And in Texas over 257,000 scores were thrown out. According to Education Secretary Margaret Spellings, excluding the scores of 1.9 million Americans is "too many."

America's education problem will be very difficult to fix, and will require many years. As a start, the huge number of overpaid administrators should be downsized. Strict accountability standards for expenditures should be implemented to eliminate fraud, while delivering severe punishment for those who use taxpayer dollars for their own needs. In addition, city officials must ensure that school boards don't have business interests for themselves or their friends.

Finally, more involvement of parents is critical. Ultimately, it's the parents' responsibility to provide a healthy family environment conducive to learning. Parents must exert a sufficient amount of effort to encourage and assist their children in obtaining a sound education. You cannot easily solve a problem that's rooted in decades of socioeconomic and institutional decline. It will take much more time and effort than money.

5

TOXIC EFFECTS OF
FREE TRADE

After WWII, the United States entered a modern industrial revolution. This period witnessed the rise of America's manufacturing dominance, creating good jobs and benefits for millions of Americans. For two decades thereafter, the U.S. was a net exporter of good across all industries. In fact, the U.S. was even the world's leading exporter of oil. As a result, foreigners paid for American-made products, which led to trade surpluses. Soon, post-war America emerged as the world's largest creditor, while Americans had a healthy double-digit savings rate with very little debt.

During the 1970s, as Asia became organized and competitive, many American jobs were exported overseas. Furthermore, large investment inflows from broad worried many Americans. Ironically, ever since 1970, America has been the world's largest debtor nation.

Today, virtually nothing of much quality or value is completely made in America. It's simply too expensive to offer the wages and benefits Americans have been accustomed to. When these costs are passed onto consumers, domestically produced goods get priced out of the market by lower priced imports. This has forced numerous industries and millions of jobs to be exported overseas.

In part, the problem stems from trying to compete with foreign companies that do not share the same employee costs as U.S. counterparts. As a result, rather than free trade, Washington willingly entered the U.S. into unfair trade. And the only benefactors have been large corporations, wealthy shareholders and overseas workers.

NAFTA was a failure from the start due to the structural differences between America's economic system and that of foreign nations. *How can America expect to receive fair trade from nations that subsidize their industries, depress wages, provide government-funded retirement benefits and healthcare, limit foreign investment and competition, and engage in counterfeiting of U.S. products?*

Clearly, these inequities have made it impossible for U.S. companies to compete with foreign peers. Since NAFTA was passed, there have been hundreds of corporate bankruptcies and the disappearance of entire industries due to the effects of outsourcing, insourcing, and acquisitions of U.S. companies by foreign interests. The effects of free trade have furthered the decline in U.S. living standards and heightened the dependency on foreign-backed credit spending.

If current trends remain intact, it appears as if corporate America will eventually be located overseas, as will many of the jobs we see in the U.S. today. Virtually every type of job offered by corporate America is subject to outsourcing, with the exception of some low-level service positions. But many of these jobs are being taken by illegal aliens via *insourcing*.

The official purpose of NAFTA was to encourage exports out of America while raising the standard of living in all member nations. Since inception over a decade ago, this goal remains a dream. Not only has the standard of living remained the same in both Canada and Mexico, but Mexico's minimum wage has been frozen at $0.50 since 1994. According to the U.S. Bureau of Labor Statistics, in 2005 Mexican labor wages were the lowest in the world next to Sri Lanka.

After fourteen years of NAFTA, Mexico's wealth is primarily controlled by about 100 corporations. And for America, NAFTA, CAFTA, WTO and other free trade policies continue to hurt low- and middle-income workers, while providing absolute benefit to corporate America and the wealthy elite. Thus, the problem with free trade isn't so much with economic growth, but how this new wealth has been distributed. It's clear that the vast majority of wealth has gone to corporations and their wealthy shareholders.

Even before NAFTA had a chance to demonstrate its damaging effects, President Clinton added fuel to the fire by entering the U.S. into the World Trade Organization in 1995. With a current membership of 149 nations, the WTO has entrenched its clout within corporate committees that advise politicians of member nations. The most restrictive policy of WTO membership is that it forbids U.S. government regulation, such as tariff protection for industries vital to its well-being.

Since the passage of NAFTA, over 5 million U.S. manufacturing jobs have been lost, over $5 trillion in trade deficits have registered, and more than $4 trillion in core U.S. assets have been purchased by foreign nations. Perhaps most disturbing is the fact that *most of the money used to purchase U.S. companies and other critical assets ultimately came from American consumers and Washington.*

You see, because an increasingly larger percentage of America's annual deficits have been financed by foreign nations (for instance, 70 percent of the deficit was financed by foreign nations in 2003 and 99 percent in 2004), *the U.S. has essentially traded core assets to satisfy its greed and addiction for non-essential consumer goods and wasteful government spending.* While Washington has allowed companies to transfer good jobs to other nations, consumers have been financing the buildup of China and India.

Thus far, China has received all of the benefits from U.S. trade relations. First, it used price manipulation to drive many of America's core manufacturing industries into bankruptcy. Next, it manipulated its currency to ensure its products would be purchased by U.S. consumers despite a weak dollar. Finally, U.S. corporations expanded into China, with the help of Bush's tax breaks, transferring investment capital and jobs.

Technology Transfer

Instead of the manufacturing job base seen during the post-war period, U.S. corporations now focus on receiving royalties from foreign companies in exchange for intellectual property rights. As well, most U.S. "manufacturers" import finished or near-finished products from Asia. This has fueled foreign manufacturing industries while exporting millions of jobs abroad.

In addition to millions of permanent job losses, Washington's "free trade" policies have resulted in the gradual loss of America's most prized possessions—its research, innovation, commercialization skills and resources. You see, outsourcing and free trade don't end with the loss of U.S. jobs. In many cases, critical innovative secrets and R&D labs have been sent overseas because they are required for manufacturing. When this happens, foreign nations ultimately share the benefits of America's most highly treasured innovative secrets. In addition to the unintended transfer of modern technologies, America is now sharing with much of the world some of its most advanced military innovations and production secrets. This alone poses a significant threat to its national security.

It should be clear that Washington in no way entered into these one-way trade agreements for the purpose of improving living conditions of working-class Americans and foreign laborers. The real motive was to provide more wealth to corporations and their wealthy shareholders. If current policies continue, more industries will be lost to foreign nations, taking jobs along with them. And America's trading partners will continue to benefit from the transfer of good jobs and intellectual property.

Along with NAFTA nations Mexico and Canada, CAFTA member-nations are serving as back-door portals for products from China, Japan, and Europe. What this means is that these nations are able to indirectly utilize the economic benefits of NAFTA and CAFTA to import goods into America duty-free.

As well, foreign nations can build production facilities in NAFTA and CAFTA member-nations where they can directly supply U.S. consumers with duty-free goods, thereby circumventing WTO regulations. In fact, the U.S. has recently seen a surge in trade from Mexico. No doubt, much of this is due to back-door entry of Asian and European goods.

Some might wonder how this harms America. Others might argue that it's beneficial for U.S. consumers. While providing lower-cost goods to consumers, the longer-term effect causes U.S. companies to be less competitive. And with no alternatives, most will be forced to lower benefits to workers, outsource, and even relocate overseas taking jobs and investment capital with them. Already, these trends are firmly in place.

With an estimated 1 out of every 4 dollars spent directly on imported manufactured goods, America is exporting its wealth overseas in exchange for non-essential consumer goods, or what I call "stuff." This doesn't even count the dollars spent on insourced products (e.g. buying Japanese cars, many of which are now manufactured in the U.S., but whose profits are sent to Japan), nor does it count money spent by Americans on goods and services supplied by U.S. companies owned by foreign interests.

America's entry into the World Trade Organization has caused even more problems. Perhaps the most insidious impact of WTO membership is the inability of Washington to invoke tariffs. Without this authority, America is trying to compete on a level playing field with nations that play by their own rules.

How can U.S. companies be expected to compete against foreign competitors that do not share the same labor costs? The only way to compete is to outsource jobs overseas. Obviously, the long-term impact of free trade will continue to exert downward pressure on employee benefits for U.S. workers, widening the gap between the wealthy and middle class until a two-class society is all that remains.

Recent improvements in technology and communications have created an interdependent system of commerce and information exchange throughout the globe, otherwise known as the New Economy. Within this economy, a fixed amount of wealth will be shared between participant nations at any given point in time. That is, you cannot create large increases in wealth overnight because all resources are of limited quantity. Thus, when one or more nations experience rapid economic growth, much of it is due to the transfer of wealth from other nations.

Many developing nations have experienced rapid increases in living standards as a result of a transfer of wealth from the U.S. Thus, by linking America into a system of unhindered and unfair global trade, Washington has solidified the trend of declining living standards for all Americans except the wealthy elite.

Best of Both Worlds

Given China's heightened stance in Washington as the top backer of U.S. debt, American companies have received little assistance to combat unfair trade practices. Most large corporations have been forced to outsource. But this has only provided benefit to America's wealthiest citizens—those who own run and own the corporations—at the expense of its working-class. But not all have fared well. Many companies lacking the ability to expand overseas (due to barriers erected by the Chinese government or by geographical restrictions) have gone out of business.

In addition, *anti-subsidy regulations that protect U.S. companies and employees from foreign subsidy programs do not apply to China because it is still considered a non-market economy by the WTO.* In accordance with WTO regulations and policies, it is illegal for the U.S. to protect its industries against Chinese subsides. In addition, WTO policy prevents the U.S. from holding China accountable for currency manipulation unless it has also established a large trade surplus with the rest of its trading partners. Of course, that's simply not going to happen as long as China keeps its currency pegged to the falling dollar.

America's Service Economy

America's high-tech companies can be considered part of the huge service industry that replaced its once dominant manufacturing infrastructure. Just a few decades ago when U.S. companies had a healthy balance of innovation and manufacturing, it was innovation that led to better products and more jobs for Americans. That was a period when more money flowed into America than out. Total U.S. debt was very low, household savings rates were high, and deficits were rare. Yet, consumer spending and investment were robust.

Today we see a much different picture. Instead of innovation creating domestic manufacturing jobs, the emphasis on intellectual property has generated a large chunk of revenues for corporate America. As well, unfair trade dynamics have severed the innovation-manufacturing bond that served America so well in the past. As a result, manufacturing jobs have been sent overseas, along with U.S. innovative secrets. An economic engine built upon innovation demands a superior education system that is able to produce an increasing population of new scientists and engineers. But as we have seen, America is falling short of these needs.

Another problem with this type of business structure is that, when extreme as it is today, it relies on a heavy R&D infrastructure that does not necessarily result in direct employment-per-dollar of revenue. For instance, in an automobile assembly plant you can correlate the number of workers needed for a certain output of cars produced.

In contrast, for a high-technology development enterprise, you cannot make these same correlations due to the reliance of technology on a variable number of services, individuals, and institutions external to the company. Many of these services are rented or paid for by other companies, university research centers, and even foreign companies. *Thus, there is a lower level of direct job creation within an innovation-based economy since there are no specific requirements to employ American workers to assist in the development of these activities.*

As a matter of fact, free trade dynamics guarantee U.S. companies will outsource much of the R&D work if possible. Once a company begins to outsource, the others must follow to remain competitive. Therefore, *companies that focus on innovation and royalty payments will ultimately end up creating very few jobs in America*, while risking the transfer of innovative secrets overseas. And because manufacturing outsourcing ultimately leads to technology transfer, nations that focus on innovation without domestic manufacturing (as America now does) are not only exporting wages overseas, but they are vulnerable to losing their innovative edge to partnering nations through the inevitable transfer of technology.

Outsourcing Trends

Modern improvements in transportation and telecommunications have expanded the labor force options available to companies. As discussed, the utility of these advances have been exploited by free trade policies. Evidence of this can be seen from recent outsourcing trends. But outsourcing is nothing new to America, having occurred for over three decades. Companies outsource their labor force as a way to lower costs, helping them deliver inexpensive products and services to the marketplace. In delivering lower-cost goods and services, companies become positioned as strong competitors, leading to higher profits and increased shareholder value.

When held in balance, outsourcing has a positive effect on the economy. Delivery of less expensive goods and services encourages consumers to spend more, which leads to business growth and expansion. Eventually, this should lead to better jobs for Americans. However, America is now experiencing the diminished returns of excessive outsourcing. The main culprit is a free trade policy that favors the exportation of American jobs. By the end of 2003 alone, 40 percent of Fortune 500 firms had already outsourced.

Let's take a look at how this can hurt America's global competitiveness. There are hundreds of examples we can use, but let's consider the computer manufacturing industry. About 90 percent of all computer parts are now made overseas, primarily in China. So, for every PC bought in America from a U.S. manufacturer, consumers are really buying imported goods slapped together to form the final product. Thus, these companies should be thought of as a foreign manufacturer of computers because most of their operating revenues go overseas, fueling more jobs.

But don't think outsourcing is restricted to blue collar workers. The outsourcing trends we see today have virtually no restrictions within the labor force. Consequently, white collar workers have been affected perhaps even more than the blue collar labor force. Companies can outsource work to a Ph.D. in India for up to 80 percent less than an American with a Master's degree. Why? Quite simply, it has to do in part with living expenses and employee benefits, which are influenced by wage growth, inflation, and interest rates.

Employee benefits account for about 42 percent of the total compensation package of the average U.S. worker; something outsourcing does not require. That means no healthcare or pension costs. As well, companies that outsource or set up facilities overseas have the added advantages of tax credits from the U.S. government, no organized labor, no Social Security or Medicare taxes, no federal or state unemployment tax, and no OHSA or EPA costs or restrictions. As a result, because *free trade transfers wages overseas, it redistributes wealth among all participant nations so that a balance of living standards is approached.* Needless to say, middle-class Americans have been the unwilling donor of this redistribution of wealth.

Obviously, while corporate America and foreign nations benefit, American workers lose during a protracted period of outsourcing. Only in the short-term do U.S. consumers gain superficial benefit through lower-priced goods. Over the longer-term, consumers end up losing due to the exportation of jobs. Without good, stable jobs providing adequate benefits, consumers can only spend on credit for so long.

Technology Transfer

When NAFTA was signed into law, it opened the door for U.S. companies to seek out the least expensive workers to supply goods and services to the marketplace. When the U.S. joined the WTO a year later, this all but assured the extinction of middle-class America due to the malignant effects of free trade.

Advocates of outsourcing point to the *Theory of Free International Trade*, published by economist David Ricardo in 1817. During the 1980s, the widespread acceptance of Ricardo's doctrine of comparative costs convinced economic policy makers that free trade with no barriers would be beneficial to all. Free trade advocates claim that the loss of U.S. industries leads to greater productivity via replacement with better jobs. Yet, they've failed to identify these better jobs.

According to Paul Roberts, former Assistant Treasury Secretary under Ronald Reagan, *in order for a comparative advantage to persist, a nation's labor, capital, and technology cannot move offshore.* This immobility of resources is mandatory so businesses do not gain an absolute advantage abroad. It turns out that when a third-world nation exchanges resources with a first-world nation for the purpose of producing lower cost goods, the third-world nation derives more benefit from the relationship due to the inescapable transfer of intellectual property. *The long-term effect of this business relationship is the transfer of income from the nation with higher wages to the nation with lower wages.*

Even when America engages in resource exchange with other first-world nations, its innovative advantage is transferred. Thus, America is in the midst of transferring its absolute advantage overseas, weakening the power of its economic engine. Back in Ricardo's day, intellectual property was barely acknowledged, much less enforced. Thus, his theory is flawed when applied to the modern economy because it doesn't account for the economic power of these assets, as well as the need to safeguard them from exportation.

Innovation and Research

When the U.S. government began to protect intellectual property, this encouraged more entrepreneurial ventures. Along with increased funding, the heightened stance on intellectual property helped stimulate economic growth through innovation rather than manufacturing. Thereafter, U.S. manufacturing output gradually declined. Aided by free trade policies that arose in the mid-'90s, domestic manufacturing has now receded to the anemic level we see today.

Despite America's dependence on innovation productivity, intellectual property laws are still not widely accepted or enforced in other nations—especially in Asia, where piracy is the norm. For many years now, tens of billions of dollars have been lost each year due to piracy. But leadership in innovation is all that America has left, making global recognition of and adherence to intellectual property laws a vital component of its economic fate.

But there are additional threats to America's innovative engine. After the devastating effects of the '80s, America's investment environment facilitated a surge in both corporate R&D and venture finance. Subsequently, private funding for research replaced much of the declining funding growth from the government. And this has shifted the emphasis on shorter-term projects which has hurt core research efforts. *What this has done is connect corporate America, along with its focus on short-term solutions and quarterly earnings statements, with academia.* As a result, the strength of America's core scientific research has been damaged.

As corporate R&D and private investment capital continues to flood into research institutions, many scientists now focus on landing research grants as a means of survival, even if quality research is sacrificed. Universities are pressuring professors to land larger grants. And because much of this funding comes from corporate America, research scientists have shifted from core research efforts to short-term studies that more directly relate to commercial goods.

Meanwhile, virtually every large university now has a technology transfer department, whose goal is to monetize as much research as possible. As a result, they have created a global marketplace for university innovation, having sold or licensed out thousands of patents to foreign companies. Similar to corporate America, university research is now for sale to the highest bidder, despite the fact that much of this research has been funded with taxpayer dollars.

Already, some of the damaging effects of America's declining innovation growth are apparent. Since 1988, U.S. patent growth has remained fairly constant. In contrast, patent applications from Western Europe and Asia have steadily increased. As of 1996, *the number of patent applications from Western Europe surpassed those from America for the first time ever.* Since then, the gap has continued to widen.

Since 1980, America's world share of new patents has declined by 15 percent while Japan's share has risen by almost 200 percent. Already, Japan has bumped the U.S. down to the number two spot in the amount of capital spent on R&D as a percentage of GDP. Furthermore, with the exception of Japan, other nations such as China, Canada, Russia, Korea, and the European Union have experienced tremendous GDP growth over the past decade, in comparison to the U.S. Therefore, this data does not account for huge increases in funding these nations have made (relative to GDP) as their GDP has soared.

Most impressive is China, which has increased its overall R&D spending as a percentage of GDP, while continuing to deliver double-digit GDP growth over the past decade. Of course, China would not have been able to post these amazing gains without the reckless spending habits of President Bush and U.S. consumers.

Given the declining production of U.S. scientists and engineers and the lack of patent growth, America will lose its technology edge within the next 15 years. And without its leadership in innovation, it will have very little to fall back on now that most U.S. manufacturing industries has either gone out of business or has been exported overseas. Furthermore, foreign dependence on manufacturing will accelerate the loss of U.S. innovative productivity through the inevitable transfer of innovative secrets.

Unlike the previous decade when America ranked third in the world, the number of new American scientists now ranks seventeenth. But the full effects of these trends have not yet registered within America's R&D base because of the lag time required to transform the next generation of young Americans into scientists. If current trends remain in place, it won't be long before America will have to import the majority of its research scientists. While importation of research talent has been occurring for decades, it has only accounted for small gaps. Even if America opens its borders amidst national security laws, the number of foreign scientists available may be insufficient.

Getting Used

Many foreign students use America's university system, only to return back to their homeland to take advantage of economic opportunities created by corporate America. This denies advanced training to young Americans while empowering foreign nations. *Therefore, permitting foreign students into American universities should be recognized as both an economic and national security issue for all disciplines.* Those spots need to be reserved for Americans or foreigners legally obligated to remain in the U.S. for an extended period after graduation.

When universities admit foreign students, this denies economic opportunities to U.S. citizens. American universities represent a substantial portion of the nation's intellectual capital. And since a large amount of university research is funded by taxpayer dollars, America needs to see a return on this investment. When foreign students return home after graduation, their share of investment returns are transferred to foreign economies.

Therefore, universities should restrict enrollment to American citizens. Universities that do not play by these rules should be stripped of all federal and state funding. After all, this funding is coming from taxpayers. And it should only be provided to universities that help create jobs for Americans. Similar restrictions should be placed on university technology transfer departments that monetize government-funded research by selling intellectual property to foreign companies.

Illusion of Value

America's service industry extends well beyond technology innovation. Over the past two decades, the non-technology segment of the services industry has grown tremendously. However, *many of these more recent service sectors focus on scavenging revenues from Americans by offering services to companies and individuals within the U.S.* For every consumer dollar of earned wages, America has a multitude of companies or independently-employed individuals looking to get a piece of the pie.

For instance, let's consider the consumer activity of buying a car. Ideally, this would involve a buyer and a seller. However, today this simple transaction can involve several service industries. If you want to buy a car, you'll probably need financing, so the financial industry becomes involved. As well, you might want to purchase an extended warranty. Again, this involves a different sector of the financial industry. Of course you'll need insurance as well. But we aren't finished. The loan you take out is resold to other financial institutions representing large investors. If you default on your loan, it might be resold to a collection agency that also stands to benefit from the original consumer transaction.

So as you can see, something as common as an auto purchase can easily involve several corporations, all grabbing for a piece of that transaction. The process is similar for consumer electronics, real estate, and many other industries. Thus, what begins as a simple consumer transaction turns into financial gains for corporate America and its wealthy investors. Furthermore, this productivity is internal, and does nothing to bring dollars into America. *The U.S. needs foreign consumers to fuel real economic growth, not domestic scavengers.*

When you have several companies taking a bite out of every consumer transaction, it requires a large volume of units to be sold in order to generate revenues for each company. *Thus far, America has been successful in operating this "scavenger economy" through credit spending.* But this can't last much longer, especially when foreign nations are less willing to finance U.S. debt due to a weak dollar.

Some would argue that this system has helped create more jobs and lowered the price of goods and services. *But it has trivialized the value that the overall workforce produces, and serves to widen the income and wealth gap, while increasing America's dependence on foreign debt.*

As it stands today, unless you are at the top of the financial hierarchy, America's future doesn't look good. It has become a nation of imports and credit-spending financed by large corporations and foreign nations. *No nation can remain strong if it imports non-essential products, while exporting valuable limited natural resources and intellectual property.* The consequences are further heightened when consumers use credit to buy these goods. *One can only consume more than they produce for a finite period before a crisis results.* For now, America is only buying time until the bubble bursts.

PART II

WEAPONS OF DESTRUCTION

6

FINANCIAL MISMANAGEMENT

Prior to 1969, America was the world's largest creditor, serving as the world's bank. Since that time, it has held the title of the world's largest debtor, with Europe and Asia as its bankers. Deficit spending has become routine policy in Washington, enabling the government to spend more than it makes, shifting the federal debt to future generations. This "buy now pay later" mentality has facilitated financial mismanagement by Washington for over two decades.

Imagine if you were able to get loans anytime you needed. But since you borrowed so much, there would be no way you could repay it, so your co-signers would be responsible for repayment. Unfortunately, the co-signers of Washington's debt are taxpayers. Today, most taxpayer dollars are used just to pay the annual interest on the federal debt. Since the majority of this debt is held by foreign nations, most of your tax dollars are going overseas to pay for Washington's ridiculous spending.

Federal Deficit

We have recently witnessed a drastic shift in the current account balance (figure 6-1) from a surplus during Clinton's last years, to increasing deficit levels during each year of President Bush's two terms. *No other member of the G-7 or any other first-tier economy has a current account deficit.* This raises the question whether the U.S. is really the world's economic superpower. Any nation can claim to be an economic superpower if permitted to run up endless debt.

The last time America experienced a similar turnaround was

during the '80s, when President Reagan was battling the Cold War with the former Soviet Union. During that period there was great concern for the economy because Reagan reversed what was a surplus of $8 billion into a $147 billion deficit in 1987. As well, inflation was high, oil was at record prices, and many jobs were being lost overseas. During Reagan's tenure, the inflow of foreign capital was seen as a threat by many. But this investment capital actually aided the nation's productivity. Rather than corporate assets being bought from America as is occurring presently, money was invested into a variety of projects during the '80s.

Thus far, recent deficits have not reached the levels (measured as a percentage of GDP) incurred during WWII, and throughout the '80s with the implementation of "Reaganomics." But President Bush's deficit trend will continue even after he leaves office because of the future liabilities he has created. Mounting liabilities for Iraq, the war against terrorism, and social insurance benefits for America's baby boomers will cause these records to be shattered within the next decade.

One thing seems obvious about deficits. While they may not matter over any given year, *large annual deficits over an extended period will increase the total debt burden of the government, causing interest rates to rise and the dollar to fall.* This will lead to a restriction in credit for consumer spending and business expansion. Unless radical spending cuts are made, it's entirely possible that America's deficit and debt trends will lead to a series of financial crises, sending the dollar and stock market lower over the next decade.

China's Role

For 2005, the federal deficit swelled to an all-time high of $726 billion, with $202 billion due to trade imbalances with China. Think about that number for a moment. That's about 9 percent of America's federal debt and almost 6 percent of the GDP. Most likely, the deficit will move higher during Bush's remaining term before any chance of trailing off. This alone will cause further devaluation of the dollar.

Over the past five years, America should have recorded a net trade surplus with China because of the dollar's low value relative to other currencies. But since China kept its currency tied to the dollar, the trade affects of a weak dollar did not manifest. Although China officially unpegged its currency from the dollar in late summer of 2005, it has allowed only a minor appreciation (about 3 percent). As a result, China's currency is still anywhere from 40 to 50 percent undervalued.

To finance the federal debt, the U.S. Treasury sells bonds, many of which are bought by foreign central banks. You see, it's in the best interest of China, Japan, and other manufacturing powerhouses to finance America's debt because these nations benefit two-fold. First, they're purchasing what are considered the safest investments in the world—U.S. Treasury bonds, which provide guaranteed interest income. Next, they're financing America's trade imbalance, thereby diminishing political pressure for trade restrictions from Washington.

Adequate financing also keeps interest rates low, which encourages consumer spending. Thus, foreign nations have been loaning the U.S. government money to ensure a favorable credit and interest rate environment to promote spending on imports. The resulting trade surpluses registered by China have been used to build its modern infrastructure. When the Summer Olympics is aired in 2008, Americans will see how they've helped transform China into a powerful modern economy that could further the decline in U.S. living standards.

Whether Washington can change this trend of record deficits or not will depend upon how much it pressures China to properly value its currency, and how much it's willing to cut spending. Washington realizes the price of deficit reduction will expose the inherent weakness of the economy because consumers are not strong enough to stand on their own without credit spending and inexpensive goods from abroad.

Washington also understands that securing access to Iraq's vast oil reserves offers a longer-term solution to America's economic fate. This endeavor alone will serve to keep the annual deficit high for many years to come, even though expenditures for Iraq are often treated as off-balance items, and thus hidden from the president's annual budget report.

Fueling China's Economy

Even a proper valuation of the Yuan will not resurrect the 3 million manufacturing jobs lost in America since 2000 as a result of China's unfair trade practices. *For every $1 of American goods sold to China in 2005, China sold $6 in goods to America.* More important, virtually none of the imports bought by U.S. consumers was absolutely needed, but only provided a lower price alternative, which stimulated consumer "bargain" spending.

What this spending did however, was create the illusion of strong GDP growth. In order to buy these inexpensive goods, many consumers maxed out their credit cards or took out home equity loans in the midst of the biggest real estate bubble in history. But GDP numbers aren't adjusted for credit spending (more on this in Chapter Eleven).

In contrast, *most U.S. exports into China consist of agriculture and natural resources; all vital ingredients for its economic revolution.* Americans continue to consume more than they produce while China keeps producing goods to feed the appetite of credit-addicted Americans. Meanwhile, China is reinvesting the U.S. portion of its trade surplus into its infrastructure, getting stronger each day, as America's competitiveness and standard of living weakens.

Bush's massive spending for Iraq and Katrina also helped GDP figures. The Federal Reserve has confessed that *as much as 40 percent of GDP growth during 2004 to 2005 has been attributable to the cash supplied by home equity loans.* Is GDP data valid if it occurred primarily by consumer credit and government spending for programs that have not improved American lifestyles? Definitely not. America's deficit has grown over the past several years while Asia and oil-exporting nations have registered annual surpluses. This trend highlights America's dependence on foreign nations.

Off-Balance Financing

In order to assess the extent of Washington's financial mismanagement, we need to consider the amount of funds classified as off-budget (off-balance) because this accounting trick is used to minimize annual deficit numbers. By allocating a large amount of expenditures to the off-budget category, the deficit will appear smaller to taxpayers, who might otherwise criticize the President's spending habits. In early 2005, you might recall President Bush approved another $82 billion off-budget for defense spending, primarily earmarked for Iraq and Afghanistan. These off-balance items don't show up when the Congressional Budget Office (CBO) releases budget data. Meanwhile, Social Security and U.S. Postal Service trust funds are considered off-balance items as standard treatment. But there are many other programs in this category, all referred to as "special items."

Furthermore, unlike public companies that are required to report liabilities in a financially responsible manner, *the U.S. government is not legally obligated to report the future value of annual liabilities generated by the annual deficit.* The CBO merely records the amount overspent each year without accounting for the expected appreciation on the debt that will accrue over the life of these loans (known as the interest expense).

For instance, over the course of 10 years, a budget deficit of say $800 billion (which is funded by selling 10-year treasury notes paying around 4.5 percent) will incur a total cost of borrowing of around $650 billion. When the same amount is funded over a 30-year period at 6 percent, the cost of borrowing (or interest expense) increases to over $2 trillion. That's $2 trillion owed in addition to the original $800 billion loan. *But these future liabilities are not reported.* This helps minimize the full magnitude of annual deficits.

As you can see from figure 6-1, the Clinton years were mainly on-budget, while the Reagan and Bush years showed large off-budget expenditures. Of course, the annual deficit disappears each year since it is transferred to the national debt. Current trends show increasing levels of both off-budget financing and annual deficits. Any improvements in the deficit and total debt will be a matter of subjective debate, since they would most likely involve cuts to critical domestic programs.

Mandatory Spending

Over the past few decades, the percentage of mandatory spending from the annual budget has increased dramatically. Mandatory spending encompasses all programs the government has promised, such as Social Security, Medicaid, and Medicare, as well as debt service payments on U.S. Treasury securities. *These spending hikes reflect the growing income gap between the rich and the poor.*

Figure 6-1. Budget Surplus/Deficit as a Share of GDP (1962-2004)

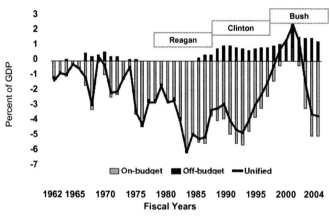

Source: Office of Management and Budget and Congressional Budget Office

As America's baby boomers reach retirement age, mandatory expenditures are going to balloon, leaving less for discretionary spending. By 2010, the percentage of American workers versus retirees will still be relatively high. By 2020, this ratio will have declined significantly due to the retirement of up to half of America's 76 million boomers. Not only will lower tax revenues from tapped out boomers drive the debt-to-GDP ratio higher, but the rapidly growing costs of Medicare, Medicaid, and Social Security benefits is going to overwhelm the U.S. budget for many years to come.

According to estimates by the budget administration, assuming all Social Security benefits are paid, and Medicaid and Medicare expenses grow by rates that are lower than current (which is remarkably conservative), *by 2050 the federal debt will be nearly 450 percent of the GDP without any tax increases. This debt ratio would place the U.S. in the same financial position as Venezuela, with over 21 percent of GDP going just to pay interest on the debt.* Currently, that figure stands at around 1.7 percent of GDP for interest-only payments.

Federal Debt

As the deficit continues to increase, it will be added to the nation's debt, which could easily surpass 100 percent of GDP over the next 5 years. Since deficits add to the total debt, we must view the federal debt as the real problem. Unfortunately, the nation's debt is certain to continue its ramped growth over the next several years, even in the midst of expected tax hikes and benefit cuts.

Thus far in America, the new millennium has been marked by record spending in defense and special situations, such as hurricane Katrina relief, three ineffective tax cuts (2001, 2002 and 2003), Part D Medicare, and the wars in Iraq and Afghanistan. Funding for these programs has come from borrowed money. This has resulted in an increase in the interest paid (at 1.7 percent of GDP) on the national debt (over 70 percent of the GDP).

As we have seen, the national debt grows each year there is an annual deficit. But even when budget surpluses are reported, off-balance items can actually cause the debt to rise. Debt also grows when the nation's budget is over-expensed, which can occur if tax revenues do not meet expectations. The problem with holding debt is familiar to most consumers who have run up large credit card bills. While access to credit can provide a "borrowed" improvement in living conditions, all debts must eventually be paid. And those who mismanage debt often end up in bankruptcy court.

Dependence on Foreign Debt

A high debt burden financed by foreign nations destroys U.S. sovereignty because its economy becomes dependent on the actions and political motives of foreign governments, much like its foreign dependency on oil. *How can America claim to be the world superpower when it is the world's largest debtor?* No person or nation can ever be truly "free" if they are a debtor, since creditors by definition have a legal claim on assets of the debtor.

For 2005 alone, $352 billion of American taxpayer money was spent just to make interest payments to holders of U.S. Treasury securities. During that same year, NASA only received $15 billion, the NIH $28 billion, the Department of Education $61 billion, and the Department of Transportation $133 billion. Clearly, the interest expense is already damaging federal funding for critical programs. For 2006, federal funding of many of America's most vital programs failed to keep up with inflation. Notably, for the first time in over two decades, NIH funding rose by only 0.5 percent in 2006.

The interest on the federal debt for 2006 was $405.9 billion and is now growing four times faster than the economy. For 2007, the interest expense on the debt is expected to reach nearly $0.5 trillion. As interest payments on America's growing national debt increase, critical domestic programs will continue to face budget cuts. As the boomers begin to qualify for Social Security and Medicare, the annual deficit and resulting national debt will soar even with major benefit cuts.

Currently, U.S. national debt held by foreign nations is just over 50 percent of total outstanding, prompting the question of who really owns America. While these debt levels have occurred in the past with no severe long-term consequences, this time things are much different. *U.S. national debt as a percentage of GDP has already surpassed 70 percent. But if one counts the total debt, (consumer, mortgage and national debt) this number is 350 percent, due to a total debt burden of around $50 trillion.* Recall as well, the liabilities needed to fund the nation's mandatory payments over the life span of the boomers, at some $51 to $72 trillion. Together, these liabilities position the U.S. in a state of insolvency unless fiscal policies are radically revised.

As China moves towards a more diverse economy, it will gradually wean itself off dependence of the U.S. consumer. When this happens, it will have no further need to finance the poor spending practices of the U.S. government. *As well, with the weakness of the dollar expected to continue, foreign governments may soon lose interest in buying U.S. Treasuries, especially if interest rates do not rise and remain high enough to compensate for the dollar's weakness.*

Finally, it is entirely possible that we could witness a global shift from a dollar-denominated world economy to a more widespread acceptance of the Euro, or in the very least a flight to gold bullion by

Asian nations looking to hedge against the fall of the dollar. For the present, it's still in the best interest of nations to continue loaning the U.S. government money. But at some point, there will be diminishing returns for foreign holders of U.S. Treasuries. Such a time might occur when consumers taper off spending and the dollar fails to rebound. This could trigger the beginning stages of a major economic disaster.

Consumer Debt

Similar to the U.S. government, consumers have embraced the "buy now, pay later" mentality. Since the onset of the most recent recession (March 2001), consumers have been utilizing inexpensive credit provided by the Fed. It's been a boom in credit spending unlike anything ever seen by anyone in America. Over the same period, real improvements in job quality and wage growth have been difficult to spot unless you live in India or China. This credit bubble has been forming for over two decades as a way for the bottom 80 percent of Americans to maintain their living standards amidst sparse real wage gains and skyrocketing costs of healthcare and higher education.

Americans don't realize the full ramifications of credit spending. They want someone to look after their pets each day, take care of their lawns, and park their cars. But most consumers who pay for these services cannot afford them, and are using this time for leisure. As a result, Americans now have dangerous levels of consumer debt. Sooner or later, overconsumption will catch up with America. It's basic arithmetic; you cannot consume more than you produce over an extended period. Eventually the interest payments alone will lead to insolvency.

Massive debt in itself will not be sufficient to cause a depression. But once extremes in this cycle have been reached, it won't take much to push things over the edge. Rather than definitive evidence of a future depression, America's record debt is but only one manifestation of the difficulties that have been growing for three decades. Similar to a company burdened with huge amounts of outstanding debt, Americans have traded their nation's assets for credit issued by foreigners.

Dollar

During the economic boom of the '90s, the trade deficit averaged about 1.1 percent of GDP. Today we see a different picture, with a *trade deficit at around 6 percent of GDP*. It is commonly accepted that when the trade deficit extends above 5 percent, the chances of major economic consequences become very high, namely a revaluation of the dollar. There is no way the dollar can mount any type of recovery at these debt levels. As U.S. debt continues its rapid growth, the dollar will continue to weaken along with the economy. Even massive benefit cuts from government entitlement programs will not reverse this trend, but would further harm consumers.

The White House would like to strengthen the dollar. But it's more concerned with keeping consumer spending strong. If Washington is successful in pressuring China to properly value its currency by at least 30 percent above present levels, this will increase the price of Chinese imports and slow down consumer spending. Slower spending would put downward pressure on short-term interest rates, increasing inflationary pressures. As well, it would expand the credit bubble even further. Any severe shocks to the economy might also cause the Fed to lower rates. Regardless of the source, lower rates would discourage foreign investment in U.S. bonds. If that were to occur, interest rates would begin a strong upward trend while the dollar sinks lower.

If on the other hand China does not value its currency appropriately and in a timely manner, the U.S. might impose tariffs on imports, which would also diminish consumer spending. But in order to impose tariffs, Washington would have to go through the WTO. This would be a difficult process. Even if successful, it would most likely cause China to buy less U.S. bonds, or at least threaten to do so. This too would cause interest rates to trend upwards, which would freeze consumer spending and weaken the dollar. Hopefully, by now you are beginning to appreciate the kind of economic mess Greenspan created.

7

HEALTHCARE

Corrupt politicians and corporate greed have reaped financial rewards from America's bubble economy at the expense of impoverished and working-class Americans. With good reason, most have lost all hope of achieving the American Dream. Underlying the complexity of America's economic decline is its flawed so-called "free-market" healthcare system. In addition to the inadequacy and ineffectiveness of this program, health coverage is strongly linked to full-time employment. Uncontrolled healthcare costs combined with free trade dynamics have forced millions of jobs overseas, while denying affordable access to those in need of adequate medical care. As a result, millions have low morale, while many others worry more about the threat of medical bills than the consequences of ill health.

Healthcare is absolutely the single biggest problem facing America today. In short, the high cost of healthcare is destroying the finances of consumers and employers alike, while compromising the health of millions. Even those with insurance are worried they'll be denied coverage due to exclusions or lifetime caps on benefits. The broad-reaching affects of America's healthcare crisis continues to damage the nation's economic outlook while select industries profit.

Employers are struggling to contain employee benefits as they battle with foreign competition. Meanwhile, healthcare costs continue to grow at three times the inflation rate and twice the rate of the economy. This has forced companies to drop coverage, shift more out-of-pocket expenses to employees, or outsource work to contractors, both domestically and overseas. As long as the United States remains without a single-payer national healthcare system, the vast majority of Americans will continue to experience declining living standards. Meanwhile, workers from developing nations stand to benefit from being added to the payrolls of America's biggest and best companies, while enjoying the security of a government-sponsored healthcare system that provides coverage for all.

Ridiculous costs and inadequate coverage for millions add more doubt to America's problematic economy, while HMOs and drug companies rake in huge profits. In 2004, the largest HMOs brought in over $100 billion in revenues, up by over 33 percent from the previous year. The pharmaceutical industry has an even longer and more robust string of profits. Even though it spends more on this vital service than any nation in the world on a per-capita, GDP and total dollar basis, the quality of America's healthcare is rather low.

All nations in Europe and Asia (as well as most of the world) have a system of universal healthcare paid for by the government. Foreign consumers have complete access to healthcare, regardless of age, income or employment status. This has registered positive economic advantages for both consumers and companies of these nations. Furthermore, within these universal programs, one finds evidence of virtually no fraud, and much less waste due to the absence of middlemen such as insurance companies, pharmacy benefit managers, and for-profit hospital management organizations—all prime players in the profiteering of America's healthcare system. Finally, all other nations of the world have price limits on prescription drugs.

Soaring premiums create enormous future liabilities for U.S. companies that offer insurance to workers. This leads to earnings uncertainty. As a result, foreign corporations are more competitive than their U.S. counterparts. This disparity in socioeconomic policy has allowed foreign nations to induce downward pricing pressures resulting in the destruction of numerous U.S. industries.

It appears as if *the free trade agreements enacted by Washington are in direct opposition to the current free-market healthcare system.* America's competitive decline is a direct result of this oversight. As a consequence, the absence of universal coverage has indirectly accounted for the growing trade imbalance and exportation of several industries, all of which have combined to heighten America's economic and job instability.

Healthcare Crisis

The United States has one of the most technologically advanced healthcare systems in the world. But the World Health Organization *ranks America's healthcare 37th among developed nations*. Despite criticisms of universal care enjoyed by other nations, you would be hard-pressed to find many Canadians or Europeans willing to trade their healthcare system for America's. For many Americans, adequate healthcare is an expensive luxury. How can America remain as the only nation that does not consider healthcare an absolute necessity available to everyone, regardless of income, employment status, age, race, or pre-existing conditions?

Many advocates of the current system insist that Americans have benefited from longer life spans over the years. Notably, the drug industry has used this argument to fight against price controls. However, *all developed nations are experiencing increased life spans primarily due to better sanitary conditions, better infant mortality rates, and wider availability of core medications, such as antibiotics and vaccines.* Yet, these critical medications make up only a very small part of total annual drug sales. In fact, most of the real breakthrough drugs were created many years ago. Today, drug companies focus their resources on producing "me-too" and lifestyle-enhancing drugs because this is the surest route to higher profits.

The United States spends far more on healthcare per person than any other nation in the world, and nearly 50 percent more than the number two spender, Switzerland. Yet, the quality is relatively low, as are the average life spans of Americans. *In 2006, America spent over $2.2 trillion on healthcare, or about 17 percent of the GDP. Yet, over 47 million or about 16 percent were uninsured* (other sources state this figure to now be near 18 percent). Ironically, America is the only nation in the OECD that does not have a national healthcare program.

In contrast, *Japanese citizens have the highest life expectancy, with total healthcare expenditures amounting to only 8 percent of GDP.* Finally, South Korean nationals have the same life expectancy as Americans, but the Korean government only spends about one-third

(5.6 percent of GDP) of the amount spent in America on healthcare. In fact, *the U.S. government spends about the same amount on its public healthcare system (5.0 percent of GDP, not counting tax deduction expenses) as S. Korea, but only provides partial health insurance for about 80 million (27 percent of the population), while S. Korea provides full healthcare for all of its citizens.*

Figure 7-1. Healthcare Expenditures as a Percentage of GDP and Life Expectancy (2003)

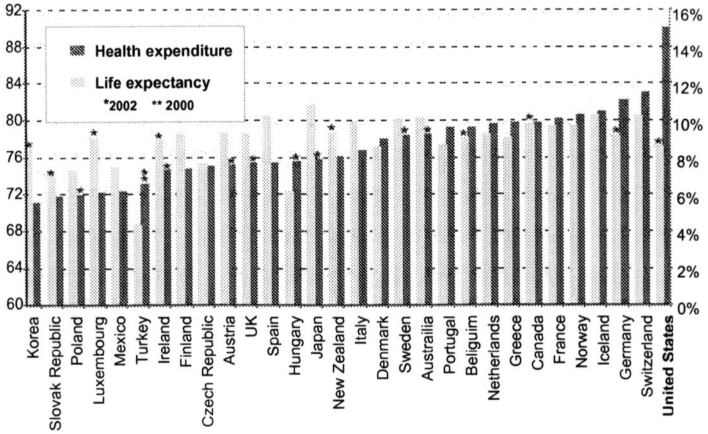

Source: OECD in Figures 2005; or see StatLink: http://dx.doi.org/10.1787/132836124886

For those in the U.S. with access to medical services, studies show that many receive more or less care than they need. As well, preventable and harmful errors are a regular occurrence. Millions are injured and tens of thousands die unnecessarily each year because of treatment errors. According to research presented in JAMA by Dr. Barbara Stanfield, *physicians are now the number three cause of death in America, with more than 300,000 annual fatalities due to medical errors.* Other experts argue these estimates are conservative.

But physicians aren't the real source of America's number one cause of preventable deaths. The main reason for medical errors is due to poor management by HMOs, whose only focus is on profits. *Quality care often takes a back seat to profits because America's free-market healthcare system has very little competition.* The division of labor approach to healthcare was created by HMOs as an attempt to make healthcare delivery more efficient. But it's been short of a disaster. In addition to a physician and nurse, hospitalized patients can be treated by ten or more secondary providers, including a nurse's assistant, physician's assistant, surgical assistant, radiology tech, cardio tech, ultrasound tech, pharmacy tech, etc. This fragmented approach combined with inadequate training of many lower level medical occupations has contributed to the explosion of medical errors, causing unnecessary mortality and morbidity.

It's critical for the primary physician to be intimately involved with the patient from start to finish. Yet, HMOs don't allow this. Instead of proper exams and referrals to specialists, managed care organizations have pressured physicians to cut costs by encouraging them to practice a pill-pushing approach and limiting them to 15 minutes per patient visit.

Healthcare shouldn't be treated like a manufacturing assembly line designed as a profit center. *When profits serve as the primary driving force behind healthcare, quality is sacrificed because caregivers are transformed into entrepreneurs who determine the final delivery of resources since patients aren't capable of evaluating all options.* This is precisely why U.S. healthcare is not operating under free-market dynamics; demand is not controlled by consumers.

The full extent of America's healthcare crisis is further revealed when noting the lack of full and adequate coverage. *Over 82 million Americans went without health insurance for at least part of 2003, while another 70 million were underinsured.* Combined with close to 50 million without any coverage, in any given year, nearly 200 million Americans are exposed to inadequate or absent coverage. In 2003, guess what country had 11.4 percent or 8.4 million children without access to healthcare. That's right; America. *All other developed nations have universal healthcare, with lower costs and still rank higher than America in total quality and accessibility of care.*

Why can't the "strongest, most powerful nation in the world" provide coverage for all of its citizens? Of course it can. Washington simply won't allow it because the industries profiting from the healthcare gravy train have the largest, strongest and wealthiest lobbyist groups sitting at the steps of Capitol Hill, ensuring things stay the way they are. No politician wants to acknowledge that the healthcare crisis is sending good jobs overseas and decreasing net wages because they fear backlash from healthcare lobbyists, as well as millions of voters linked to this industry. Most Washington officials care little about the people they were elected to serve. They only care about reelection. And being added to lobbyists' most favored lists is the best way to ensure a long tenure on Capitol Hill.

Despite the strong link between healthcare and employment, loss of coverage can occur by ways other than losing a job. Life events such as divorce, chronic illness, pre-existing medical conditions, and even a felony conviction (due to the inability to find reasonable employment) can leave one without health insurance. I find it amazing that most Americans lack adequate coverage, but prison inmates have full access to medical services. Employment is also linked to one's credit history. So if you have bad credit you could be denied access to the most affordable healthcare conduit in the U.S.—full-time employment.

Healthcare Costs

Healthcare costs are rising at double-digit rates and increasing their share of the economy without commensurate increases in quality of life. Across the board, while quality is increasing at 2.8 percent annually, costs are increasing at a rate of 8 percent. In *1960, America only spent 5.1 percent of GDP on healthcare. During that period, HMOs didn't exist.* Government estimates indicate that by 2014, total healthcare costs will reach 20 percent of GDP. I expect this number to be reached by 2011 without drastic changes.

For several years now, Europe has been spending only about one-half as much as the U.S. relative to GDP, but has delivered more effective healthcare with fewer medical errors, virtually no fraud and very little waste. Europeans also have longer life spans and everyone is guaranteed coverage. How can America spend far more on healthcare than any other nation in the world, yet the number of uninsured is so high, while quality and access is relatively poor? Where is this money going?

Health Insurance Costs

Over the past few years, health insurance costs have increased by several hundred percent over wages, resulting in a hidden source of inflation no one in Washington mentions. Even more troubling is the fact that insurance premiums are now growing faster than healthcare expenses. In 2004, employer health insurance premiums increased by 11.2 percent, representing a growth of 400 percent over inflation.

Many experts agree that the high cost of employer-sponsored health insurance is undermining the competitiveness of the U.S. economy and eliminating good jobs. The Kaiser Family Foundation and the Health Research and Educational Trust report that premiums for employer-sponsored health insurance in the United States have been rising by an average of five times higher than median wages since 2000. And because companies are struggling to compete globally, they have shifted most of the increases to workers. As a result, the employee portion of premiums increased by 126 percent between 2000 and 2004.

But employers have been decreasing healthcare benefits to employees for nearly two decades to lighten the burden of higher premiums. Some have dropped coverage altogether. Overall, the percentage of employees covered by insurance at work has declined from 75.5 percent in 1987 to 68.6 percent in 2003. Today, *30 to 40 percent of employers offer no insurance at all.* Finally, the number of companies with 200 or more employees offering health insurance has decreased by 50 percent since 1988.

In 2004, the annual premium charged to employers for a plan covering a family of four averaged $9,950, or $829 per month; workers contributed $2,661, or 10 percent more than they spent in 2003. For single coverage, workers contributed an average of $558 towards the $3,695 annual premium. Health insurance premiums are expected to rise to an average of more than $15,000 for family coverage in 2007, representing an increase of 80 percent since 2001.

The average benefits package for the average full-time worker in America can amount to about 42 percent of the total compensation package, with as much as 75 percent of this being due to healthcare benefits. Therefore, it's not difficult to see how U.S. corporations are struggling to compete with foreign peers who do not bear the burden of healthcare costs (see figure 9-4).

It has been said by many figureheads in Washington that small businesses represent the driving force behind the U.S. economy. Today, more than 25 million Americans own a small business. But since small businesses and the self-employed aren't able to purchase insurance as cheaply as large corporations, rising healthcare costs make it increasingly difficult to afford basic coverage for their employees and families. As a result, *workers in small companies are three times more likely to be uninsured as workers in large companies.*

As money continues to be pumped into healthcare, tens of thousands of distraught workers are switching careers, opting for high-paying, low-skill medical service jobs. It's no wonder why so many are headed for the healthcare industry. With no price controls and record spending, a career in healthcare can provide a nice life, often with minimal training. According to the BLS, wage and salary employment in the healthcare industry is projected to increase by 27 percent through 2014, compared to 14 percent for all industries combined. Overall, healthcare employment growth is expected to account for 3.6 million new jobs—19 percent of all wage and salary jobs added to the economy over the 2004 to 2014 period.

Why Are Costs So High?

Certainly, skyrocketing premiums have pushed more Americans out of the healthcare loop. But historically, the fastest growing component of healthcare costs has been due to increases in prescription drug prices. As a way to deliver earnings growth, pharmaceutical companies have focused on two strategies. First, the big drug makers now market many of their drugs to enhance one's lifestyle. First there was Rogaine, then Prozac, Viagra, and a host of others. The success of lifestyle-enhancing drugs has grown due to manipulative marketing campaigns from drug producers.

Rather than promote anti-psychotics for severe debilitating disorders, drug companies have marketed their use for typical "down" periods that are normal in one's life. According to them, no one should ever feel down (depressed) because they have great treatments for you. The fact is that transient depression is normal. And until it becomes chronically debilitating, it cannot be diagnosed as depression. *But most physicians do not take the time to perform an adequate diagnosis of depression due to time and cost constraints mandated by HMOs.*

Recent studies from Columbia University now confirm what many drug critics have suspected for years—up to 25 percent of all Americans taking antidepressants have been misdiagnosed. In fact, many studies have linked the cause of depression to many commonly used antidepressants. Finally, numerous studies reveal increased suicidal effects of these drugs. But the drug industry has done much to trivialize this research and suppress it from the mainstream media.

Today, most patients come to physicians convinced of a depression diagnosis based upon television ads by drug makers. They even request the name of the drug they want (or feel they need). And physicians are ever so happy to provide them with their drug of choice. It makes their job a lot easier, and sends the patient home in no time so the physician can see more patients. This approach benefits HMOs, physicians and drug makers. That's why drug companies spend billions to make their products household names.

The second strategy used by drug makers is to focus on producing "me-too" drugs because it yields higher profits with less risk. You see, when a company develops a drug, a new market becomes established after it spends millions on ad campaigns. But other drug companies want in on this growing market. And it's relatively easy for alternative drugs to be made for this "disease." All that's needed is to design a different mechanism of action by studying the biochemical pathway of the drug. Before you know it, you see numerous "me-too" drugs in the marketplace.

Due to the corrupt ties between big pharma and the FDA, many of these "me-too" drugs are approved despite evidence of being less effective. In many cases, these copy-cats have more severe side effects. Evidence can be seen from a review of the medical literature. It's a waste of human and financial capital when you have too many of these copy-cats. But it becomes a tragedy when these drugs provide more health risks than benefits.

If the FDA was doing its job to protect consumers, hundreds of drugs would not be on the marketplace today. The most obvious examples of drugs with terrible risk-benefit ratios are birth control pills and patches, drugs for erectile dysfunction, and sleeping aids. What's the benefit in using a contraceptive drug that causes damage to the cardiovascular system? Should an elderly man be taking a drug that enhances his libido if it could potentially cause a heart attack?

As a result of manipulative marketing techniques and overuse, Americans consume over 3 billion prescriptions annually. In 2004 alone, they spent in excess of $200 billion on prescriptions drugs. Americans pay more for prescription drugs than any other nation even when the drugs are produced by U.S. companies because Washington permits it. In contrast, because other nations have government-sponsored healthcare, they've set limits to what drug companies can charge. Thus, *Americans are actually subsidizing the cost of prescription drugs for other nations since, it is the only nation with no drug price controls.*

In the early 1990s, drug spending kept pace with increases in other healthcare spending items. But ever since the mid-1990s (when the FDA started receiving all of its funding from big pharma), increases in drug spending rose by 200 to 500 percent greater than expenditures for hospital care and physician services. Prices have increased an average of 7.4 percent annually from 1993 to 2003.

Even after several product recalls, the pharmaceutical industry was *300 percent more profitable at 15.8 percent than the median of all Fortune 500 companies* at 5.2 percent (figure 7.2). Investors in the big name drug companies need not worry for long, as Part D Medicare promises to catapult the industry back into the top position over the next few years.

Figure 7-2.   Profitability Among Pharmaceutical Manufacturers

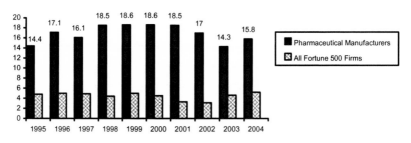

Source: Ibid, The Henry J. Kaiser Family Foundation

Uninsured in America

According to the U.S. Census Bureau, nearly 50 million (18 percent) Americans did not have health insurance in 2006. As well, estimates show that an additional 150 million Americans lost their insurance for part of the year or were underinsured. Surprisingly, *eighty percent of the uninsured are working or are in families with current workers.* Since healthcare in the U.S. is linked with employment, free trade promises to increase the uninsured rate in the coming years. Alternatively, most Americans will be underinsured without realizing it.

When you factor in public healthcare, America's uninsured rate is magnified, given that Medicare covers the disabled and elderly, while Medicaid covers many of the indigent. Since most elderly Americans qualify for Medicare, the percentage of uninsured Americans under age 65 stands at nearly 19 percent. Astonishingly, the *uninsured rate among seniors 65 and older is 17 percent, despite the estimated 80.2 million (2005) Americans who are considered insured by Medicare and Medicaid.* Most likely, America's total real uninsured rate is over 20 percent.

As the state of the crisis continues, it has shown no particular preference, touching the lives of Americans from all backgrounds, regardless of race, ethnicity, income, education, employment, and age. While more than 80 percent of the uninsured belong to working families, 66 percent come from low-income households. However, about *30 percent of the uninsured come from households with incomes exceeding $50,000. About 50 percent of the uninsured work at small businesses or are self-employed.*

For the most costly healthcare expenses, such as those incurred during chronic illnesses, many are uninsured as well. For instance, about 11 percent of cancer patients under the age of 65 are uninsured, as are up to 20 percent of minority cancer patients. Even those with full insurance might experience a rude awakening when seeking care for one or more chronic diseases, due to lifetime caps, limitless premium hikes, or being denied coverage upon changing of jobs due to preexisting conditions.

Most uninsured Americans are unable to pay for medical treatment, yet they do not qualify for Medicare or Medicaid. These unfortunate citizens are refused treatment by hospitals unless they are in the critical stages of illness. As it turns out, these are often the most costly of all healthcare expenses. Thus, *by denying Americans basic healthcare and preventative treatments, those without any form of insurance are actually placing a larger financial strain upon the system.*

To make matters worse, those without insurance are charged the most by hospitals. Does it make sense that those with the least ability to pay for a basic necessity like healthcare are the ones who are charged the highest prices? According to a state agency in Pennsylvania, *health insurers only pay only $0.38 for each dollar of healthcare used by its policy holders due to the large discounts offered by HMOs and PPOs to insurers.* The response from insurance and hospital spokespersons is that volume discounts are "the norm in any industry."

This illustrates the squandering of U.S. healthcare at its best. Make no mistake; I fully support the benefits of a free-market economy. It's what makes America great. However, the uniqueness of healthcare renders it incapable of achieving the supply-demand dynamics essential to operate effectively within a free-market system. As a result, it remains highly susceptible to fraud, waste and exploitation, causing lives to be lost for the benefit of profits.

Medicaid

In 1965, Congress created Medicaid for low-income and disabled Americans who were unable to afford health insurance. Over the past 40 years, Medicaid has provided healthcare for about one in six Americans. However, by the admission of the Department of Health and Human Services, "Medicaid does not provide medical assistance for all poor persons."

While each state varies in its Medicaid program, funds are provided by a 50-50 split between state and federal governments. Despite numerous holes in coverage, Medicaid has become the fastest growing expense for states, accounting for over 20 percent of state government spending. Overall, Medicaid costs command the number two spot after education. Even though most states are cutting benefits, by 2009 Medicaid will most likely take over the top spot of most budgets. Clearly, it has become the biggest challenge for state budgets across the nation.

Medicare

In 1965, Medicare was approved by Congress to provide medical insurance for the elderly. It was expanded in 1973 to cover some disabled Americans under age 65. Today, Medicare provides medical expenses for over 35 million elderly and 6 million disabled Americans.

To fund Medicare, each American worker pays 1.45 percent of wages, matched by the employer for a total of 2.9 percent. *Unlike the case with Social Security taxes, there is no cap on wage taxes for Medicare,* so each worker is taxed 1.45 percent on every dollar of earned income. Medicare has had about 3.3 workers paying taxes for every recipient for the past 30 years. However, baby boomer retirements will reduce that to 2 workers for each recipient by 2040.

In the 1930s, when Washington defined the retirement age at 65, most Americans didn't live that long. Since then, life expectancies for women have increased from 66 to 79, and for men from 61 to 77. Meanwhile, the birth rate has dropped from 25 per 1,000 residents in the 1950s to just 15 today. The lower birth rate means fewer workers are paying taxes to finance Social Security and Medicare benefits for the rapidly growing population aged 65 and over.

As Medicare recipients are growing older their lifetime healthcare costs are also rising. Much of this has to do with the surge in chronic diseases. As a result, annual medical costs for an 85-year-old are double those of a 65-year-old. And the costs for those 65 and older are four times more than that of a younger adult, and as much as seven times more than a child. Overall, up to 90 percent of lifetime healthcare costs occur for people 65 and over.

Medicare costs are also being strained by HMOs, which tend to recruit healthy members while using creative tactics to encourage sick patients to opt for Medicare. According to the CMS, in 2006 federal spending per Medicare recipient averaged about $7,500. By 2050, the CMS estimates that Medicare will be responsible for paying $26,683 per recipient (in 2004 dollars). It is highly likely that without any changes, these expenses will be reached much sooner. *Overall, the costs for Medicare and Medicaid are increasing by up to 6 times faster than Social Security.* This trend will continue to accelerate as the boomers get older, live longer and healthcare costs remain uncontrolled.

Figure 7-3. Projected Medicare Spending Per Person

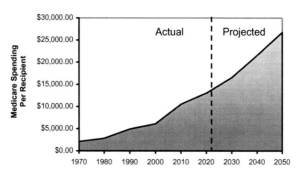

Sources: Health and Human Services Centers for Medicare and Medicaid Services

Bills for Your Grandchildren

Combined with inadequate planning, (boomer phenomenon and longer life spans) uncontrolled care costs will stifle public healthcare within the next decade if radical solutions are not found. According to the Urban Institute, a married couple entering their final year of work earning the median income of $46,400 will retire the following year with a joint Medicare benefit valued at $283,500 on a present value basis. Over this couple's life expectancy, this amount will of course be much higher.

Over the years in which this same couple had worked, they only contributed a total of $43,300 in Medicare taxes, for a deficit in Medicare of $240,200. With this example alone, it's easy to see how America's youth will be faced with the enormous burden of funding Medicare benefits for the boomers.

As we shall see in the next chapter, Social Security benefits of the boomer generation will add to the annual debt. For instance, this couple also qualifies for $22,900 in annual Social Security benefits. The present value of $22,900 is estimated at a lump-sum amount of about $326,000. But the total amount of Social Security taxes paid over the couple's lifetime was only $198,000, resulting in a deficit of $128,000 for Social Security. Therefore, the total loss to taxpayers for this couple's Medicare and Social Security benefits is $368,200.

But the children of today will be entitled to receive even higher benefits due to general inflation and healthcare inflation that affects Medicare benefits. When the children of this couple retire they will receive total benefits that are 45 percent higher than their parents, or $884,000 versus $609,500 (present value).

Conclusions

Until America's healthcare system is fixed, the majority will remain without affordable, continuous and complete access to healthcare. Job benefits will suffer and continue to decrease net wage growth. More U.S. companies will relocate overseas. And the financial security of Americans, especially in their Golden Years will remain questionable. The only reasonable solution is to create a national healthcare plan structured within a single-payer system. All other alternatives will be inadequate. Only then will America be prepared to compete globally.

Removing the healthcare middlemen alone would save hundreds of billions annually. A single-payer system would save billions more due to administrative cost savings. The public healthcare system has an administrative overhead that is up to 70 percent less than that found in the private system (on a per-dollar basis). Disintegration of unrestricted price hikes by drug companies would make healthcare costs even more affordable.

Some Americans haven't had the time or money to wait for needed changes to the system. With no other choices, the less fortunate have been forced into bankruptcy due to medical bills they cannot pay. Others have gone overseas to have procedures performed at huge discounts. India, Singapore, and South America are among the hottest spots for healthcare outsourcing, saving them up to 80 percent of the costs charged at home. Many of these hospitals have been specifically built to profit from the effects of America's healthcare crisis.

But don't think these foreign hospitals are in some way deficient. The physicians found in these healthcare outsourcing centers are just as good as those in the U.S. In fact, many of the hospitals resemble 5-star hotels equipped with a full array of high-tech medical facilities and the latest therapeutic devices. What's left for America when its citizens have to travel abroad for affordable healthcare?

No nation can claim to be great when one-fifth of its population is without access to healthcare. With a badly damaged economic scaffold, America must construct a new foundation if it intends to remain the world superpower. And healthcare will be the primary component of this foundation. This transition will consume many years and require numerous hardships, but if initiated now, it will be less painful to current and future generations.

8

SOCIAL SECURITY DEBACLE

Perhaps the greatest achievement in U.S. domestic policy has been the formation of a social insurance system that provides a core income and healthcare benefit base to less fortunate individuals. This entire system consists of Social Security, Medicare, Medicaid, Workers' Compensation, and Unemployment Insurance.

Among these programs, Social Security has been the most successful. In addition to providing a needs-based subsidy, it's a true entitlement program, since people earn the right to participate by contributing payroll taxes to the fund. As it stands today, Social Security remains as America's only social insurance program providing a basic level of income to prevent poverty, while allocating benefits (although reduced) to higher-income retirees who have paid into the system. Because of its uniqueness, Social Security has provided for the well-being of millions during good times and bad, and has no private market comparable. Thus, its preservation is critical.

When FDR signed the Social Security Act (SSA) in 1935, the Great Depression had taken its toll on the nation. Millions were unemployed, had no savings, and risked losing their homes. At the time of inception, payroll taxes used to finance Social Security were only 1.0 percent each from employers and workers, capped on the first $3000 of annual earnings. Yet, even before the first benefit was paid, payroll taxes were doubled to 2.0 percent in 1938. By 1989, taxes had increased to 12.4 percent, where they have held constant to this day. This represents a tax increase of over 600 percent in just over five decades. But benefits don't provide the same level of buying power as they once did. During this fifty-year period of Social Security tax hikes, corporate taxes have declined, serving to spotlight the rising power of corporate America over this nation amidst a declining middle class.

In 2007, the Social Security program covered 53 million Americans, mostly retired workers. But it also provided benefits to widows and widowers, those with one of more disabilities, and severely disabled adult children of deceased, retired, or disabled workers. In total, about 1 in 6 Americans, or 1 in every 4 households receive Social Security benefits each year.

Cost-of-Living Adjustments

In 1972, President Nixon signed into law a 20 percent cost-of-living adjustment (COLA) to combat the effects of inflation. However, since the late '70s, Social Security benefits have failed to keep pace with inflation. During the inflation crisis of the late '70s and early '80s, benefit growth was decreased due to economic conditions and fears of insolvency for future beneficiaries. Consequently, in 1983 a cost-of-living adjustment (COLA) was delayed, up to half of the benefits became taxable, and payroll taxes were increased.

During the same year of his COLA delay, President Reagan added a gradual increase in retirement age to be phased in at 67 for those born in 1960 and thereafter. While the original early retirement remained at age 62, benefits for those born in or after 1960 were reduced from 80 to 70 percent. And those opting for the new early retirement age of 65 would only receive 86.7 percent of full benefits.

Thus, while the Reagan administration was successful in curbing double-digit inflation, appropriate adjustments for Social Security were never made due to massive expenditures for the Cold War arms buildup. Today we see the effects of benefits that have much less buying power. In 2007, the maximum Social Security benefit for a single person age 65 was $25,392, representing about 25 percent replacement of average wages.

This gradual loss in wage replacement has been magnified by a heightened dependency on Social Security due to losses in the stock market, poor savings rates, and declining living standards. As a result of these trends, most Americans opt for early Social Security retirement, decreasing their annual benefit amount, despite the fact that life expectancies continue to increase.

Eligibility

To fund Social Security, eligible workers pay 6.2 percent of their annual earnings up to a maximum of $97,500 (2007). This is part of the payroll tax known as FICA (Federal Insurance Contribution Act). The other half of this tax is paid by the employer, resulting in a total tax of 12.4 percent.

Elderly Americans born before 1960 qualify for full retirement benefits at age 65, or partial benefits at age 62 for early retirement. In order to qualify for retirement income, a typical worker must have earned 40 Social Security credits. This means they must have worked 40 quarters (10 years) in a job that was covered by Social Security (i.e. one where payroll taxes were paid). Some disabled Americans or minors who have lost a parent may also qualify for benefits with no age requirements.

Current Status

For several years workers have been paying more into Social Security than has been paid out in benefits. This has generated annual trust fund surpluses. Because Social Security was designed as a pay-as-you-go plan, annual deficits and surpluses were to be expected due to changing demographics.

Regardless, it is the deficit expected in 2017 which has caused many to be alarmed. But it's really not a reason for concern since the annual surpluses throughout the years have accumulated into a large fund of several trillion dollars. This surplus fund has been invested in interest-bearing U.S. Treasury securities ("special interest") that will fund annual deficits for several years.

To date, these securities have yielded an average annual return of 6.0 percent which has been added to this special account. The interest income alone from this multi-trillion dollar surplus fund will be sufficient to pay benefits for several years. Thereafter, the fund will be gradually liquidated to pay benefits. Consequently, the surplus fund will have been exhausted by 2040, leaving current payroll tax revenues as the only source of funds for beneficiaries.

At the end of 2006, estimates by the Trustees report showed trust fund reserves (surplus fund) at about $2.035 trillion. This amount is expected to grow even larger since annual surpluses will continue over the next ten years (although declining each year). Together with accruing interest, the surplus fund is expected to generate a total reserve base of $4.186 trillion by 2015. By 2016, Social Security inflows and outflows will break even.

Beginning in 2017, the tax revenues flowing into the fund will be less than the total benefits flowing out, creating an annual deficit. This deficit will grow larger each year as more boomers reach retirement age, stacked against fewer workers paying into the trust. Therefore, this $4.186 trillion surplus fund will be used to make up for annual deficits beginning in 2017. This fund will be sufficient to pay for these deficits through 2040. By 2040, the surplus fund will be empty, leaving Social Security to rely only on current payroll taxes. After 2040, the incoming payroll taxes will fund about 73 percent of the benefits needed. The Congressional Budget Office has estimated that the surplus fund will be able to pay full benefits until 2052, while payroll taxes will provide for about 80 percent of benefits thereafter.

The Real Problem

Since inception, Social Security has helped millions avoid poverty, as defined by the U.S. government. But as we have seen, the government's definition of poverty is in need of updating. Current criteria are simply too low and have not kept up with inflation of basic necessities such as energy and healthcare. Therefore, *it is the buying power of Social Security that is of most concern.* If Washington used proper variables to calculate cost-of-living expenses needed by seniors it would overweigh inflation due to healthcare and would count food and energy, rather than merely indexing annual adjustments to wage inflation.

The increased reliance on Social Security for retirement income highlights the weakening financial position of the average American, who has fallen victim to a nation in decline. This has been reflected by low household savings rates, high debt, low retirement savings, and an overpriced and inadequate healthcare system.

Even prior to the entry of America's baby boomers into the system, *Social Security already accounts for nearly three-quarters of the income of middle-income Americans aged 65 and older.* As well, it accounts for nearly one-half of the wealth of the middle 10 percent of Americans aged 55 to 64 (table 8-1). Almost 66 percent of Americans over 65 receive half or more of their income, and 20 to 30 percent receive all of their income from Social Security. People from all around the world view America as the wealthiest nation. They'd be shocked to learn that most of its elderly rely on Social Security as their primary source of income. These trends will strengthen as the boomers enter retirement, most with very little savings.

During a period when energy and healthcare costs are at record highs and expected to continue their ascent, Social Security will increase its importance as a security blanket against poverty. Unless adequate COLA adjustments are made, the only thing that will prevent the majority of boomers from slipping into impoverished conditions might only be the government's outdated definition of poverty.

Figure 8-1. Non-Earned Retirement Income of Those 65 and Older by Source, Middle Income Quintile (2004)

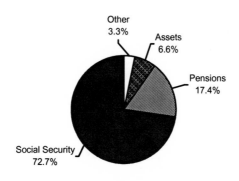

Source: Munnell, Alicia and Sunden, Annika "401(k) Plans are Still Coming Up Short. Figure 2. CRR Number 43   March 2006. Calculations based on *Current Population Survey*.

Table 8-1. Wealth Holdings of a Typical Household Prior to Retirement

Source of Wealth	Amount	% of Total
Primary House	$125,208	21
Business Assets	$10,370	2
Financial Assets	$42,014	7
Defined Contribution	$45,244	8
Defined Benefit	$96,705	16
Social Security	$251,983	42
Other Nonfinancial Assets	$26,402	4

Note: The "typical household approaching retirement" refers to the mean of the middle 10 percent of the sample of households headed by an individual aged 55-64. 2004 data

Source: Ibid. Table 1.

Bush's Solution

In 2001, President Bush appointed a group to study the merits of a voluntary program by which *individuals under the age of 55 would have the option of investing 2 to 4 of the 6.2 percentage points of their Social Security payroll taxes into personal accounts.* This portion would be invested in a conservative group of investment products, such as stock and bond index funds. These funds are expected to have a higher long-term appreciation potential than annual COLAs. This is the basis of the privatization plan that would transform Social Security into an investment account rather than the security blanket it was intended to serve.

Consequences of Privatization

One of the main flaws with privatization is that is does nothing to address the solvency problem since it does not call for any contributions to be made into the trust. As a matter of fact, it actually makes the trust fund less solvent at an earlier period since the money needed to fund private accounts will come from trust reserves (the surplus fund). Additional consequences of privatization are an increase in the national debt, a decrease in the amount of guaranteed benefits, and a decrease in benefits for certain groups.

More Rapid Insolvency

The formation of private accounts would not change the amount of revenue entering the Social Security Trust Fund. Therefore, it would *not resolve the insolvency issue* that Bush has claimed is of most concern. Rather, *privatization would actually increase government spending* since the federal government would need to immediately begin funding private accounts and continue funding them annually.

Decreased Guaranteed Benefits

The President's plan is expected to decrease guaranteed benefits by as much as 60 percent. *Even those who do not choose to participate in private accounts will see a major benefit reduction.* Thus, privatization transforms the social insurance component of Social Security into an investment account that *rewards high-wage earners with uninterrupted work histories.* We already have several retirement-based investment accounts available to workers that work in this manner.

Increased Federal Debt

Funding private accounts would increase federal spending, leading to higher annual deficits. Transitioning those currently in the Social Security program into private accounts would require that a portion of earned benefits be paid to all participants immediately rather than waiting for each individual to retire. Thus, the increased borrowing needed to fund these accounts would increase both the national debt and the cost of interest payments on the debt. Specifically, *Bush's plan would create $17.7 trillion in additional debt by 2050, representing a 19.3 percent increase relative to GDP.* As a result, privatization would require Americans to rely on the rest of the world to finance a significant portion of their retirement income.

Higher Risk

Younger Americans are excited by the possibility of converting their Social Security earnings into an investment account. Television ads by online brokers have led many to believe that they can "do it themselves" and "investing is fun." But investing is extremely difficult, even for seasoned professionals. Unless you're truly an experienced and disciplined investor, you might regret trying to invest on your own.

It's easy for those with high-paying jobs and stable careers to conclude that privatization would be the best solution. However, life is full of uncertainties, and we can never know what might happen. Having a social insurance system as a safety net for unforeseen circumstances is critical to prevent poverty.

Increased Administrative Costs

The administrative fees for Social Security are about $0.01 for every dollar of benefit received. Because privatization would create millions of individualized accounts administered through retail (for-profit) entities, expenses are expected to increase by up to $0.15 per dollar of benefit in commissions, management fees, and other expenses. *With an estimated $950 billion in fees and management costs for privatization, the financial industry is already drooling.*

Severe Damage to Specific Groups

Under the President's privatization proposal, those receiving disability benefits would be subject to the same regulations for private accounts as everyone else. Consequently, *disabled Americans would be severely disadvantaged in cases where their disablement occurred early in their work career* since they would not have contributed much income to their private accounts. Thus, they would face much lower returns not only from their private accounts, but also due to the reduced guaranteed benefits that have been traded for these accounts.

Similar to everyone else who would have private accounts, *the disabled would not be able to access these funds until reaching retirement.* And as you might appreciate, the importance of Social Security in the everyday lives of disabled Americans is a critical portion of their entire pre-retirement income.

Finally, *women and minorities would stand to lose through privatization.* These groups are particularly dependent on Social Security. Because they tend to have lower incomes and larger gaps in unemployment, they would receive a small percentage of benefits under privatization due to the reduction in guaranteed benefits.

Alternatives

As previously discussed, if Washington does nothing at all, the Social Security Trust Fund should be sufficient to pay all benefits including all estimated COLAs up until at least 2040. Thereafter, it will be able to pay 73 to 80 percent of benefits even if no changes are made. Thus, *it should be relatively easy to make minor adjustments now that will enable Social Security to pay full benefits indefinitely.*

As we have seen, privatization is not the solution to providing solvency, stability, or extending the longevity of Social Security. In contrast, it will partially relieve the government's commitment to provide a base level of assistance for otherwise impoverished Americans. In fact, privatization would really only benefit Wall Street at the expense of millions who rely exclusively on Social Security.

While Social Security is certainly in no desperate shape, it does need some fine tuning to ensure its strength and solvency throughout the second half of the twenty-first century and beyond. But these changes must be made now, or else the problem will grow exponentially. Some have proposed increasing the retirement age to 70 or beyond. But this would not be well received by voters. Others have proposed an increase in the FICA tax. But raising FICA would hurt low-wage earners the most.

There are many other viable options to improve solvency. For instance, newly hired state and local workers could be entered into the system. Another solution would be to earmark other taxes for Social Security. Perhaps the most reasonable solution would be to raise the limit by which Social Security is taxed on wages, currently at $97,500.

If Social Security is indeed a social insurance program, it does not make sense that wage earners making $2,000,000 are only taxed on the first $97,500 of wages. While a tax up to the full amount of one's salary is a bit extreme, I do feel that the limit could be raised from $97,500 to $160,000. With only 6 percent of the American workforce earning more than this wage cap, it would not affect the disposable income of most.

One of the problems is that a higher payroll tax cap would cause higher income wage earners to get double-taxed. That is, because

Social Security income is taxable, those who make above the poverty level must pay taxes on benefits. Therefore, if the payroll cap is raised, the tax rate for Social Security benefits should also be adjusted so double-taxation is curtailed. Finally, while addressing the solvency issue may be achieved by one of many modest changes, this in itself will not alter the trend of diminishing buying power and increased reliance on Social Security benefits.

Why Privatization?

After demonstrating that privatization is a no-win scenario for most Americans, why would President Bush and other members of Congress propose these changes? There are several possible reasons why Social Security has been one of the biggest topics for Bush's political agenda—as a way to help the stock market, to draw attention away from the healthcare crisis, and as a way to execute the Republican Party's commitment to minimize "big government."

First, privatization of *Social Security would help minimize the effects of a potential stock market decline when baby boomers retire.* Remember, most boomers will retire broke, and will need Social Security to keep them out of poverty. Therefore, many who have retirement assets in the stock market will need to sell these securities at in order to survive. However, *privatization would add trillions to the stock market over several years and would continue to on an annual basis.* This would neutralize boomer redemptions of stock funds and would most likely cause the market to soar.

In addition, consider that republicans have always been against social programs. Rather than big government controlling Social Security, republicans prefer to release the liability and risks of this program to individuals. Privatization is the first step towards achieving this goal. Finally, Bush's focus on privatization creates the perception that he is providing value for Americans. Similar to Medicare Part D, privatization creates the illusion of improvement when in fact it only benefits corporate America, and allows him to avoid addressing America's biggest problem—healthcare.

9

Retirement Blues

All seniors rely on a solid foundation of resources to provide a graceful transition into retirement and ensure the longevity of their Golden Years. There are four resource categories thought to function as structural "retirement pillars," providing the foundation upon which a quality retirement depends. When just one of these pillars is compromised, episodes of instability appear, similar to a three-legged chair. And when two of the pillars are dislodged, like a large building that collapses, a retired person can lose the stability needed to sustain their livelihood.

The first pillar of a stable retirement plan is health insurance. It would seem reasonable that every developed nation should be able to provide a system of affordable healthcare to all its citizens. Healthcare is a basic necessity for any developed nation. Yet, the United States is the only developed nation in the world without a national healthcare program. We have already seen how America's healthcare system has diminished the global competitiveness of its workforce and positioned millions with neither jobs nor health insurance.

Currently, 17 percent of retired Americans do not have any presence of this pillar. And for as much as 50 percent of the elderly, this pillar will be weakly constructed due to underinsurance, lifetime caps, and exclusions. When the boomers retire, the percentage of uninsured over age 65 could easily reach 25 percent, while underinsured rates might exceed 70 percent. At the very least, public healthcare benefits will be slashed upon entry of 76 million boomers into the system, resulting in a weakened pillar for millions.

The second retirement pillar consists of continued earnings from work. This is a fairly recent addition to America's retirement pillars and itself highlights the current problem with retirement in modern

America. A few decades ago, retirement actually had a meaning. But declining living standards have prevented many from saving the needed income that would guarantee a permanent retirement from work.

Mandatory employment income almost excludes one from enjoying their Golden Years. Unfortunately, most Americans will have to delay retirement and continue working because they never imagined they would face the current high costs of basic goods and services. Others will continue to work in order to obtain health coverage. Thus, this pillar serves to absorb some of the deficiencies in the others. It can only be circumvented if all other pillars are strongly intact.

Without the ability to work in a job that provides some type of benefit, whether personal gratification, income, or health insurance, many retired Americans will lack this pillar. As it stands today, it is very difficult for those over 65 to obtain meaningful employment due to the stereotypes faced by the elderly.

America's third retirement pillar is Social Security. Unlike decades in the past, Social Security has become nearly as important as it was when first utilized towards the end of the Great Depression. For several decades after WWII, many workers with pensions thought of Social Security as a source of bonus income. But today, most of America's 35 million elderly rely on it as their primary source of retirement income. This dependence will only grow for the boomers. Combined with increased dependency on this program for retirement income, this pillar has several vulnerabilities. And if privatization is passed, the guaranteed benefits afforded by Social Security will be compromised.

The fourth and final pillar of retirement consists of personal savings and retirement plans. Unlike the post-war period when Americans were amongst the world's best savers, they have since mirrored the government's debt patterns, having been transformed into the world's worst savers and largest debtors. As life spans have increased, few have saved enough to ensure a retirement period, free from financial concerns. The problem of America's dwindling savings trends are further magnified by staggering levels of consumer debt. It's very difficult to save if you have a large debt burden. This is especially true during a rising interest-rate environment since credit card interest payments rise. This poor savings rate has harsh consequences for the newer 401(k)-type savings plans since contributions are voluntary.

Only about one-half of the private workforce is covered by some type of retirement savings plan. Therefore, *up to one-half of America's 76 million baby boomers will rely on Social Security as their only source of retirement income, adding further stress to this pillar.* For the more fortunate half of the American population, two-thirds are covered by a 401(k)-type plan, while the remaining one-third have a defined benefit plan.*

Figure 9-1. Personal Savings Rate (% of Disposable Income)

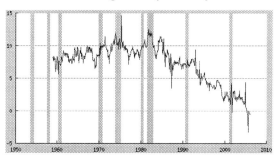

Source: U.S. Department of Commerce: Bureau of Economic Analysis.
Prepared by: Federal Reserve Bank of St. Louis: research: stlouisfed.org
Shaded areas indicate recessions as determined by the NBER

As *of 2005, only about half of all Americans aged 55 had an average balance of $50,000 in their 401(k)-type plan.* In addition, over 18,000 private pension plans remain underfunded. As a result, most boomers will face a diminished lifestyle, adding further emphasis on the employment pillar. Any way you look at it, the transition to retirement for the majority of the boomers will be difficult. And for some, their Golden Years might be best remembered for the time they spent under the golden arches of McDonalds trying to make ends meet.

---

* Note that the terms "pensions" and "defined benefit plans" are used interchangeably. Strictly speaking, a defined benefit plan is only one component of a pension plan. Other components include disability, healthcare and other perks. It just so happens that most companies with a defined benefit plan also have one or more of these other perks, accounting for the synonymous use of the terminology.

The combined effects of healthcare costs, Social Security dependency, pension plan uncertainties and risky 401(k) assets will lead to a major economic slowdown lasting many years. In this chapter, I focus on the fourth pillar that involves retirement assets.

Overview of the Pension Crisis

Over the past two decades there has been a dramatic change in the funding structure and stability of retirement assets in America. The consequences of these changes could result in a financial crisis for the majority of boomers. In order to fully understand these issues, we need to distinguish between the current pension plan crisis and the growing reliance on 401(k) plans.

Problem #1: Underfunded Pensions

America's pension system is currently in a state of disarray. On the one hand, most pensions are financially unstable. They have become underfunded due to increasing life spans, rising healthcare costs, and the recent correction in the stock market. As a result, most companies and government entities do not have sufficient funds to pay full benefits over the expected life span of retired employees. You can think of underfunded plans as having annual deficits.

The problem is only going to get worse. To a large extent, it's a snowball effect—pensions become underfunded due to poor performance in the stock and bond markets, resulting in smaller pension returns, leading to insufficient funds to pay current benefits. This decreases consumer spending, which trickles back down to the stock market, causing further declines in pension assets. Even with a sustained rise in the stock market, there will be fewer new workers to fund the pension benefits of retired workers.

Problem #2: The Shift to 401 (k) Plans

A different but even larger problem is the shift by employers from defined benefit plans (pension plans) to the newer defined contribution or 401(k) retirement savings plans. This trend is not a consequence of the underfunded pension problem. It is more of a consequence of the high costs incurred by companies that offer defined benefit plans. Over the past two decades, many companies began replacing defined benefit plans with less costly defined contribution plans, commonly referred to as 401(k)-type plans. This trend has recently accelerated due to the underfunded defined benefit pension problem.

Unlike the mandatory participation requirements of defined benefit pension plans, *401(k) participation is voluntary.* So many employees either do not participate at all, or do not contribute enough to amass the recommended 10 to 12 times annual salary needed to ensure sufficient retirement funds. Wage growth and disposable income have not grown at rates seen prior to the 1980s, causing many to save less (figure 9-2). As a result, many have been short-changing their retirement because they do not understand the importance of planning ahead and/or they do not have the discipline to save.

Figure 9-2. U.S. Median Family Income Growth has Slowed Since 1980[a]

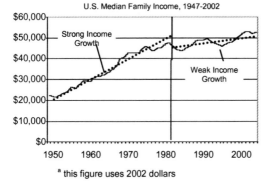

U.S. Median Family Income, 1947-2002

The best-fit straight (dotted) lines have been drawn through each period before and after 1980. The slope or rate of growth for the post-war period up to 1980 is 62%, while that after 1980 is 16%. Therefore, the rate of growth in the median family income has declined by nearly 400% since 1980. Note these are rough estimates.

[a] this figure uses 2002 dollars

Source: U.S. Bureau of Census. Created by Munnell, Alicia H. Hatch, Robert E. Lee, James G. "Why is Life Expectancy So Low in the United States?" Figure 11, CRR Number 21. August 2004.

Growth of Defined Benefit Plans

Defined benefit plans surged in popularity during the uncertain wartime period. The Wage and Salary Act of 1942 put a freeze on wages in an attempt to control inflation during the war. As an incentive to attract and retain employees in a very tight labor market, businesses began offering employee benefits, namely pensions. These plans were the perfect solution for attracting high-quality, dedicated workers since they rewarded employees based upon their years of service. Finally, since company contributions were tax-deductible, this shielded these expenses from high wartime tax rates.

Over time, defined benefit plans began to include healthcare benefits during a worker's employment years. And in exchange for several years of service, many employers provided workers with full healthcare benefits for themselves and their spouse after they retired. Upon entering retirement, workers had no worries about healthcare costs and knew exactly how much income they would receive for as long as they lived.

The stability and financial security of pension plans provided much of the financial strength that helped the middle class emerge as the main force driving the U.S. economy. From 1940 to 1960, the number of Americans covered by private pension plans increased from 3.7 million to 23 million, representing 30 percent of the labor market. By 1970, participation had increased to 45 percent and peaked at just over 50 percent a few years later.

Rise of 401(k)s

In 1981, Johnson Companies introduced the first 401(k) plan. This was the first defined contribution plan allowing employees to defer a portion of their pre-tax salary for retirement. Only when they retired and began withdrawals would this account be taxed (a deferred tax retirement contribution). Shortly thereafter, the IRS officially approved this tax-deferred retirement savings plan, encouraging many companies to begin offering a 401(k) plan, in addition to other defined contribution and defined benefit plans.

But ERISA never intended 401(k)-type plans to serve as a substitute for pension plans. They were created primarily as a means for self-employed workers and small companies to have a less expensive retirement plan. And for large companies, 401(k) plans were intended to serve only as supplemental retirement assets to defined benefit plans.

But now, due to rising healthcare costs and corporate failures, 401(k)-type plans are being offered as the exclusive retirement plan by most small companies and many larger ones; that is if they even offer a retirement plan. While defined benefit plans still exist, the number of companies offering them to new employees has been declining rapidly over the past decade. As a result of this trend, many workers are now faced with a pool of less stable and uncertain retirement assets that are directly affected by the performance of the capital markets.

From 1980 to 1999, (the most current and reliable data available) the number of defined benefit plans in the U.S. decreased by over 70 percent. In contrast, the number of 401(k) plans increased by 100 percent. According to the Employee Benefit Research Institute, as of year 2000, only 20 percent of workers were covered exclusively by a defined pension plan. I expect this number to continue its decline for many years to come, due in large part to the competitive effects of free trade. These trends are very disturbing. A change from defined benefit to defined contribution or 401(k)-type plans should be interpreted as the expected inability or unwillingness of corporations to provide full benefits to retirees.

Figure 9-3. Participation in Workplace Retirement Plans: Defined Benefit vs. Defined Contribution (1983-2004)

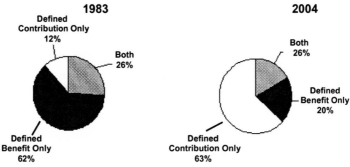

Source: Munnell and Sunden (2006)

What are the Differences?

While both defined benefit and contribution plans are thought to increase employee tenure, these affects are minimal for employers offering a defined contribution or 401(k)-type plan. This has to do with the way these plans are funded. In the case of 401(k) plans, employer contributions (termed matching) are paid in full and deposited into the employee's account (after vesting has been satisfied), with no future financial commitments. However, employer funding is optional.

In contrast, employers offering a defined benefit plan do not transfer any benefits into the employee's legal possession until they retire. The contributions are merely documented as company liabilities in the name of the employee. So if the employee changes jobs before some set period, he could lose most or even all of the employer contributions that have been set aside for his pension. And if the company files for bankruptcy, pension assets are in jeopardy of forfeiture. Thus, the most vulnerable element of a defined benefit plan is the financial strength of the employer. To help make them more stable and secure, the government provides insurance to pensions via the PBGC. But 401(k) plans have no insurance against their most vulnerable variable—the performance of stock and bond markets.

Unlike pensions, 401(k) plans do not provide other forms of employee benefits such as healthcare and disability insurance. According to the NCPSSM, three out of every ten 20-year olds will become disabled prior to reaching 67. Yet, *75 percent of the private workforce has no long-term disability insurance.* This trend is partly due to the declining use of pension plans.

> **Defined benefit plans** have a "defined benefit" for employees so they know ahead of time what their lifetime benefits will be based upon their wages and years of service. **Defined contribution or 401(k)-type plan benefits** are variable and depend upon both the amounts contributed by the employee (as well as employer matching if applicable) and the investment returns.

Workers who change jobs can take their 401(k) plans with them, including all employer contributions (except for funds that have not satisfied vesting criteria). This portability feature has been viewed as a huge advantage by employees. However, it favors employers much more since they are showing an unwillingness to commit to a long-term career for their employees. Hence, *the rise of 401(k) plans in America signifies the growing trend of job insecurity that has accelerated since the acceptance of free trade by Washington.*

No longer is corporate America concerned with employee retention as a means of securing profitability. Today, the world is an open marketplace that's made cheap labor accessible to any company. Therefore, employee retention is no longer seen as a valuable attribute by most U.S. companies. Companies value profits, not people.

Similar to Social Security, defined benefit plans specify the benefit amounts workers will receive in advance, thereby providing strong assurances of retirement income—as long as these promises are kept. This is not the case with 401(k) plans. If workers happen to retire during a secular bear market, they could face major financial difficulties. Thus, with 401(k)s, more of a future retirees' income will be directly dependent upon the stock and bond markets, which can show periods as long as 18 years of little or no growth. In contrast, *because defined benefit plans are designed to provide for perpetual benefits, fund managers can take a longer-term approach and can better weather a bear market, while providing benefits to retirees.*

401(k) Plans Eliminate Employer Risk

Employers that sponsor defined benefit plans provide guarantees of benefits in advance and must keep these promises unless they file for bankruptcy. But once again, most of these plans are insured by the PBGC against company bankruptcy. With 401(k) plans, employers leave the returns up to the worker, who has the freedom (and responsibility) of selecting the funds offered by the financial company administering the plan. 401(k) plans have no insurance because the funds are made available to employees as contributions are made.

Employers offering 401(k)s do not have to worry about increasing life spans of workers. In addition, 401(k)s allow employers the flexibility (but not obligation) of paying annual matching funds with no further obligations in the future. Thus, 401(k) plans have a wider variability of payout that depends on employee and employer contributions and the performance of these investments, which are the responsibility of employees.

Flexibility & Control of 401(k)s

For the employee, 401(k)s provide better transparency and more direct control of where and how their retirement funds are invested. Thus, the shift to 401(k) plans provides a way for employees to become more involved with their retirement investments. And when they leave for another job, they can roll their 401(k) into an IRA, which will enable them to buy and sell stocks as they chose. IRAs provide the ultimate control of one's retirement investments. However, *such responsibility requires a sophisticated and disciplined investment approach, which most people lack.*

A unique characteristic of 401(k) plans is that they can be used as a source of funds for certain expenses such as a first-time home purchase or medical bills, as long as these funds are paid back by a specified period. Although most employees view this as advantageous, it introduces an added layer of risk due to fees and penalties associated with non-compliance of repayment. *When Americans have to use their retirement savings as a credit card to purchase a home or pay medical bills, it paints a troubling picture of their living standards.*

Why 401(k) Plans are Bad

Because participation in 401(k)-type plans is purely on a voluntary basis, many workers don't contribute at all. And even when they do, most contribute only a fraction of that needed to ensure sufficient retirement assets. Several studies have shown that *the average participation rate for companies that offer 401(k)-type plans is 75 to 80 percent.* In other words, between 20 and 25 percent of workers who have a 401(k)-type plan do not participate. Thus, while 20 to 25 percent of employees are jeopardizing their retirement security, they are costing the employer zero expenses since no matching can occur if employee contributions are not made.

Part of the problem with participation rates is that most workers are being squeezed with slower wage growth, fewer benefits, and more out-of-pocket healthcare costs. As wages fail to keep pace with inflation, workers tend to contribute less to these plans because they are fighting the effects of America's declining standard of living. And when they retire with inadequate funds, they will have to face greatly diminished living conditions.

Pensions Perform Better and Cost Less

Alicia Munnell has estimated that the average defined benefit plan outperformed the average defined contribution plan by 0.8 percent per year from 1981 to 2001. When compounded, this difference yields a total in excess of 20 percent.

There are significant cost differences as well. The Investment Company Institute determined the expense ratio of defined benefit plans was on average 40 basis points (0.4 percent) lower than that for defined contribution plans. When 12(b)-1 fees are added from mutual funds within 401(k) plans, the cost can add an additional 25 to 50 basis points (or 0.25 to 0.50 percent). Brooks Hamilton has determined that defined benefit plans cost about 1 to 3 percent of payroll to administer annually, while 401(k) plans cost 6 to 8 percent.

Over time, these differences add up to large expenses due to compounding. *For an employee who has had a 401(k) plan for four decades, estimates are that nearly 80 percent of the plan balance has gone to fees, leaving them with only about 20 percent of the gross investment returns;* a total fleecing of retirement assets by the financial industry. This difference in fees stems from the fact that 401(k) plans are managed by the retail financial industry, while defined benefit plans are not, so there is no middle man.

The Pension Problem

It has been estimated that *over 50 percent of Fortune 1000 companies' defined benefit plans are underfunded.* In other words, there's not enough income from pension assets to pay benefits to retirees. Many companies are also freezing pensions as a way to transition to less costly 401(k) plans or to cut costs. Together, these trends will cause more retirees to depend on Social Security income.

The Big Freeze

At any time and for any reason, companies can freeze their defined benefit (pension) plan unless they are under some type of collective bargaining agreement, such as a labor union contract. If there is a bargaining agreement in place, companies must first obtain approval from the union prior to making any changes. As you might imagine, the percentage of companies with labor unions has diminished to a very small number over the past several decades due to free trade.

Thus, without labor unions, companies can freeze their plans at any time to new employees and recently hired employees (called a *partial or soft freeze*). Alternatively, they can freeze their plans to all employees (called a *full or hard freeze*).

A partial freeze means new employees will not be entered into the plan at all, but current employees will continue to accrue future benefits from the plan. When a hard freeze is declared, not only are new employees restricted from inclusion into the plan, but current employees will no longer accrue benefits. They only retain their right to payment of previously earned benefits upon retirement.

Freeze versus Termination

The main difference between a pension freeze and termination is that in the former, companies cannot take away any of the future benefits that employees have earned prior to the announcement of the freeze. The plan also remains in operation which means it can be reinitiated at a later time. In contrast, *plan terminations* remove the company from the responsibility of paying benefits, and plan operations are shut down. If the company can demonstrate to the PBGC that is has sufficient funds to pay all benefits to plan participants, it can end the plan using a *standard termination*. Under this situation, the company purchases an annuity for the employees.

If the company is financially unstable, it can apply for a *distress termination*. This would be granted by the PBGC only if it is shown in a bankruptcy court that the employer cannot remain in business unless the plan is terminated. In this case, the PBGC would assume the responsibility of providing for retiree benefits, often at reduced rates. However, *the PBGC does not provide healthcare coverage.*

How a Freeze Effects Employees

While a full pension freeze is not thought to result in severe consequences for younger employees, it shortchanges the retirement benefits of workers who have been with the company for a longer period. This is because defined benefit plans are structured with an accelerated compensation schedule towards the last few years prior to retirement. Therefore, *when a company places a hard freeze on its plan, employees who may have worked there for 20 years, yet may only be age 55, will be missing the majority of future benefits.*

Due to their older age, it's much more difficult for them to make up these shortfalls with a 401(k) plan since they're self-funded, self-directed, and require many years of participation in order to build up a sizable asset base. In addition, if the stock market happens to perform poorly over the remaining period or just prior to retirement, the investment returns can be small.

Why the Freeze?

In the past, pension freezes have been a normal part of bankruptcy protection. But a newer, growing trend is the freezing of pensions by healthy companies looking to cut costs. As it turns out, *the most common reason companies are freezing pensions is to decrease the future liabilities of healthcare costs.* Quite simply, management has chosen to steal benefits promised to employees in order to increase corporate profits. Skyrocketing healthcare premiums have made this decision more easily justified.

Since 1970, U.S. companies providing health insurance within pension plans have seen healthcare costs rise by more than 350 percent; much more than any other expense. As figure 9-4 demonstrates, *the underfunded liabilities of defined benefit plans have been dwarfed by healthcare liabilities.* Unlike the case with underfunded pensions, healthcare liabilities will only get larger regardless how well the stock market performs due to the America's uncontrolled healthcare industry.

Figure 9-4. S&P 500 Retiree Healthcare Funding and Defined Benefit Funding Shortfall

(2000-2004)

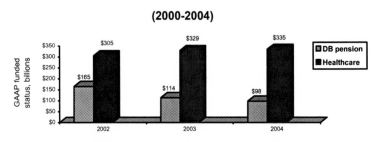

Source: A. Munnell, F. Golub-Sass, M. Soto, F. Vitagliano. "Why Are Healthy Employers Freezing their Pensions?" March 2006, Vol 44. CRR.

Companies receive many other benefits by freezing their pensions. Some have frozen their plans as a way to help them become more funded since liabilities do not accumulate (during a full freeze) or only add based upon workers already in the plan (during a partial freeze) while the plan is frozen. However, frozen plans are still subject to market performance, which can affect the funding status.

As well, some companies freeze plans to lower overall compensation as an alternative to cutting salaries. Many companies also state that defined benefit plans make them less competitive with smaller companies that never offered such plans, or due to foreign competitors whose pensions are funded by their government; all effects of free trade. While it does not immediately impact future retirees, (unlike pension underfundedness and terminations) the current trend of pension freezes will strengthen the momentum of replacing defined benefit with 401(k) plans.

Underfunded Pensions

Due to oversights in ERISA laws, companies are not required to fully fund their pensions for any given year. In extreme cases, some companies use current cash inflows from incoming employee contributions to pay benefits to retirees; a very risky practice. Of course, when the stock market experiences a period of poor returns, a huge problem can arise, namely, a pension that is underfunded.

That's precisely what happened to thousands of companies after 2000. And it's resulted in a potential $450 billion shortfall in private pension benefits. But this doesn't even count the huge healthcare benefits promised to employees of these plans. Healthcare benefits are funded from current cash flows (and are not counted on the pension liabilities section of the balance sheet).

As of 2006, more than 18,000 corporate pension plans were underfunded by over $450 billion. And public pensions are underfunded by an additional $460 to $700 billion; a total of around $1 trillion in liabilities for current and future retirees that's unavailable.

When pensions become underfunded for a period of two years, ERISA regulations state that benefit payments to retirees must be suspended. In the past, underfunded plans had three years to become funded. But the deadline was recently extended from seven to twenty-five years. Since Washington also redefined a fully funded plan from 80 to 100 percent, it's going to be difficult for underfunded plans to gain solvency without a sustained surge in the stock market. As you might imagine, the underfunded problem could be another incentive for Bush's Social Security privatization plan.

With so many pensions in the red, millions aren't able to receive retirement benefits. In the last four years, more than 600 companies have weaseled out on pension obligations, topped by United Airline's pension fund failure of $9.8 billion; the biggest since the government began guaranteeing pensions in 1974. These failures add to the large pool of retirees counting on Social Security to provide up to 100 percent of their income.

Conclusions

America's pension system is facing huge challenges that will not be easily solved. Studies have shown that the average worker aged 60 to 65 has only about three times current salary in retirement funds. In order to achieve the recommended 10 to 12 times annual income by retirement, workers need to save anywhere from 15 to 18 percent of annual wages. But as we have seen, this is rarely done due to the trend of diminishing net employee compensation, combined with the massive inflation in basic necessities. Thus, as more enter retirement, the fate of Social Security will become an even greater concern.

When the boomers enter retirement, many will be forced back into work, mainly in low-paying jobs. This will not only serve to destroy the morale of the largest group of Americans, but it will also have a chilling effect on younger workers who will begin to wonder if their Golden Years will be a filled with a period of living concessions.

Washington is ultimately to blame for millions of boomers expected to retire with inadequate funds. Our elected officials permitted the corporate raid on employee benefits. They also allowed America to enter into free trade arrangements that force companies to outsource in order to remain competitive. Washington tells us that Social Security was never meant to serve as the primary source of retirement income. But these same politicians have permitted corporations to eliminate pension plans in favor of 401(k)s—plans that were never intended to serve as the primary source of retirement income.

As it stands today, we are witnessing the disappearance of America's most stable and secure retirement savings program, as Washington and corporate America shift the responsibility of a secure retirement to each American. If you have a 401(k) or other defined contribution plan, you're basically on your own, with no guarantees of retirement benefits. You and your 401(k) or IRA will have to face the stock and bond markets, along with the high management fees of mutual funds. Good luck.

10

REAL ESTATE BUBBLE

Millions of Americans have bought a home during the last stage of the housing bubble thinking it will pay off if they can "hold on." When the bubble deflates, many speculators will be stuck with properties they won't be able to sell for a long time. Even worse, many won't be able to continue mortgage payments due to millions of variable-interest rate loans that have repriced upwards.

In many parts of America, home prices have risen as high as 150 percent in just a few years. Despite an inherently weak economy, home ownership rates are the highest in U.S. history, at 70 percent. You might recall that household ownership in equities approached the highest point ever during the peak of the previous stock market bubble. And of course we all know what happened shortly thereafter.

According to estimates made in 2002 by the Center for Economic Policy Research (CEPR), the housing bubble correction will drop the value of the average home by 11 to 22 percent, evaporating between $1.3 and $2.6 trillion of paper wealth. Since that time, there has been an 18 to 25 percent increase in median home prices, which would imply an even larger decline when the bubble deflates.

At its bottom, I expect a 35 percent correction for the average home. And in "hot spots" home prices could plummet by 55 to 60 percent from peak values. I expect the fallout in home prices to affect different regions at different time periods. This will be one of the confusing dynamics that will cause some to think the correction is over. It's likely to move in waves, from region to region as a repeating cycle, sucking in more blind investors with each repeating wave.

You might be thinking that a correction won't really destroy wealth for those who plan to live in the same home for many years, but you'd be wrong. Once you agree to a price for a home and take out the mortgage, you're stuck with the final sales price (the total cost of the mortgage over the period financed), unless of course you refinance at a lower rate. Even if you were able to refinance, it's not going to lower the price you paid for your home. It would only lower the interest portion of the loan.

Most likely, there will be no more refinancing opportunities for many years since we are just coming out of the lowest mortgage rates in decades. In fact, I expect long-term rates to move higher over the next few years due to the weak dollar and mounting national debt. When that happens, it will add further downward pressure on home prices. And of course, this is going to deal a severe blow to consumer spending. Finally, millions of defaults will cause a meltdown in financial institutions holding these junk mortgages, resulting losses well exceeding those from the Savings & Loan Crisis of the late '80s.

Mortgage Mania

The past few decades have witnessed an explosion of creative financing options available to home buyers. Just over three decades ago, an adjustable-rate mortgage (ARM) was rare. But when interest rates soared during the '80s, the use of ARMs exploded. By 1984, ARMs peaked at 60 percent of loan originations.

ARMs have recently increased in popularity as a way to decrease the total home purchase price since short-term rates were so low. ARMs were less than 2 percent of all mortgages in 2001, but peaked at 34 percent in 2004 when short-term rates were at their lows. *Yet, in the first three months of 2005 when short-term rates were much higher, ARMs managed to top 19 percent.*

Record low rates have also caused a boom in interest-only loans. Use of these risky loans has been the only way many can afford housing in San Diego, Los Angeles, Boston, San Francisco and dozens of other cities. *The use of interest-only loans during record-low rates is like burning money since you are not paying off any principal. And when interest rates rise, these mortgages create negative amortization.*

Finally, there are even riskier mortgages that allow one to pay less than the current short-term interest rate. These are referred to as option-ARMs. Also known as cash-back financings, these mortgages create the illusion of home ownership while accelerating a negative amortization schedule. In other words, each month you're paying the mortgage, the total amount owed on your home actually increases. It's nothing short of financial suicide. Option-ARMs are truly the epitome of desperation utilized to take advantage of what many feel will be a great investment in real estate. While most statistics do not count option-ARMs as home equity loans, they have a much worse affect since home equity is depleted rapidly.

Because of the way they work, *ARMs are usually popular when the yield curve is steep* (short-term rates are much lower than long-term rates). Although the yield curve remained steep for much of 2004, even when it flattened thereafter, the share of ARM originations remained fairly constant.

How can we explain this? Due to the huge appreciation in homes over the past few years, many first-time buyers could only afford a home if they used ARMs. And aggressive sub-prime lending helped ARMs account for 20 percent of sub-prime loans in 2004.

As of mid-2006, nearly 25 percent of American home owners had an ARM of some kind. It's no wonder why home ownership hit a record 70 percent. Most Americans don't understand the concept of compounding interest. So it's safe to assume that most home owners with ARMs and other sub-prime loans do not fully understand how they work, and thus have no idea how risky they are. But soon they will.

Table 10-1: Interest-Only Loans	
Metro Area Loans	Interest-Only (as a share of total, 2004)
San Diego	47.6%
Atlanta	45.5%
San Francisco	45.3%
Denver	43.4%
Oakland	43.1%
San Jose	41.1%
Phoenix-Mesa	38.8%
Seattle-Bellevue-Everett	37.2%
Orange County, CA	37.0%
Ventura, CA	35.3%
Sacramento	34.9%
Las Vegas	33.7%
Stockton, CA	32.0%
Washington, DC	31.4%
Charlotte, NC	29.1%
W. Palm Beach-Boca Raton	28.0%
Portland, OR	27.8%
Los Angeles	26.7%
Salt Lake City	25.6%
Nation-wide	**22.9%**

ARMs are linked to some type of economic index, typically short-term interest rates. So they adjust up and down along with this rate. Because borrowers assume the risk of rising rates, they are offered lower initial interest rates than fixed-rate mortgages (FRMs). More important, ARMs are much easier to qualify for since the debt holder has a shorter duration of repayment, thereby lowering the risk to the lender. Given the extremely low rates provided by 30-year traditional mortgages, one would expect FRMs to dominate the housing market. But soaring home prices made ARMs the only possible choice for many who were unable to afford a home.

Perhaps the most disturbing trend in mortgage data is that *the majority of the 10 million ARMs outstanding were issued towards the end stages of the housing boom, and after short-term interest rates were already on the rise (i.e. between 2004 and 2005).* Over the years, Americans have become greedy. The credit-based economy has trained them to always overextend themselves and make up the difference with credit. Subsequently, excessive use of ARMs has been a reflection of consumer greed and financial irresponsibility that has reached dangerous levels in America.

According to First American Real Estate Solutions, of the *7.7 million Americans who took out an ARM from 2004 to 2005*, up to 1 million could lose their home through foreclosure over the next 5 years due to rising mortgage payments. *I expect anywhere between 40 to 50 percent of these mortgages (or around 3.5 million) to face foreclosure during the next three years (revised 2007).* This estimate doesn't include the other types of non-FRM mortgages, nor does it include other foreclosures from the sub-prime market, or the average foreclosures expected even without a real estate bubble.

Over the next 7 to 9 years, I expect *10 to 12 million foreclosures (including pre-foreclosures) to hit the housing market without substantial government intervention.* Most of the homes lost to ARMs will have occurred by the end of 2009. Thereafter, foreclosures due to FRMs will account for the majority of defaults.

Of course, the ultimate outcome will depend on how Bernanke handles inflation. The higher rates go over the next 3 years, the more

ARM-related foreclosures we will see. *But there is a strong force acting to keep rates high and push them even higher—the need to create an incentive for foreign investors to buy more U.S. Treasury bonds, needed to support Bush's deficit spending.* This upward force on rates is further accentuated by the weakness of the dollar.

Even for those who are able to hold on, many will owe more than their home is worth for several years. Imagine making payments on a mortgage you took out for $600,000 and having your home worth only $450,000 ten years later. This scenario is possible and it doesn't exactly do much to help consumer sentiment.

The Real Estate ATM

According to the Federal Reserve Board, American home owners extracted $600 billion in equity from their homes in 2004, spending half of this money on goods and services. *This $300 billion accounted for 40 percent of the GDP growth in 2004.* Figure 10-1 illustrates the effects of mortgage equity withdrawal on GDP growth from data reported by the Federal Reserve. Between 2003 and 2004, the Fed estimates that consumers tapped into over $1 trillion of equity from their homes using home equity loans, refinancings, and cash-out purchases at closing. Alone, these cash-out financings have been estimated to account for a significant portion of inflated values.

Mortgage Money Machine

How has the mortgage industry been able to lend so much money to so many under-qualified consumers? Even back in the late '90s when the economy was at its peak, it was more difficult to obtain mortgages than today. With few options remaining, *Washington has permitted this industry to engage in irresponsible lending practices to increase access to credit for the purpose of fueling the phantom recovery.* This has served to enhance consumer spending which has boosted many industry wages; fees and commissions of brokers in the real estate and mortgage industry, commercial banking salaries, and revenues in all industries as a result of reckless credit spending.

Figure 10-1. The Effects of Mortgage Equity Withdrawal on GDP Growth

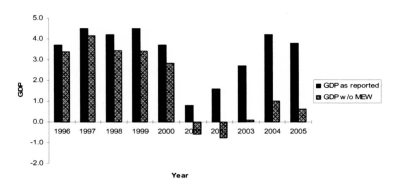

Source: Mortgage Bankers Association of America and Federal Reserve Flow of Funds

Hence, without this real estate bubble, there would be very few signs of improvement in the economy since 2003. As well, remember that the majority of government discretionary spending items since 2003 have been for Iraq, Afghanistan, Katrina, and Homeland Security—none of which resulted in a net improvement in living standards, as normally implied by GDP numbers. Therefore, if we adjust for the effects of spending due to credit released from the real estate bubble and due to government expenditures that have not resulted in an improved economic benefit, America has actually registered negative GDP growth since 2003. Instead, Greenspan's release of credit helped create the illusion of a recovery.

Secondary Mortgage Market

Virtually all consumer and business loans in America are analyzed and packaged into a pool along with hundreds or even thousands of other loans, then rated for default risk by some outside agency. This is the basic process of *securitization*. And once the process is complete, these securities are considered *collateralized*, since they are backed by cash flow payments of the borrowers.

When this debt has been securitized from auto loans, collection notes, business credit, royalties, TV syndication deals, or virtually anything else with a revenue stream (except mortgages) they are known as *asset-backed securities*. These securities are resold to institutional investors outside of the stock and bond markets in what is known as the asset-backed securities (ABS) market. Mortgage loans securitized in a similar manner are known as *mortgage-backed securities* (MBS) and are bought and sold by the same investors on the mortgage-backed securities market. Collectively, these securitized loans trade on what is known as the collateralized securities market.

The majority of MBS exist due to the upstream liquidity provided by Fannie Mae, Freddie Mac, and Ginnie Mae (the GSEs). Together, these three government agencies are responsible for securitizing and marketing the majority of the $11.5 trillion outstanding residential mortgage debt in America. Once packaged and rated for credit risk, institutional investors supply the downstream liquidity needed to keep the cycle running through their purchase of these securitized mortgage products from the GSEs. Meanwhile, loan origination companies get cash to issue more loans. In short, *the collateralized securities market serves as a perpetual money machine that has fueled the massive credit and real estate bubbles seen today.*

Over the past two decades the rapid growth of America's financial system has led to a changing trend in which most banks that originate loans sell them to other companies in exchange for cash flows to originate more loans. This has given rise to the *mortgage servicing industry*, which is now larger than the *loan origination industry*. Together, both industries comprise the *primary mortgage market*.

Closely associated with the primary market is the *secondary mortgage market*. This segment of the industry specializes in buying and selling mortgages packaged in bulk on the MBS market. The mortgage servicing industry works closely with the providers of MBS (in theory) to ensure these investment products meet certain standards, as well as a timely collection of payments.

The MBS and ABS markets have exploded over the past two decades and now are considered amongst the biggest investment markets worldwide. Most consumers aren't aware of them because these securities aren't publicly traded like the stock and bond markets. But since the primary companies involved in securitization of ABS and

MBS are publicly traded, (Freddie Mac, Fannie Mae, and Ginnie Mae for MBS; Sallie Mae, Citigroup, Chase, Washington Mutual and Bank of America and many others) a significant portion of mortgage and consumer debt is indirectly linked to the stock and bond markets. Thus, investors should be very concerned about the fragile MBS market.

Figure 10-2 shows a breakdown of the huge collateralized securities market. The entire pie excluding the ABS slice makes up the $9 trillion MBS market (note 2007 data is nearly $11.5 and $4 trillion for MBS and ABS respectively). The ABS market includes not only credit card and auto loan securitization debt, but also student and home equity securitized debt.

Figure 10-2. Composition of the Collateralized Securities Market

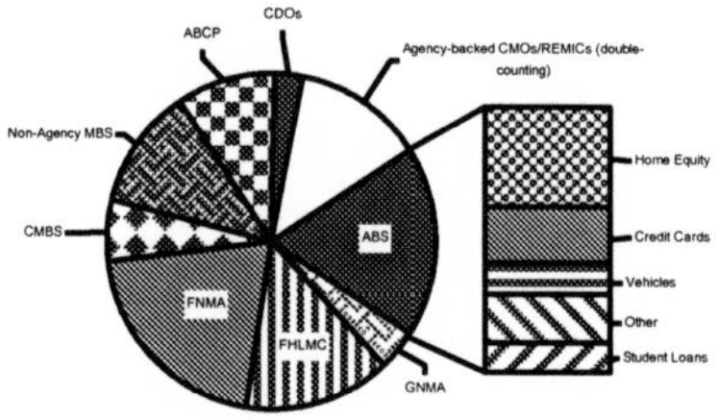

Based on a total $9.02 trillion total as of September 30, 2005

Figure 10-3 illustrates the size of the ABS and MBS markets relative to all publicly traded bond markets. As you can see, the $10 trillion MBS market alone (Agency MBS and Agency debt, private MBS, and ABCP) is larger than the corporate and U.S. government bond markets individually, and nearly as large as both combined. When you add the $1.9 trillion ABS market to the MBS market, the entire $12 trillion collateralized market is larger than the U.S. government and corporate bond markets combined.

As of September 17th, 2007, the estimated value of the collateralized securities market stood at about $15 trillion, while the total value of the U.S. stock market stood at around $13.5 trillion. Thus, the collateralized securities market (primarily made of mortgage debt) is the biggest investment market in the world (with the exception of the global credit derivatives market). It's also one of the riskiest.

Figure 10-3. U.S. Capital Debt Markets (as of September 30, 2005)

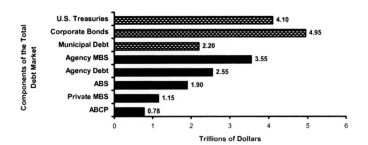

Risks of Collateralized Securities

The great thing about securitization is that it creates liquidity and makes credit widely available to consumers and businesses at competitive rates. This helps drive economic growth and investment. Thus, securitization is an invaluable resource generating abundant credit needed for economic expansions. But it can also lead to busts if a sufficient number of consumers default on payments.

While securitization seems like a nice way to sanitize consumer and mortgage debt, the reality is that the process creates a deceptive investment with many hidden risks. *Even the riskiest of these loans can be manipulated into AAA-rated debt* and sold to pensions and other large funds because the same standards that apply to corporate debt are not applied to collateralized debt products.

Government-Sponsored Entities

The GSEs were created by Congress to increase Americans' access to mortgage loans. There are three GSEs and several related agencies: the Federal National Mortgage Association (Fannie Mae), the Federal Home Loan Mortgage Corporation (Freddie Mac), and the Federal Home Loan Bank (FHLB) system.

The intended purpose of the GSEs was to provide affordable housing to the private sector. But Freddie and Fannie have been supplying funds to the overall market. Thus, *the GSEs have been a significant stimulus for the rapid growth of sub-prime loan market that has contributed to the enormous risks within the real estate bubble.*

Because Fannie and Freddie lack sufficient government oversight, they have not maintained adequate capital reserves needed to safeguard the security of payments to investors. And due to their exemption from the SEC Act of 1933, they are not required to reveal their financial position, nor are they required to register debt offerings with the SEC. In fact, *they are the only publicly traded companies in the Fortune 500 exempt from routine SEC disclosures required for adequate transparency and investor accountability.*

Derivatives Exposure

Furthermore, the GSEs have created very risky derivatives exposures for themselves and many financial institutions. Fannie Mae has taken about half of its MBS and pooled them into another security called a Real Estate Mortgage Investment Conduit (REMIC), otherwise known as a restructured MBS or Collateralized Mortgage Obligation (CMO). These mortgage derivatives are considered very speculative.

Consider what might happen if one or more GSE got into financial trouble. Not only would investors get crushed, but taxpayers would have to bail them out since the GSEs are backed by the government. Everyone would feel the effects. With close to $2 trillion in debt between Freddie Mac and Fannie Mae and several trillion dollars held by commercial banks, *failure of just one of these companies could create a huge disaster that would easily eclipse the Savings & Loan Crisis of the late '80s.*

Conclusions

There is indisputable evidence that most Americans have been buying homes as an investment vehicle for over a decade. This behavior is a primary characteristic of a real estate bubble. GSEs have added to the real estate boom by providing endless liquidity, thereby encouraging the growth of the risky sub-prime market. But just as Greenspan denied any existence of an Internet bubble a few years back, he has also denied any trace of a real estate bubble. He even recommended that consumers consider financing home purchases with

ARMs in January 2004, just a few months before he began raising rates by nearly 400 basis points.

Since 1997, the U.S. total residential mortgage debt outstanding has risen by over 165 percent to about $11.5 trillion. With an estimated *75 million home owners* and over $4 trillion of increased residential real estate value in the past few years, there should be no doubt that the real estate bubble has peaked. At least 30 percent of the $11.5 trillion residential mortgage debt market will correct downward leading to record foreclosures, which will affect the MBS and ABS markets.

Under normal conditions, anywhere from *25 to 30 percent of the U.S. economy is directly affected by the housing sector.* However, due to exaggerated asset prices from the housing bubble, this share is significantly higher. *Housing prices have up to two times the effect on consumer spending when compared to declines in the stock market.* Consequently, if housing prices decline by 25 percent, the economic impact will be as if the stock market declined by 50 percent.

Based on today's grossly overvalued housing prices, a 35 percent correction on average seems very likely. And in some areas, declines of up to 60 percent are possible. Combined with millions of foreclosures and massive losses in the financial industry, you should expect several shocks to the economy. Most likely, it will take several years for the washout to be completed. We can only hope that the MBS market doesn't experience its first blow up since inception, but don't bet on it.

Update

By early spring 2007, clear signs of a correction in the housing market were evident. After a brief sell-off, the stock market shrugged off issues with some of the mortgage companies as if the problems were over. But as predicted, several more consequences of the meltdown materialized a couple of months later. By August, the DJIA declined by 1500 points in less than a month, as many more mortgage companies faced bankruptcy. Again, the markets rebounded and more problems appeared a couple of months later.

In 2007 alone, we have already witnessed over 100 mortgage company bankruptcies, two notable MBS hedge fund blow-ups, a loss in value between 30 to 100 percent for most brokerage, banking, and mortgage-related stocks in the U.S., and extreme swings in stock market volatility. In the fall of 2007, America's largest banks pooled funds to create a $100 billion bail-out fund, but this won't help much. As 2007 winds down, it appears as if the nation will report in excess of 2 million foreclosures. The devastation will only get worse over the next couple years.

In order to prevent a complete halt in consumer spending over the Christmas Holidays, President Bush authorized a bailout for those with ARMs, with a plan to hold rates fixed for up to 5 years. But this is expected to protect only about 500,000 homeowners in danger of foreclosure, leaving millions in harms way. Already with nearly $100 billion in sub-prime losses and official estimates north of over $400 billion before it's all over, the financial industry is in a panic. By the time the correction ends, I expect total direct losses at $600 to $800 billion, not counting the paper losses for those who are able to keep their home.

The Fed responded by dropping interest rates by 100 basis points (1.00 percent) to help restore liquidity. In fact, it appears as if 2008 may well see more rate cuts, judging by statements made by Bernanke. However, this will only make the credit bubble worse. Providing liquidity to banks can be achieved by lowering the discount rate without touching the Fed funds rate. This will ultimately cause more pain down the road. Attempts to avoid a recession will be met with more severe consequences down the road. Regardless, there is nothing the Fed can do to counter the effects of slashed property tax revenues. Soon, state budgets will be in deep trouble as they struggle further with rising Medicaid costs.

In total, nearly $1 trillion has been released into the global banking system (by the U.S. Federal Reserve and the European Central Bank) in 2007 to help provide needed liquidity. This is only the beginning of what promises to be the most severe collapse in real estate in U.S. history, easily dwarfing the $150 billion in losses from the Savings & Loan Crisis. And it could very well trigger the initial stages of America's financial apocalypse.

PART III

GREED, DESPERATION & DECEIT

11

WASHINGTON'S DECEIT

Washington has several ways to hide liabilities and reduce benefits for many government programs. In Chapter Six, I discussed the federal deficit problems and noted how liabilities are hidden through the use of off-balance financing. While the deficit is often cloaked by accounting tricks, Washington cannot hide the national debt.

If held to the same standards as corporate America, Washington's off-balance financing tricks would be considered accounting fraud by the SEC. But alas, this is the United States government, leader of the richest, most powerful nation in the world, capable of raising taxes anytime it needs and printing as much money as it chooses. After all, the world must accept the dollar regardless how low it declines. But soon, the dollar may lose much of its international clout. If that happens, America's financial apocalypse will be official. Already the dollar remains weak and will continue its slide for many years to come.

The annual budget and trade deficits add to the problem of America's unmanageable debt burden—all direct consequences of excessive consumption and the unwillingness by consumers to concede diminished living standards. Mismanagement of the annual budget, trade deficit, and total debt burden reflect America's weakened economic position and declining global competitiveness.

Bush's Dirty Little Secret

In preparation for his reelection campaign against Democratic Party Nominee Senator John Kerry, President Bush instructed Secretary of Treasury Paul O'Neill to commission a study to determine how much the U.S. government owed for the fiscal year 2004. As a part of this study, Dr. Jagadeesh Gokhale, senior economic adviser to the Federal Reserve Bank of Cleveland and Dr. Kent Smetters, an economics professor at the University of Pennsylvania, examined Social Security, Medicare, and Medicaid. The results of this study revealed that the total present value of liabilities needed to pay the boomers for Social Security amounted to $22 trillion. When Medicare and Medicaid were added, this obligation totaled $43 trillion. Adding Part D Medicare brought the total to $51 trillion—all after accounting for expected payroll tax revenues over the deficit period.

Independent groups later studied this same data. It turns out that the estimates by Gokhale and Smetters were conservative, with total liabilities reported as high as $72 trillion. How much is $72 trillion? Well, it's much higher than the $48 trillion (revised 2007) in total assets held by all Americans, liquid and illiquid (cash, securities, real estate, autos and collectables). As well, it easily surpasses the $50 trillion total debt held by the U.S. government and consumers (i.e. America's total credit bubble). Finally, these liabilities exceed the total GDP of the world.

While the *present value* of these mandatory spending liabilities is somewhere between $51 and $72 trillion, (table 11-1) the *future value* of over the next five decades is around the $120 trillion. In other words, if Washington funds these programs as they're needed and without any benefit cuts, the total deficit over the benefit period could be as high as $120 trillion, depending on when these expenditures are funded. Therefore, by delaying the fiscal solutions, the present value will increase each year, only making matters worse.

Of the three liabilities, the greatest challenge by far is with Medicare, with a growth rate six times faster than Social Security. So what are some of the solutions to fix these shortfalls? In the report written by Gokhale and Smetters, four options were identified as the only solutions to provide for these gigantic liabilities. The list is as follows:

1. Increase the payroll tax by over 100 percent immediately and forever from a current 15.3 percent of wages to nearly 32 percent

2. Raise income taxes by nearly 70 percent <u>immediately and forever</u>

3. Slash Social Security and Medicare benefits by 45 percent <u>immediately and forever</u>

4. <u>Or eliminate forever</u>, all discretionary spending, which includes the military, Homeland Security, highways, courts, national parks, and most of what the federal government does outside of the transfer of payments to the elderly

Technically speaking, America is already bankrupt. Each day Washington allows these liabilities to persist, America's financial problems get worse. Meanwhile, foreign nations gain more control of the United States since they are the financiers of its record debt. Hence, the unwillingness of foreign nations to continue financing America's reckless spending sprees could cause a major collapse of the dollar.

When the White House read the study commissioned by O'Neill, Bush called for his resignation and removed these findings from the final report. The official word is that O'Neill's resignation was due to disagreements with Bush's tax cuts. But it's reasonable to assume it was more directly related to the study by Gokhale and Smetters, since the tax cuts were contrary to the recommendations made in the report.

Table 11-1. Studies on U.S. Government Social Programs

Study	Estimate of Present Value of Obligations For Social Security, Medicaid and Medicare
Gokhale & Smetters	$51 trillion
International Monetary Fund	$47 trillion
Brookings Institution	$60 trillion
Government Accountability Office	$72 trillion

Economic Numbers

The problem with deciphering the nation's economic data is that it's so voluminous. As well, appropriate frames of reference are rarely provided. And many assumptions are not disclosed when the data is reported to the public, making interpretation problematic. This leads to reporting by the media that mirrors what the "experts" state about the economy. But this deception has a purpose. For Wall Street and off-beat financial institutions, it provides more confidence to investors who shuttle more money into the stock market, leading to increased business. For corporate America, it provides higher profits because consumers spend more credit thinking their future is promising.

For several years now this financial deceit has kept the economy running. Perhaps if consumers are kept in the dark long enough the economy will rebound; or so Washington figures. But where will future spending come from now that home equity loans and credit cards have been maxed out, interest rates and inflation are higher and rising, there's no net job or wage growth while outsourcing increases each day? *How will Washington convince foreign banks to continue financing its record debt against the weak dollar, while U.S. diplomacy continues to create global discontent?*

Discouraged by the Economy

The government and related agencies are responsible for reporting the nation's economic data. Thus, they're in the driver's seat to manipulate this data or dump so much of it onto consumers that they can't possibly analyze what's really going on. Each day, "critical" economic numbers are released by one or more agencies connected to Washington. And consumers look to Wall Street and the media to make heads or tails of the numbers. Of course, Wall Street is always going to paint a rosier picture for its own benefit. Meanwhile, mainstream media merely serves as a puppet for Wall Street.

The problem is that by the time this data has been reported it's already been manipulated. And when Wall Street gets a hold of it they make matters worse, tugging and pulling on the meaning of the numbers. This creates market volatility, which generates a lot of trading commissions. Virtually every economic indicator has been altered by the government and its affiliated economic organizations for over three decades. I argue that this has occurred to distort the realities of America's economic picture.

For instance, when Washington reports unemployment data it *makes no distinctions between part-time workers who want full-time work but cannot find it;* they're considered "employed" which is assumed to mean fully employed. A much better measure of employment is to look at the *underemployment rate*, which is always much higher. While this data is available, you'll never hear about it from Washington because it demonstrates America's declining job quality and competitiveness.

Government employment figures also count workers that are employed in what are known as "non-standard jobs" with no distinctions. Typically, these jobs include temp workers, independent contractors, part-time workers and the self-employed. The main problem with counting these individuals as "employed" is that *non-standard jobs rarely include employee benefits such as healthcare or retirement plans.* And because America's labor force depends upon a large percentage of employee benefits for the total compensation package (up to 42 percent of the median wage earners total compensation), a proper analysis of employment trends must consider non-standard employment data. However, this data is not included.

As well, non-standard jobs are much less secure than traditional jobs, so they don't provide the assurance and benefits of a stable career, making it difficult for these workers to plan for the future. *In addition, employment data does not indicate how long workers have been with a particular employer.* But this information is also very important for understanding the financial security of workers. Even before the last recession, estimates show that over 25 percent of the U.S. workforce was engaged in non-standard employment. With little doubt, this percentage is significantly higher today due to the competitive effects of free trade.

As another way to make employment numbers look more

promising, Washington economists came up with a new designation a few decades ago called the "discouraged worker." Such a person is thought to have "thrown in the towel" after six unsuccessful months searching for work. What happened to these discouraged workers? Why aren't they counted? *What is it about the economy that has caused these workers to be unable to obtain a job after an extended period?*

Knowing the number of discouraged workers is vital to understanding trends in the overall competitive landscape of the economy. But these individuals are simply dropped from the list as if they no longer exist. Why was there no such thing as a discouraged worker fifty years ago? Back then, Americans who were willing to work found stable jobs so there was no need to hide the truth. As we have seen, the economy was much better back then. Imagine what would happen to consumer confidence if more comprehensive employment data was reported.

Poverty

Among the government statistics that are inaccurate, twisted or misleading, poverty has escaped scrutiny. Inaccurate reporting of poverty data saves Washington billions since this information is critical for determining how much should be spent on programs providing basic necessities and outreach—for Social Security, Medicare, Medicaid, and other programs.

The big weakness in the government's definition of poverty is how to define basic living expenses and how to measure financial well-being. For instance, the poverty calculation includes only cash income before tax deductions, excludes capital gains taxes, and doesn't factor in accumulated wealth or assets such as securities or property ownership. *How can poverty calculations neglect figures for net worth and capital gains?*

Despite more reasonable definitions used by outside organizations, the Office of Management and Budget determines how poverty is measured to determine benefits. Currently, the official poverty level for a family of four is $19,307, and $12,334 for a family of two (2006). Hence, a family of four might have a total income of

$20,000 and be considered above the poverty line. In contrast, a person with a $5 million investment portfolio and a $2 million home who takes a year off of work would be considered impoverished since he earned no income that year. By definition, poverty is the extreme opposite of wealth. And *because wealth is measured in terms of net worth, it's unreasonable that the government's definition of poverty only includes income.*

GDP Myths

Up until the 1980s, the Gross National Product (GNP) was used as the predominant measure of economic growth in America. The GNP measures the total amount of goods and services produced by a nation's citizens regardless of the location of production. Thus, GNP includes corporate profits that multinational companies earn overseas. As an example, the profits earned by General Electric's facilities in China are counted towards America's GNP rather than China's.

As globalization began to alter America's economy, GDP (Gross Domestic Productivity) became accepted as a more reliable indicator of economic growth. Since the '80s, economists have pointed to GDP as the single most reliable indicator of economic strength. *This proclivity has led to a kind of "follow the leader" mentality, with few to question its accuracy.* But as we shall see, there are major problems with the way GDP is calculated and accepted as a measure of economic growth and standard of living.

Released quarterly (at 8:30am EST on the last business day of the next quarter) by the Department of Commerce, *GDP is defined as the total value of goods and services produced within a territory during a specified period, regardless of ownership.* GDP differs from the GNP through exclusion of inter-country income transfers, thereby attributing to a territory the products generated within it rather than the incomes received in it. *In other words, GDP only counts goods and services produced within a nation's geographic borders.*

GDP = Consumption + Government Expenditures + Investment + Exports − Imports

Going back to the earlier example, all profits earned by General Electric's facilities in China would not be counted towards America's GDP, but China's. However, America's GNP would benefit from these profits, as previously mentioned. Therefore, unlike GNP, the *GDP is thought to provide information on domestic economic growth after adjusting for trade deficits or surpluses.*

At first glance, it might appear as if the use of GDP provides an accurate measure of domestic productivity since it doesn't count earnings from multinational corporations. In fact, one might imagine that GDP excludes earnings made overseas, say from outsourcing. However, this isn't necessarily the case for several reasons. In short, *the complexities of global production and commerce make it relatively easy for companies to alter how much of what gets made or serviced where.*

First, consider that multinational corporations and other companies that outsource can shift earnings and expenses from one business unit to another without detection. Next, companies that outsource services packaged as a part of a total service or product can assign arbitrary earnings and expenses to the portion of the services or products that have been outsourced.

For instance, let's assume that General Electric has operations in China that are responsible for the production of a component used in refrigerators. Not only will the effect of an undervalued Yuan cause these costs to be understated, but the expenses involved with the production of this component can be assigned an artificially high value. Next, the component can be shipped to America for final assembly in order to receive more favorable tax treatment. For services such as IT, random assignment of expenses can be even easier to conceal.

Finally, as we will see in Chapter Fourteen, a significant amount of U.S. assets and companies have been purchased by foreign interests. When such purchases have not been in full, domestic revenues from these assets are treated as components to the U.S. GDP, when in fact a significant portion of these earnings are leaving U.S. borders and entering the hands of foreign owners. There are many more problems with GDP data, as we shall see.

Problems Measuring Living Standards

GDP only provides an overall measure of economic output of a given nation, and speaks nothing of individual living standards or the overall well-being of a population. Quality of life is determined by other factors unrelated to finances, such as life span, work week, minimum required vacation days, government entitlements, social factors, and many other variables. For example, the United States is the only developed nation without required vacation days in the workplace.

Failure to Account for Deficits

Because consumer spending accounts for about 66 percent of the GDP, and since a large percentage of goods purchased in the U.S. are produced overseas in full or in part, *GDP growth indicates the extent of exportation of America's asset base when it's running large annual deficits.* In order to better understand this rationale, recall that each federal budget deficit is added to the national debt, which is financed by selling U.S. Treasury securities. Over the past five years, foreign nations have financed about 80 percent of this debt. Thus, *even if GDP data reflects net productivity, this data does not factor in the deficit incurred as a result of government spending or the trade imbalance— all of which adds to the national debt and decreases America's net worth or wealth.* In short, America has been trading ownership rights for imported goods.

Many point to America's annual 5.0 percent GDP growth rate over the past decade as a sign of its continued stability and economic dominance. During that same time period, *America's trade deficit has grown by over 25 percent per year, household debt as a percentage of disposable income has doubled, and the household savings rate has declined by 75 percent.* What does that tell you? To me it says America's "growth" has been fueled by credit spending that's been grossly disproportionate to such growth. Credit spending or debt is certainly no indicator of wealth, but lack thereof.

Failure to Account for Savings and Debt

Calculation of GDP also neglects to factor in the external effects of saving versus spending. Japan's case is particularly illustrative of this point. The savings rate in Japan has been high ever since the NIKKEI collapsed nearly decade ago. As well, Japanese companies have been investing large amounts of capital overseas (e.g. auto facilities, insurance and media in the U.S.) resulting in a much lower GDP than one might expect.

In the case of America, decades of declining savings and increased debt are not factored into GDP data. But borrowed money falsely inflates the GDP. Likewise, *economies experiencing asset bubbles (eg. real estate and the stock market) tend to show falsely inflated GDP figures since consumption is higher than can be maintained over an extended period.* During these asset bubbles the total credit bubble grows along with the GDP. This is the current state of America.

Failure to Adjust for Net Output

Another shortfall of GDP is that *it measures output that produces no net change or productivity,* such as that seen for reconstruction of New Orleans after hurricane Katrina. While capital was pumped into the region to help restore the living standard, no net improvement was made relative to before the disaster (unless you count the estimated $1.5 billion stolen from FEMA by some). In fact, most victims of this disaster are still much worse off than before the storm. Yet, GDP data assumes these expenditures led to a net improvement in living standards.

GDP data counts government spending at all levels, from the war in Iraq and hurricane Katrina, to Homeland Security. Basically, the government has been borrowing money to pump into the economy without registering commensurate returns. *If these investments had been successful, America would have net job and real wage growth, affordable energy, utilities, and healthcare.* But we see a much different picture, despite record federal and trade deficits, as well as record consumer and national debt levels. The overall impact of these trends can be seen by the weakness of the dollar.

Thus, it's easy to see that *a nation increasing its debt can show healthy GDP numbers,* when in fact the picture isn't as rosy as reported. This is especially true when credit spending has accounted for a large amount of the GDP growth, as in America's case. Therefore, when examining GDP data, one should investigate where and how the productivity occurred, whether there was a net improvement, and what costs (debt or deficit) were incurred, rather than focusing on the magnitude of the number.

Failure to Report Year-Over-Year Changes

When the Commerce Department reports GDP figures each quarter, the data isn't presented like a corporate P&L statement. When a corporation provides an earnings statement, it shows comparisons of revenue, earnings, etc. from the same quarter in the previous year (called year-over-year reporting). In contrast, the U.S. *government reports changes in GDP relative to the previous quarter.* And each *quarterly GDP figure is annualized or multiplied by a factor of four, which implies this figure will continue over the next three quarters.*

As far as I am aware, all other developed nations report GDP changes as year-over-year. Why does this matter anyway? Consider that year-over-year numbers minimize the effects of business and economic cycles. The fact is that all businesses (and therefore government operations) experience changes in business health and earnings due to seasonal or business cycle fluctuations inherent to their industry, the dynamics of the company, and the economic cycle. In order to minimize the effects of these variables, companies report the year-over-year changes, as do all governments except the U.S.

To illustrate the significance of year-over-year reporting, let's use Mattel as an example. As you can imagine, because Mattel is a toy manufacturer, it generates the majority of revenues during the month of December. Let's assume the fourth quarter is responsible for 70 percent of its annual earnings (an accurate assumption), while subsequent quarters contribute 10 percent equally to earnings. If Mattel reported fourth quarter earnings like the U.S. government, it would appear as if growth was exploding during first quarter earnings announcements. Thus, because each quarterly GDP figure is extrapolated over 12 months, it's virtually impossible to detect GDP trends accurately even if the numbers, when reported were accurate. But as we shall see next, accurate reporting is rare.

GDP is Inaccurate for up to Five Years

Keep in mind that *the government provides GDP revisions for up to five years* after the data was first reported. That's why you often hear adjustments to GDP numbers long after they were reported. It's also why the Washington often changes the dates of recessions several months and sometimes many years later. While these adjustments might be a valuable exercise for historians, they do nothing to alert consumers and investors of the current and future expected economic environment.

The official definition of a recession is two consecutive quarters of negative economic growth, as measured by GDP data. As a recent example of the inaccuracy of GDP numbers, on July 30, 2004, the Bureau of Economic Analysis (BEA) issued its revised GDP data for 2001. *According to the definition of a recession, we now know that there was none during 2001, since the latest numbers do not show two consecutive quarters of declining GDP growth.* As a matter of fact, the economy was reported to have grown by 0.8 percent in 2001.

Hedonic Pricing

How is it possible that inflation has remained low over the past decade while housing, healthcare, energy and higher education costs have skyrocketed? Does that seem reasonable to you? How has the government been able to conclude that inflation doesn't present a problem for the economy? Furthermore, how can the government report inflation without measuring food and energy costs? Does that seem reasonable?

Washington makes selective use of core and non-core CPI when it wants to hide the effects of inflation. But all inflation data is subjected to a very deceptive and inaccurate adjustment by a method known as hedonic pricing. The primary use of hedonic pricing is to identify price factors based on the premise that price is determined both by internal and external characteristics of goods and services. This may sound confusing but you're probably more familiar with hedonic pricing than you realize.

The most basic application of hedonic pricing is commonly seen in the housing market. Using this method, the price of a developed property is determined by the characteristics of the house (size, age, appearance, features, condition) as well as the surrounding neighborhood (accessibility to schools and shopping, crime rate, level of water and air pollution, noise, traffic, etc.). You might recall a realtor pointing to the enhanced value of a home located in a good school district, with a low crime rate, and so on.

Washington's use of hedonic pricing explains why both core (includes healthcare but not food and energy) and non-core CPI (includes food and energy) numbers haven't been high considering the fact that healthcare and energy costs have skyrocketed. *Washington has used hedonic pricing to hide the effects of inflation as a way to boost consumer confidence.* Even Bill Gross, fund manager of the world's largest bond fund has stated that the manner by which the government calculates the CPI is a "con job" due to hedonic pricing. Many others are also aware of Washington's manipulation of data.

Let's look at a real example of hedonic pricing so you can decide for yourself if it seems reasonable. Tim LaFleur from the Bureau of Labor Statistics conducted a price analysis of television sets for the purpose of calculating the CPI in 2005. He noted that the price remained at $329.99 over several months. However, significant improvements were made such as a better screen. Using hedonic pricing, LaFleur concluded that these improvements resulted in an increase in valuation of these television sets by more than $135. Thus, when determining inflation data for this product, he reduced the price value of these television sets by 29 percent (a deflationary effect) due to improvements, although the sales price remained at $329.99.

The same methodology is used by the Washington for many other goods and services, from computers to autos. *But, it's inaccurate to assume that product improvements will enhance consumer appeal of goods in the same manner as a price cut, unless we assume that consumers have an endless supply of money.* Maybe you can begin to understand now why the inflation data over the past few years has been low, while energy, healthcare, higher education, and many other costs have soared.

Converting Inflation into Debt

When you consider the trade deficit with China, it's easy to appreciate the effects of hedonic pricing. While Chinese imports have been inexpensive, (due to currency manipulation) Washington subsidized these costs by incurring a record trade deficit, which was financed largely through the purchase of U.S. Treasury bonds by China.

Thus, *Washington has been able to keep consumer spending high during stagnant economic conditions by passing out credit and transferring part of the costs of Chinese imports (using hedonic pricing) into the national debt.* In short, Washington has used hedonic pricing to transfer inflation into debt. Perhaps this is the New Economy we've heard so much about.

Why Distort Inflation?

It should be obvious why Washington would want to inflate GDP data. But why would it care to suppress inflation data? Consider that annual Social Security (via CPI-W) and Medicare benefit increases are earmarked to the CPI. With these programs already in trouble, Washington is doing all it can to minimize cost of living adjustments. The CPI is also used to adjust for annual changes in lease payments, wages in union contracts, food-stamp benefits, alimony, and to determine tax brackets. Suppression of inflation data would also decrease the future liabilities of mandatory expenditures. But one can only play games for so long before the bottom falls out.

12

GREED & FRAUD

Fraud is often the consequence of extreme levels of greed. Although it's been present for decades, corporate fraud continues to reach new heights because of the strong links between Washington and lobbyist groups. On the rare occasion executives are caught, most are faced only with fines levied against the company. Rarely do those in charge go to prison. This is precisely why the fraud continues. Never before has corporate America been so powerful in Washington. Never before has Washington been so corrupt. Perhaps the only comparable period was during the Roaring '20s. And this was one of the contributing factors that led to the Great Depression.

Corporate Insiders

When Wall Street analysts favor a company, they issue "buy" ratings and raise price targets, which causes the stock price to move up. This ultimately generates more cash for the company. You see, all companies own variable amounts of their own stock (known as *treasury stock*) used for stock options compensation and business acquisitions. Once a company owns its own shares, this treasury stock is no longer considered part of the *float,* or the number of shares readily available for trading in the stock market. Therefore, treasury shares are not used to calculate per-share figures, such as the price-earnings ratio, often distorting the real picture of a company's business health. And this can mislead unwary investors.

Thus, when buying a large portion of its own stock, a company can create the illusion that earnings are growing. While merger and acquisition activity has not been particularly brisk since the fallout of the Internet bubble, stock repurchase plans have hit record levels, helping boost profits while exporting jobs overseas.

Because companies know better than anyone what their short-term fate will be, they are truly the ultimate insiders. Corporate treasury departments can time the purchase and sale of their stock as long as they abide by certain minimal restrictions mandated by the SEC. Hence, unknowingly, *shareholders lose when companies purchase treasury stock.*

As well, there are very few restrictions for insider purchases of company stock. Don't you think CEOs and CFOs know their company's business prospects over the next few years? Of course they do. Yet, the holding period for exercising stock options is remarkably short. *This legalized insider activity has accounted for the bilking of billions of dollars from investors.* In most cases, the timely liquidation of stock options is transacted legally, although representing an unfair advantage and what I consider *legalized insider trading.*

Executive management cares only about one thing—earnings growth, because it leads to a higher stock price. This makes their stock options more valuable. But it also makes the corporation's treasury stock more valuable in a variety of ways, whether through the effects of increased buying power, or by providing a source of collateral for loans. And of course, management stands to benefit from higher bonuses and more stock option awards.

Today, CEOs are much too powerful and overcompensated, largely due to unchecked stock option programs. They stand to profit from overly generous stock option awards when the company performs well even on a short-term basis. Oddly enough, they do not share a proportionate decline in compensation when performance lingers. As a matter of fact, even the most abysmal performance often provides them with an 8-figure severance package. Thus, it is greed rather than the fear of underperformance that provides incentive to cook the books. It's really not a big deal for them because they know they won't go to jail even if caught. Enron and WorldCom serve only as rare examples of prosecution due to fraud, but only because these scandals received so much media attention. Unfortunately, widespread fraud will continue as long as corporate America controls Washington.

America's Most Powerful Industries

If one examines the twenty most profitable companies in the world, this elite list is dominated by two industries, mainly U.S.-owned. Care to venture a guess what these two industries are? oil and finance. From this list, twelve of the world's largest companies are from the U.S. But many of the non-U.S. companies receive a significant share of profits from the U.S., such as Royal Dutch Shell, BP, Total, and UBS. Likewise, 42 of America's 50 most profitable companies are also oil and finance-related. Both industries are exploiting consumers with the help of corrupt politicians and their lobbyist friends in Washington.

Oil companies are holding consumers hostage by manipulating inventories, causing oil prices to soar. Financial firms have things figured out as well. They've created the perfect business because they've got the best possible customer; the American credit-junkie. Washington allows banks to disregard responsible lending criteria so they can help consumers get their "credit fix."

Can you guess the third most profitable industry for 2005? pharmaceuticals. Remember, this industry has only slipped to the number three spot due to recent drug recalls. Prior to that, it was number one for over a decade.

Oil Industry

Oil is unique because it is only modestly affected by the law of supply and demand. While a limited supply will cause an increase in price, demand will only diminish so low because a certain amount of oil is required for basic living conditions. As a result, when the price of oil goes up consumers have no choice but to pay what is asked. And while we might begin to ration, we can only cut down so much before feeling the effects in our lives. Thus, *those who control oil have an unhindered ability to extract wealth from nations and people because it is the lifeblood of all modern economies.*

Oddly enough, as oil prices have risen, so have the profits of this industry. *In no other industry will you see this odd relationship that appears to be exempt from the law of supply and demand (except healthcare).* Similar to healthcare in the U.S., oil producers are not exposed to the full relationships typically found within a free market system. In reality, both industries operate as virtual monopolies.

It's common knowledge that oil companies manipulate inventory levels in order to raise prices. When catastrophic events occur, they manipulate inventories more drastically, creating the illusion of scarcity. But the big oil companies have contracts with suppliers which allow them to lock in rates below market prices. This ensures that any unexpected price increase will boost profits. Most large oil companies also refine their own oil and add another markup to consumers. Wall Street traders and other financial institutions know this. That is precisely why oil stocks trade up when hurricanes are expected to damage drilling rigs or refineries.

Why does Washington help the oil industry maintain its monopoly, rather than opt for a strong commitment to alternative energy? Washington realizes that any diminishment in the importance of oil would help deemphasize the dollar-oil link, which would devastate America's credit-based economy. *The control exerted by the U.S. oil industry keeps the world dependent on oil.* And this helps support the dollar as the global currency, with help from the Saudis. In return, the Saudis make huge profits selling U.S. oil companies crude while Washington stands ready to support the Royal Family if needed. The oil industry has shown its appreciation for support from Washington through very generous donations to both parties, especially over the past five years, overlapping its most profitable period in history.

All of these factors aside, I find it ridiculous that oil, gas and utilities companies—companies that provide some of the most basic necessities for human life—can be publicly traded or for-profit monopolies. Every time Exxon reports a $10 billion quarterly profit, that represents $10 billion that was overcharged to working-class and impoverished consumers who are struggling to keep their home warm, lights on, and a way to get to work.

Energy spokesmen argue that these companies need to be public so they can secure adequate financing for operations and risk-taking ventures. I can tell you that this argument is bologna. First, there is not one single electricity company in America that engages in the kinds of risk-taking activities that cannot be financed by municipal bonds. Power grid expansion projects can be tied to future revenues, so they're relatively low risk ventures. In fact, these companies often issue corporate bonds for these projects. But this financing avenue provides even more opportunity for fraud. We have already seen what happens when an electric company is provided with enormous capital from investors—Enron.

As for oil companies, while higher-risk ventures are certainly required, there is no need for them to be structured as for-profit entities. They would be able to secure adequate financing through municipal underwritings and private investments from financial institutions via private equity. *Being structured as a public and/or for-profit company allows energy industry executives secure their $400 million retirement packages and $50 million annual salaries, like Exxon's CEO has done.* Who do you think is paying for that? Think about that the next time you fill up your SUV or truck with gas.

Financial Industry

As a result of its change from manufacturing to a service economy, America has become a nation dominated by consumer finance companies that have addicted consumers to credit like a drug dealer does to a junkie. Think about it. *What does a large U.S. company do when it has reached its limits of growth? It forms a consumer finance division!* Why might expansion into consumer finance be seen as a lucrative way to grow earnings? Two reasons: lack of true regulation by Washington and a huge pool of credit junkies struggling to compensate for declining living standards.

As Americans have increased their dependence on credit, *corporate America has shifted from making products to making interest.* Think of America's largest companies and there's a good chance they're involved in the consumer finance business. Over the past three decades, America has been transformed into a credit-based society, whereby *the government encourages and rewards consumers for spending, while punishing them for saving.*

Even in 2005, President Bush passed a law that allows taxpayers to deduct sales tax from consumer goods—another desperate attempt to stimulate the economy by rewarding consumers for spending more of what they don't have. During the same period, Bush passed bankruptcy reform. Now and in the future, millions won't qualify for bankruptcy due to a hardship stemming from the effects of free trade and the healthcare monopoly.

America's "supply-side" economics began to spin out of control when the U.S. government realized it could print as much money as it needed, knowing foreign banks would finance its deficits (debt). Without foreign loans, interest rates would rise, making credit spending prohibitive. And since U.S. consumers rely on credit, they would be less willing to buy imports. It all seemed like a nice scheme in the beginning. Washington could spend what it wanted and foreign banks would finance the gap. Consumers would use credit to buy imports and the U.S. economy would appear strong due to credit-based spending. In fact, this economic system resembles a pyramid scheme.

What will happen when interest rates rise making credit less attractive? Already, rates are much higher than in 2003, yet they still aren't high by historical standards. You can bet rates are headed much higher over the next several years. As credit risk in America continues to increase, foreign investors will demand higher rates of return for investing in U.S. bonds. *It's going to be very challenging to convince Japan and China to keep buying U.S. Treasuries when consumers run out of credit to buy their goods.* Add the weak dollar, and soon no nation will want U.S. Treasury bonds; that is, unless long-term rates soar.

Record Profits

Washington has provided corporate America with access to the cheapest labor pool in the world by advocating its free trade policies. While this has served to keep many large corporations competitive, smaller companies have not been able to survive. As well, these policies have actually caused the death of many U.S. industries due to their inability to take advantage of the tools afforded by free trade.

You might reasonably assume that America's economic progress has been missing in action since slipping into the post-bubble correction phase of the stock market. On the contrary, corporate America has done exceptionally well throughout this period. As a matter of fact, *it delivered its best four and one-half year performance period in nearly six decades.*

Since the beginning of what was previously labeled the last recession (March 2001), production as a share of national income has increased by nearly 60 percent as of June 2006. This represents the largest increase since tracking of this data began in 1947. During this same timeframe, production as a percentage of national income has risen from 7.0 to 12.2 percent at the beginning of 2006.

Even profit margins for U.S. corporations are at record levels. In the first quarter of 2006, margins represented 8.4 percent of the nation's income for a 65 percent gain over the post-war average of 5.5 percent. Keep in mind these records come at a time when most companies have underfunded pensions, while many others have terminated or frozen their pensions. Other companies have filed for bankruptcy protection.

So what's going on? How were corporations able to deliver record production with fierce competition overseas? The answer should be clear: outsourcing. *Since labor costs are thought to comprise about 70 percent of corporate expenses, and given that labor unit costs rose by only 0.3 percent, the only reasonable conclusion is that companies cut total labor costs by outsourcing, lay-offs, and a reduction in benefits.*

As we have seen from earnings data since 2001, if you define the economy as corporate America, then the U.S. economy is booming. But as we all know, the economy is driven ultimately by consumers. Certainly consumers can appear strong when provided with endless credit. But this credit bubble has reached its limits. Over the longer-term, the effects of diminished job quality, record household debt, poor savings, and soaring inflation will expose the true state of consumers.

Corporate Tax Relief

The U.S. tax structure has been gradually tweaked over the past two decades to favor wealthy individuals and corporations at the expense of middle-class Americans and the poor. Of recent note, President Bush's tax cuts have been much more gracious to corporations. In fact, corporate America has paid fewer taxes than in prior periods despite record profits. As a result, *corporate taxes as a percentage of GDP have been at their lowest levels since the post-war period.*

Between 2002 and 2003, corporate tax revenues were only enough to contribute about 6 percent of total government expenses. While corporate revenues have contributed to the GDP more so than any period in the past five decades, its share of taxes is at record lows. This has led to the overall low tax revenues versus GDP.

During Bush's leadership, 275 of America's largest companies reported pretax profits from operations exceeding $1.1 trillion (from 2001 to 2003) but were only taxed on half of this amount. In addition, 28 of these companies paid absolutely no taxes on profits of almost $45 billion. Some might argue that low corporate taxes stimulate the economy. However, when favorable tax treatment occurs at the expense of American jobs and in the face of record profits, unnecessary pension freezes and corporate scandals, this creates a problem for both consumers and the government.

13

CONSUMERS & THE CREDIT BUBBLE

Consumers are the strongest force in the economy, accounting for roughly 66 percent of all economic activity. Therefore, the single most revealing indicator of the nation's economic health is the strength of the consumer. When consumers feel good about the economy (as gauged by interest rates, job security, wage growth, and inflation) consumer sentiment is high. This is reflected by increased consumer spending, which boosts business demand, leading to job creation and increased business spending. When they feel bad or uncertain about the economy, consumer sentiment declines, as does spending. Companies respond with job cuts and decreased investments. Thus, consumer spending ultimately affects business profitability and employment. Even when these activities are merely anticipated they cause the stock market to react.

As we have seen, Washington has many ways to inflate GDP data to provide the illusion of growth. Combined with government expenditures for mandatory programs and military operations in Iraq, the Fed's loose credit policy has created illusive GDP data. But most of this money has been borrowed from foreign nations. Thus, growth is an illusion when the source has been massive debt. But it fools consumers into thinking that the economy is strong. And that keeps consumer spending high.

The expansion of consumer credit over the past three decades has done well to mask America's loss of wealth and decelerating real wage growth. But credit spending can only go so far. Over the past four years, consumers benefited from very low interest rates. Now that rates have risen, there will be no more inexpensive credit. As well, debt balances will be more difficult to pay off as rates continue to rise.

Already, credit card companies have mailed out "changes to terms and conditions" to feast on the carnage of consumer misfortune. Aided by bankruptcy reform, finance companies are now well-positioned to hold indebted consumers hostage, raising rates as high as they want, regardless of credit scores. Many companies have raised rates to 35 percent for over-the-limit accounts and late payments.

Financial institutions were bending over backwards to give you credit when rates were at their lows. Their strategy was to entice you to raise your debt balance to unmanageable levels, knowing that President Bush would approve bankruptcy reform. Now the lions have come to feast. This alone could be the tipping point triggering a series of disasters over the next several years.

Boomers Are Coming

When baby boomers begin the early retirement benefit period in 2008, Social Security claims will start to increase rapidly. When 2011 arrives, the first group of boomers will become eligible for full Social Security and Medicare benefits. By 2017, Washington will get a dose of reality when trying to fund these programs. Each year thereafter promises only to get worse, as more boomers enter retirement age.

Over the next two decades, approximately 76 million baby boomers will have entered retirement. By 2025, Medicare and Social Security benefits will consume an enormous percentage of mandatory expenditures. As we have seen, only a small portion of these expenses will be accounted for by current tax revenues from the labor force.

Even if adequate increases to the payroll tax cap are made to prevent insolvency, Social Security must be strengthened further to keeps up with inflation of basic living expenses. And as we know, Medicare presents a much greater challenge to Washington because it will be hit with 76 million boomers combined with uncontrolled healthcare costs.

One way to temper the economic effects of the boomer gap is to legalize millions of illegal aliens. This is currently a hot topic of debate in Washington. Would this pool of 20 million or so be enough to reverse the diminished productivity expected over the next decade? No way. Consider that the majority of illegal workers, even if made citizens, would pay very little income taxes due to their relatively low wages. While they might prove to be good consumers, their payroll taxes won't make a dent in future payments needed by Social Security, Medicaid, and Medicare. As a matter of fact, legalizing millions will add to the future liabilities of these programs.

Boomer Myths

By now, you should appreciate the potential economic impact of the boomers. However, boomer demographics aren't confined to America. They actually extend throughout the globe. As a matter of fact, most nations will suffer more severe consequences from their own boomer trends. This global phenomenon is going to cause even more problems for the U.S. economy.

Furthermore, many critics have pointed to this demographic change as a short-term trend that will correct within the next few decades. But current boomer demographics actually represent more permanent trends. Why is this distinction relevant? Because there are many who claim that the boomer generation will only cause temporary financial setbacks. However, *the elderly are going to comprise an increasingly larger proportion of the world population for the foreseeable future.* And this has numerous economic implications.

Entry of the world's baby boomers into retirement could result in a global economic meltdown unless radical solutions are devised. Solving the economic problems of America's boomers won't provide a total remedy for the U.S. economy because it's become dependent on foreign credit. As the global baby boomer crisis winds down, the elderly population of the world will begin to harvest their investments overseas. This means less foreign credit will be available for America to fund its enormous liabilities.

World Boomer Crisis

As a first point of discussion, let's address America's boomer

142

crisis relative to the rest of the world. As you can see from figure 13-1, the United States is actually in pretty good shape compared to the rest of the developed world in terms of the ratio of young workers to an aging workforce. As well, America has a higher birth rate than most developed nations. So it's producing for more workers to fill the boomer gap.

What do these forecasts imply about America's future? Could they serve to rebalance the cheap labor markets in Asia in twenty years when younger workers become less populous? Will America become the nation of cheap labor used by corporate America? Could the rest of the developed world also encounter a crisis due to the liabilities each foreign government will face, such as healthcare and pensions? Given the impact of a world boomer crisis, who will have the money to buy U.S. Treasuries over the next two decades?

Figure 13-1. The World-wide Baby Boomer Phenomenon (2000 and 2020)

Ratio of population aged 65 and over to the labor force

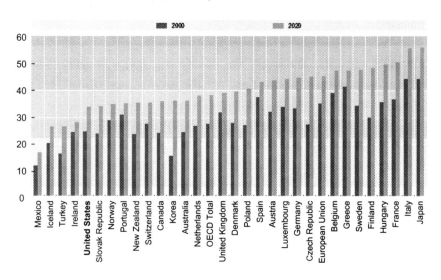

Source: OECD 2005 Factbook.

Boomers Are Here To Stay

Next, let's address the myth that the boomer phenomenon will disappear within the next few decades. But first, let's see how and why the boom in births happened. According to proponents of the "baby boom" theory, the post-war period reunited soldiers with their wives, which led to an increase in birth rates. If reunification alone accounted for America's birthing boom, one might assume the surge in birth rates would have ended after a couple of years. However, it extended for two decades.

As previously discussed (in Chapters One and Five) because its infrastructure was unscathed, America emerged as the global leader in manufacturing, leading to higher living standards. Human nature dictates that when people feel good about their future ability to provide for themselves and their family, they will have more children. Hence, it was primarily due to this period of heightened economic growth and stability that the baby boom period extended for two decades in the U.S. In contrast, much of the developed world suffered from the lasting effects of invasion and military occupation. As a result, war-torn nations experienced a much shorter birthing boom.

In 2000, approximately 12 percent of America's population was 65 or older. By 2025, this percentage will rise to 19 percent, making America a "nation of Floridas." Yet, by 2080, when the youngest boomers have reached 116 years of age, the percentage of Americans 65 or older will not have declined by much. Thus, the boomer demographics we see today will remain for at least several generations after the last of the current boomers have died. And as we have seen, these demographic trends will extend throughout the globe.

Double-edged Sword

The danger to the U.S. economy is that its boomer population may in fact turn into a double-edged sword. As boomers retire, they will have less income and fewer consumer needs, causing a gradual decline in consumer spending. Younger generations are not nearly as populous and will be unable to provide the same level of consumer demand as the boomers. In addition, due to their smaller numbers, younger workers won't be able to generate the needed tax base to supply government benefits to the boomers. Thus, it is likely that the economy will experience a gradual meltdown from these effects alone.

In response, many U.S. industries will be forced to target foreign consumers as their top priority. Given the potential customer base and healthy savings rates of nearly 3 billion Chinese and Indian consumers, it would appear as if Asia will soon represent the bulk of many industry revenues from U.S. companies. And this will further increase overseas expansion and outsourcing activities.

Credit Bubble

Previously I've discussed the real estate bubble and mentioned its effect on the total credit bubble. Throughout this book, I've emphasized America's weakened economic position by focusing on factors that have contributed to its declining living standards. As it turns out, *the growth of the credit bubble is a direct corollary of these economic changes, all of which have been accentuated by the malignant effects of free trade.*

As a result of Greenspan's credit bubble, the average American family is highly indebted, and not just for their home. Data from the Federal Reserve shows a total U.S. debt level (consumer, mortgage and government) of $50 trillion—some $600,000 for a typical family of four, or about 350 percent of America's 2006 GDP. As you will recall, this massive credit bubble has already surpassed all previous highs.

While average consumer debt for credit cards, autos and other assets are at record highs, U.S. banks and automakers continue to offer credit with numerous incentives. Some consumers even finance auto purchases for seven or eight years to lower the monthly payments. Due to extended financing terms, most owe more on their car than it's worth. The same situation will occur for millions of homeowners due to cash-out financings and a large correction in housing prices. Higher interest rates threaten to implode the $11.5 trillion dollar mortgage debt bubble, where home values are estimated to be at least 35 percent overvalued. Any severe shock to the real estate bubble would ultimately lead to higher interest rates which would stifle consumer spending. And if the Fed lowers rates to reduce the pain, it's only going to increase inflation, ensuring a more severe correction down the road.

America is now at a crossroads. While inflation is increasing, the Fed really can't afford to raise rates above 5.75 percent over the next three years without breaking the back of consumers. Already, short-term rates have risen 17 consecutive times since June 2004, peaking out at 5.25 percent. Recent problems in the real estate credit squeeze have caused Bernanke to lower rates to 4.25 percent; a bad move.

Regardless of the continued effects of the real estate meltdown, interest rates cannot go much lower. Now the Fed is trying to decide which is worse—inflation or a halt in consumer spending. If the Fed continues to downplay inflation as it has since oil crossed the $50 mark, Bernanke might lower rates to stimulate spending or as an attempt to prevent a recession, which appears to be almost certain in 2008. However, this will only cause the credit bubble to swell further, assuring a more severe correction.

Housing Bubble Affects Everyone

The run-up in real estate prices has created nearly $4 trillion in housing wealth compared to the previous decade. This period of real estate increases is unprecedented and *accounts for nearly one-half the paper wealth created by the previous stock market bubble.* But unlike the stock market, *the wealth attributed to the real estate bubble is more evenly distributed across America, so it may have larger implications than the bursting of the Internet bubble.* In 2005 alone, mortgage debt increased by $885 billion. Since 2001, $3 trillion worth of mortgages have been refinanced. Add to that over $2 trillion in home equity-type loans (including cash-back financings) and you can see where consumer spending came from. Adjusted for inflation and declining employee benefits, wages have actually declined for several years.

Will Asia Keep Buying Treasuries?

When bond investors lose confidence in Greenspan's bubble economy, (inherited by Bernanke) the only support for low rates will be the willingness of Asia to buy U.S. bonds. But Japan's economy is not exactly booming. And China is trying to wean itself from the dependency of U.S. consumers and the weak dollar. Soon, no nation will want to increase its amount of U.S. Treasury bonds for investment reasons alone because the dollar will remain weak for the next several years. And America is not exactly the diplomacy champion as of late. If America has difficulty financing its irresponsible spending habits, long-term rates will soar. Regardless, rising inflation promises to increase rates over the next few years.

Irresponsible Credit Spending

Ever since the banking industry began deregulation in the late '70s, credit card companies have increasingly preyed on consumers using a variety of deceptive sales and marketing practices. Specifically, two Supreme Court Rulings opened the doors for exploitation of consumers. Today, *29 states have no limit on credit card interest rates.* They're free to charge any rate they want at any time, as long as they comply with consumer disclosure laws, which amount to sending you a notification letter.

We all know these disclosures aren't written in plain English. As well, the print is small and the documents can amount to three pages, encouraging most to discard them without knowing of any changes. This is just one of the gimmicks banks use to exploit consumers. Even when you realize they plan to raise your rates, you're stuck in a bind since all other credit cards increase their rates as well.

Since 1989, credit card debt in America has risen by nearly 400 percent and is now over $1.5 trillion. Greenspan's reckless monetary policies have helped this debt increase by over 50 percent in the past six years alone. With over 1.5 billion credit cards in America today, each household has an average of twelve. But that's only part of the picture, as another estimated $2 trillion was extracted from home equity since 2001, much of it to pay off credit card debt. While this might appear to be a financially savvy move, consider that *those who substitute credit card debt for home equity debt have now transformed unsecured into secured debt*, all but guaranteeing it will take up to 30 years to repay. And these debt service payments can add up to huge expenses over this period. It's no wonder why the household savings rate in near zero. Would-be savings are fueling the profits of credit card companies.

For the majority of Americans, the use of credit cards can be considered a destructive rather than productive use of debt. The transfer of credit card into home equity debt has only enabled America's credit junkies to spend more. Of the 40 percent of home owners (30 million) who refinanced or took out a second mortgage from 2001 to 2004, more than 50 percent used the cash to pay down credit card debt. But the Center for Responsible Lending (CRL) survey data indicates that the use of home equity loans to pay off credit cards did not lead to reduced levels of credit card debt. This implies households quickly used more credit after paying down their credit card balances.

Credit Cards for Lost Wages

While many consumers use credit to buy things they don't need, a growing trend is the use of credit cards to pay for basic necessities they can't afford. Why are consumers relying on the use of credit card debt so much? According to a survey by the CRL, *71 percent of low- and middle-income families now rely on credit cards to pay for basic necessities* such as food and utilities, or for unexpected expenses such as medical bills and living costs after a job loss. Table 13-1 shows other possibilities for increased dependence on credit.

Exploitation and Deceit

The credit card industry is unregulated because Washington considers it a powerful resource to assist consumer spending. But the unfair and misleading business practices used by this industry are destroying the finances of working-class Americans who have no other way to pay bills during an unexpected emergency.

Credit card companies exploit their customers at every opportunity, charging high penalties for late payments and raising interest rates by as much as 300 percent for exceeding the credit limit by even $1. It's obvious they created these ridiculous rules and

148

penalties in order to trap consumers so they can feel justified in raising fees at their will. They use the tactics of psychological warfare on consumers to get them to become their victims. And they know most consumers don't fully understand the terms, fees, penalties, or the effect of compounding interest.

Credit card companies bombard consumers with direct mail offers until they submit to temptation, or financial desperation. Capital One has been notorious for this (in my personal experience). Yet, there is no way to be put on some "no spam mail" list similar to email. Even if you could prevent these countless solicitations, they have hundreds of other manipulative marketing tactics to get your business.

Table 13-1. Why Credit Cards America's Most Popular Safety Net

	Then	Now
Unemployment Benefits Maximum duration	15 months (1975)	6 months (2004)
% Workers Covered by Pensions	40% (1980)	20% (2004)
Federal Budget for Job Training	$27B (1985)	4.4B (2004)
% Workers with Employer-provided Health Insurance	72% (1979)	60% (2004)

Source: Demos, "The Plastic Safety Net: The Reality Behind Debt in America."

Many banks offer cards with images of your college, favorite athletes, or business name, knowing you'll be more willing to use the card as a sign of school pride, fan loyalty, or business acknowledgement. They also "reward" customers with higher credit limits even when the cards have never been used. This makes card holders feel wealthy (a phantom wealth effect). And when you finally start using the card, they send out changes to terms (i.e. higher interest rates, late fees, and confusing conditions) buried along with credit card checks and other junk mail, hoping you'll discard the notification without looking.

The Federal Reserve has defended credit card companies, stating they do a good job of assessing customers' ability to repay debt. In fact, the Fed has stated that there is no correlation between credit card debt and bankruptcy rates since companies assess their customers' ability to repay debt. Wrong. It's impossible to provide a continuous assessment of one's ability to repay debt by checking a credit report since things change; people get laid off and medical emergencies happen.

Fees Galore

The fastest element of revenue growth in the industry is now with fees, such as over-the-limit, late payment, overdraft, cash advance, and others. From 1995 to 1998, revenues from late fees grew from $8.3 billion to $17.9 billion while the average late fee more than doubled to an average of $29. Currently, the average late fee is around $35, but many companies charge in excess of $50.

Unlike the early '90s, when the grace period for late payments was on average 14 days, most companies have since eliminated this period to ensure more revenues from late fees. Most consider payments late if they arrive after 2:00pm on the due date. To make matters worse, they change the terms every few months and send customers written disclosures buried within all the rest of the junk mail they bombard you with each week, causing consumer confusion or neglect.

Credit Reporting Agencies

The credit reporting system is another scam that holds consumers hostage to companies that fail to deliver promised services. It's supposed to be regulated, but the fact is that it's not. Consumers have no idea how the rating system works since the rules aren't published. So they're unable to safeguard their credit score.

Based upon my knowledge of the rating formula, it appears to have been designed by either an adolescent or a crook. You can decide for yourself. Rather than providing benefit to consumers, the credit reporting system punishes consumers unfairly for the benefit of debt collection agencies and corporate America. As a result, millions have bad credit scores that are inaccurate. As we know, low credit scores increase rates for insurance and loans. It can even cause you to lose employment opportunities, as if it reflects one's ability to do a job.

The fact is that the credit reporting system has been put in place as a resource for the credit industry. But lack of real regulation has caused the system to emerge as a leading force of consumer destruction. Corporate America uses the system to further extort money from consumers. If you sign a contract with a cable, wireless phone or other provider who fails to provide the promised services, the entire sum of the contract will be sent to collection agencies which will report delinquencies on your credit score. And consumers can do little to remedy the situation. Your credit score can also go down merely by closing unused credit card accounts, or by applying for financing.

Today, nearly every business feels the need to check your credit. Every time you authorize a credit check you're opening the door to identity theft; another crisis Washington ignores because the credit industry makes huge profits selling identity theft services. These are the same companies that "lost" your records in the first place! As a result of this unchecked and abusive system, the debt collection industry has boomed over the past decade.

Household Savings and Consumer Debt

Household savings is the main domestic source of funds to finance investment in America, serving to promote its long-term growth. Savings can also serve as an emergency fund to provide security for unexpected events such as a job loss. But today, most Americans have neither savings nor an emergency fund. *Up to one-third of boomer households (about 25 million) have no savings, no investments, and no pensions. As a result, they are counting on Social Security as their only source of retirement income.*

While America's household savings rate has averaged around 1 percent over the past few years, nations that have obtained net benefit from the U.S. economy have posted much higher rates. As a consequence of poor savings, America's consumption-based economy has been transformed into a nation of debt, while Europe and Asia have become its creditors. The European Central Bank (ECB) head economist states, "As a result of the high level of savings in Europe we have two different worlds...European households are clear savers and net lenders while U.S. families are net borrowers—this has huge macroeconomic implications." Europeans tend to save around 10 percent of household income. Consumers in Asia save even more. China's savings rate is 25 percent of annual income. In South Korea the savings rate is 24 percent; in Japan it's 12 to 15 percent.

Figure 13-2. Comparison of Current Savings Rates As a Percentage of Disposable Income

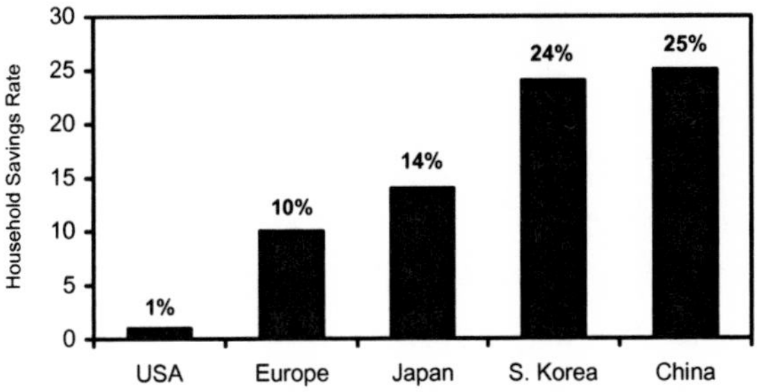

Even during the high inflation of the early '80s, U.S. savings as a percentage of income was more than 10 percent annually. Since then, the savings rate has steadily declined and is now oscillating between low single-digit positive and negative numbers. *In the 1950s, we saw a drastically different America, with household savings close to 12 percent. That was a time when the economy was booming with no need for credit, two-income households, or inexpensive labor from illegal aliens. That was the period when America was the world's largest creditor.* That was also the period when America led the world in manufacturing and oil exports.

Conclusions

America's New Economy is the result of advances in technological innovation, and a more rapid and efficient exchange of information. Free trade is also part of this economy, which was promised by Washington to deliver improved living standards, and it has—for everyone except working-class Americans. Thus, far, America's New Economy has been characterized by outsourcing, insourcing, declining employee benefits and job insecurity for all categories of wage earners except upper management. America's lack of preparation for the New Economy has resulted in a weaker link between workers and employees, while strengthening the bond between healthcare access and employment.

With a credit bubble swollen at its seams, we must wonder where consumer spending will come from over the next several years. Approximately one-third of the U.S. population will be struggling just to pay for healthcare, food, and utilities. Already, the cost of most consumer goods and services has increased by over 200 percent in the past two decades. In contrast, wages have failed to keep pace with inflation. *Since 1959, real wages (wages adjusted for inflation) across the board have risen by only 1.7 percent.*

So far, America has been able to borrow from other nations to fill this gap in wages. But in the near future these funds will no longer be available because America is not the only nation facing a baby boomer crisis. And the weakness of the dollar is not exactly attractive to foreign investors unless interest rates head significantly higher. As inflation continues to mount, we will soon see much higher rates.

Within the next decade, as the global boomer crisis begins to take effect, government-sponsored pensions in Europe could be in deep trouble. What that means is less investment capital for America; in other words, fewer buyers of U.S. Treasury securities, higher taxes, more benefit cuts, higher inflation and interest rates. As well, with over 10 percent of the U.S. stock market owned by foreigners, it seems likely that much of these holdings will be liquidated to provide for the retirement needs of European and Asian boomers.

Americans buy today what they plan to pay for tomorrow. But they consume so much of what they cannot afford, they end up paying for these items for several years. This has made the financial industry one of America's largest and most profitable businesses. Similar to its dangerous dependence on oil imports, America's dependence on credit has become its Achilles' heel.

14

FOREIGN PLAYERS

America for Sale

During the 1980s, Americans were troubled by Japanese investment into the U.S., prompting many to proclaim that America was "selling out" to foreigners. As we now know, these investments actually helped pull the economy through that difficult period. While the '80s witnessed a period of foreign investments into the U.S., the '90s ushered in the trend of foreign ownership. As powerful as corporate America has become, these companies are always for sale to the highest bidder.

Over the past decade alone, ownership of some of America's most valued assets has been transferred to foreign interests. During this short stretch, foreign interests in terms of loans, investments and asset acquisitions have totaled four times the foreign investment inflows from the '80s. Even more disturbing has been the source of these funds. In the previous ten years, the BEA estimates that *up to 40 percent of foreign investments were funded by channeling U.S. money into the hands of foreigners due to their financing of $4 trillion in trade deficits.*

Foreign nations have been anxious to finance America's credit bubble. Limitless credit means uncontrolled consumer spending on imports. Combined with the free-trade transfer of incomes overseas, exported capital from import revenues has fueled the modernization of China and India. It's a simple relationship. Foreign nations sell Americans inexpensive goods; U.S. deficits and trade imbalances are leveled by financing from the same nations. Foreign cash arising from interest payments on U.S. federal debt and trade surpluses have gone towards the savings and reinvestment programs of these nations. In short, we are witnessing a transfer of wealth from the U.S. into Asia, due to excessive consumer and federal spending. This is how developing nations have been able to mount double-digit savings rates while improving their living standards. This is precisely why the dollar has remained weak relative to most currencies.

You see, America has what other nations don't—strong consumers and an enormous agricultural engine. For several years now, much of the strength of the U.S. consumer has been due to the wide availability of credit provided by the U.S. banking system. But much of this credit comes from foreign central banks and overseas investors. Foreign nations also provide another essential element missing from the U.S. economy—cheap manufacturing labor.

Washington wants consumers to spend in order to fuel the economy. A strong economy encourages foreign investment into the U.S. Among other things, it finances deficit spending. But since America no longer makes much of anything anymore, much of this consumer spending is for imported goods. Combined with mounting debt, free trade boosts Washington's illusion of productivity, when in fact it's transferring jobs and capital abroad, serving to strengthen participant nations.

China keeps its currency devalued, so it slides along with the dollar. This ensures it will have the world's best customers—Americans, who buy Chinese imports, either directly or indirectly from U.S. corporations. This spending adds to the GDP. But America needs something it doesn't have to continue its growth—money to finance its reckless spending. So in return, China buys U.S. Treasuries to finance America's excessive consumption. Likewise, China and other Asian nations need something to continue their growth—natural resources.

The problem is that natural resources like food, oil, timber, and metals can be supplied by nations other than the U.S. Thus, it is easy to appreciate how dependent America has become on Asia. And when Asia needs vital assets, they've bought them from America's corporate auction block, courtesy of its capital markets.

Foreign nations are getting the money to buy U.S. assets from the reckless spending habits of consumers and Washington. As a result of this relationship, America is mortgaging off its most vital assets while receiving very little in return, other than a heightened dependence on imports and credit. A similar relationship exists between the U.S. and the Middle East, where America trades crude oil for ownership of U.S. assets.

America's foreign oil dependence coupled with high oil prices has created large current account surpluses in all oil-exporting nations. And because the dollar is weak, these nations can buy U.S. assets at bargain rates. But unlike China, whose trade revenues benefit from financing U.S. deficits, the Middle East has nothing to gain by financing America's debt, since the U.S. will buy its oil regardless how weak its economy is. Therefore, rather than buying U.S. Treasuries, Middle Eastern nations prefer investments in hard assets. In 2007 alone, Middle Eastern nations purchased an estimated $70 billion of U.S. investments, including large stakes in banks, real estate, franchises, and business units of large companies.

During the past decade alone, while U.S. deficits have been financed by $4 trillion of foreign cash, over $3.2 trillion of foreign trade surpluses were used to acquire U.S. corporate assets, including 8,600 takeovers in energy ($116 billion), transportation equipment ($146 billion), printing and publishing ($56 billion), insurance ($85 billion), electronics ($61 billion), and pharmaceuticals ($60 billion). As a result, many of America's most critical industries are now largely owned by foreign interests (plastics/rubber: 47 percent, financial services: 36 percent, machinery: 32 percent, chemicals: 30 percent, transportation equipment: 27 percent, publishing: 27 percent, cement: 81 percent, motion pictures: 69 percent, consumer television and electronics: nearly 100 percent).

If in fact corporate America controls Washington politics, we must question to what extent foreign nations will gain influence over Washington as this trend in foreign acquisitions continues. Finally, we must pose this question as it relates to U.S. national security. Most economists agree that foreign investment into America is good for the nation's growth. But everything has a point of diminishing returns. Already, foreign nations have financed America's total national debt by over 50 percent. The most recent portion of this debt was financed by foreigners to the tune of 98 percent, (in 2004 and 2005) mainly China.

Foreign nations continue to buy U.S. assets using trade surpluses generated from America's import-based economy. There's a big difference between lending a nation money and buying its assets. As you might suspect, these trends have major ramifications for America's ability to execute foreign policy. Unlike in the past, *America is no longer able to tell the world what to do because the world has a significant ownership in its empire*, and could cause its collapse by selling or refusing to buy U.S. Treasury bonds. Furthermore, with significant ownership of U.S. corporations, foreign nations are extracting more of America's intellectual capital and innovative infrastructure, in addition to the inevitable transfer of technology that occurs with America's free trade partners.

Peak Oil

Global oil demand continues to surge due to the rapid development of Asia. China and India are expanding their automotive industries so that they too can begin to enjoy the benefits of a modern economy. With nearly 40 percent of the world's population, these nations are expected to post huge increases in demand for fossil fuels as they continue their aggressive expansion. By 2030, the EIA expects a 47 percent increase in world oil demand relative to 2003. And 43 percent of this increase will come from non-OECD Asia (which includes China and India).

When oil experts discuss crude reserves, they distinguish between conventional and non-conventional crude. This is a very important distinction since our ability to mine and refine non-conventional crude is limited by technology and cost constraints. While the volume of conventional crude reserves was originally equally dispersed throughout the world, each region now differs in the amount remaining, quality, cost of production and refinement, and the estimated time until a decline in production will be reached.

Many experts believe that about 90 percent of the total conventional oil available on earth has already been discovered. In other words, we can only count on another 100 billion barrels of conventional crude to be discovered in the future. What does this mean? More discoveries of conventional crude must be made at a faster pace, or the world will rely on lower quality, higher-priced non-conventional crude. Since it is becoming harder to find new reservoirs, this guarantees that *oil prices will continue to remain high for a long time since much of the current exploration is off-shore or extracted from mining non-conventional crude, both which are very expensive.*

When the major oil companies are asked about the future global oil shortage, they insist the world has enough reserves to supply demand for several decades to come. However, inaccurate and inconsistent reporting of reserves, misleading data, and misconceptions of Asia's continued growth paint a very different picture. Regardless, *it is not the total oil reserves potentially available that are important as much as the maximum mining output per unit time, otherwise known as the peak oil production capacity* (Peak Oil Theory).

Because oil becomes more difficult to extract from each well when less than half of the original volume remains, the peak production is thought to occur when half of the oil within a specific reserve has been extracted. Upon entry into its peak oil production phase, (when half of the volume remains) crude is extracted at a maximum rate, but drops off permanently until the well finally dries up or is no longer economically or technologically feasible to continue mining. When this point has been reached, the reservoir is "peaked out."

Peak production behaviour has been described by a bell-shaped curve first introduced by geophysicist Marion King Hubbert in 1956. According to Hubbert's Peak Oil Theory, the time period of peak production is highly variable and unpredictable. It can last a few months or several years. Thus, peak production can demonstrate a long time plateau or a rapid spike of maximal output, followed by a variable rate of declining production. Once peak production has expired, crude output begins to decrease. And there is no way to know how long the well will last before running dry.

Most U.S. officials and oil optimists usually refer to oil reserves rather than peak oil. This mischaracterization undermines the problem of expected oil shortages over the next decade. Once again, the amount of oil reserves is irrelevant. *You can have 10 trillion barrels of oil in the ground. But if you have no way to extract it rapidly or economically, it is equivalent to not having abundant supplies.* And the supply-demand curve will necessarily increase the price of crude.

Knowing when peak oil will occur is all that matters, since this signals future permanent rates of declining output. But as we have seen, peak oil can only be verified many years after it has occurred. So by the time peak oil has been verified, output will have declined significantly. Thus, if global peak oil occurs prior to adequate transition into alternative energy sources, this would create a global oil crisis, sending the price of oil to astronomical levels. Because most nations depend on oil for economic growth, there would be a major war, as each nation fights to secure its economic sustenance.

Several highly respected geological experts and organizations without ties to the oil industry feel that peak oil will be reached globally by 2010. There are significant signs that this period has commenced. But once again, there is no way to know for certain until production declines for several years.

Regardless of one's support of Peak Oil Theory, what must be scrutinized are the assumptions which underlie the application of this theory. Consequently, oil companies have advocated overly generous estimations in order to protect their own interests. If Americans are alerted that the world will soon experience a decline in the amount of oil produced per day, (i.e. the post-peak oil period) this would prompt more investment into alternative energy technologies.

The big oil companies have no interest in developing alternative energy because this would threaten their monopoly. The aversion of alternative energy by oil companies is similar to drug companies that insist on higher drug prices to ensure better products, while shunning alternative remedies because they're more focused on preserving their monopoly than providing value. It's all about profit preservation.

Many nations appear to be concerned about peak oil. These concerns have stimulated billions of dollars of investment capital into the Canadian oil sands region from across the globe. In fact, many oil companies are now relying on Canada to provide most of the unconventional crude needed to make up for declines in conventional finds over the next three decades. But *the Canadian oil sands are not only very difficult to mine, but the oil is of low quality and requires a large expenditure of capital to provide adequate mining facilities. As well, volumes of natural gas are required for the intensive refinement process.* Finally, refinement of the Canadian oil sands emits significant pollutants into the atmosphere. Aside from these difficulties, even this huge non-conventional supply won't meet global demands.

America's Oil Dependence

The U.S. is by far the world's largest consumer of oil, at over 23 million barrels per day, followed by China (8 million), Japan, and Germany. With only 5 percent of the world population, the U.S. consumes 25 percent of the crude and over 45 percent of the gasoline produced on earth each day.

Prior to 1994, the U.S. was able to produce half of its oil needs. Since 1994, it has steadily increased its percentage of imported oil, in part due to rising demand, but also due to diminishing production of existing oil fields and the relative lack of new finds. This trend is expected to continue until Washington makes a strong commitment to alternative energy. The U.S. now imports over 14 million barrels per day (million bpd), or about two-thirds of its daily consumption.

During the post-war period, the U.S. was the leading exporter of oil. It was the abundance of oil that helped fuel this post-war boom. Ever since the post-war expansion, the U.S. has exhausted most of its 600,000 reservoirs, each producing on average a few barrels daily. Since reaching peak oil production in 1970, the U.S. has continued to spend more money to produce less oil, driving the cost up. Its ranking as the world's #3 producer is primarily due to the rich but dwindling reserves in Alaska, and its expensive off-shore exploration projects in the Gulf of Mexico.

America's growing thirst for fossil fuels has continued to outpace its productive capacity for over three decades. This accelerating trend has resulted in a large portion of its imbalance of payments, which has contributed to its recent federal budget deficits. *Thus, similar to its credit industry, oil has become America's Achilles' heel.*

Even when Washington finally decides to commit to absolute energy independence, America will never escape its need for oil. Oil provides much more than a combustible fuel supply. In fact, we use products made from crude on a daily basis. Virtually every plastic-based product is made from crude, as well as many chemicals used in manufacturing, special textiles, paints, fertilizers, pharmaceuticals, and hundreds of other products. Therefore, replacing oil with alternative energy can never completely eliminate its importance to the economy. So *when Washington politicians and economists mention U.S. national security, oil must be part of the equation since it's so dependent upon this natural resource.*

The Middle East contains a handful of oil wells that produce the bulk of their crude. *Approximately two-thirds of the world's reserves are concentrated within five Middle Eastern countries—Saudi Arabia, UAE, Iran, Iraq, and Kuwait. These nations also boast the majority of the world's largest oil fields.* While Saudi Arabia has the largest oil field in the world, Iran has three and Iraq has two of the world's top ten largest oil fields. Finally, these reserves are associated with the lowest production costs in the world. As the world's top consumer of fossil fuels, the U.S. is looking for alternative sources of inexpensive crude to fuel its economic engine. It should be apparent that the Middle East is the primary focus of America's quest for oil.

Figure 14-1. World Proved Oil Reserves by Geographic Region

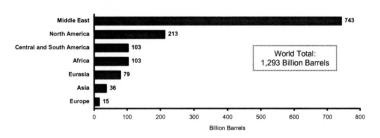

Source: Energy Information Administration, International Energy Outlook June 2006.
Note: North America's reserves consist mainly of Canada's oil sands, which are non-conventional and have a high cost of mining and refining per barrel.

Threat of OPEC

Ever since the oil crisis in the '70s and '80s, OPEC has been viewed as a political organization. OPEC demonstrated its support for Palestine's conflict with Israel by raising prices. This led to worldwide shortages. Sensing an opportunity to gain market share, non-OPEC nations increased exploration and production efforts. Today, non-OPEC oil accounts for the majority of production.

OPEC Members
Algeria
Indonesia
Iran
Iraq
Saudi Arabia
Kuwait
Libya
Nigeria
Qatar
United Arab Emirates
Venezuela

As an alternative to combat higher prices, many developed nations increased energy production from nuclear plants. But when the accident occurred on Three Mile Island followed by the meltdown at Chernobyl a few years later, the U.S. halted all new nuclear energy projects. Despite this, France produces 99 percent of its energy needs by nuclear means.

With oil prices at record highs, non-OPEC nations will most likely increase oil production even more, since they are less profitable when oil is below $30 per barrel. In contrast, because most OPEC nations have production costs under $5 per barrel, their profit margins are always high regardless of price. Because oil prices have been high, non-OPEC nations have been mining at full capacity to lock in these profits. However, this is causing a more rapid depletion of non-OPEC reservoirs. And when non-OPEC reservoirs become depleted, OPEC will control the world crude market.

Even now, Saudi Arabia or Iran could easily cause a financial crisis, using oil as a tool for economic and political extortion. In the past, America has indicated it will go to war for oil. Iraq and Afghanistan are just the latest in a long series of oil-crusade activities by the U.S. military. *If access to oil drives economies, it appears as if OPEC will soon hold the U.S. economy hostage unless it gains access to a huge amount of oil, or rapidly commercializes viable forms of alternative energy.*

Consider the following scenarios:

1. Middle Eastern nations, influenced by individuals tied to Al-Qaeda, strike deals with China, while leaving the U.S. out. As China continues to grow, America will no longer represent a dominant oil consumer for OPEC. The consequences of upsetting the U.S. will not have as much significance as in the past. This has happening now.

2. With about 39 percent of all non-OPEC oil reserves (proven plus undiscovered) in Russia, it could join OPEC for a share in the control of the world's oil supply.

3. OPEC could begin demanding non-U.S. currency for its oil, which if successful could cause a major financial catastrophe in the U.S. if OPEC follows suit. Iran is already trying this.

Iraq's Role

We should consider the possibility that Iraq will serve as America's access to badly needed oil. Iraq's oil reserves are extremely attractive for investment and development due to its high quality, huge supply, and low production costs. By some estimates, *Iraq could hold the world's largest oil reserves at up to 400 billion barrels since only 10 percent of the nation has been explored.* Thus, it appears as if Iraq holds the key to America's escape from OPEC oil dependence and political agendas. That might explain why Washington has already committed over $2.4 trillion to Iraq's recovery over the next decade.

What's Next for Oil?

Even when oil surpassed the $60 mark, many experts felt prices wouldn't go higher. I even made what turned out to be conservative forecasts in early 2006—crude at $85 by 2009, passing $100 by 2012. As of late 2007, oil is closing in on the $100 mark. While much of the recent price surge is being driven by the falling dollar, it is still greatly ahead of itself, in part due to continued tensions with Iran. Regardless, I am raising my target price for oil to $120 per barrel by 2010. If military actions break out between the U.S. and Iran, oil could easily surpass the $170 mark. Before the transition to alternative energy has been made, those nations with the largest oil reserves stand to gain tremendous benefits, financial and diplomatic.

China

Similar to America's economic revolution after WWII, China is benefiting as the victor from the free trade war which began over a decade ago. Even before China's entry into the World Trade Organization (2001), it benefited at America's expense. For nearly two decades, China's economy has delivered an annual growth rate of 9 percent. And since its election of PNTR status with the U.S. in 2000, it's posted double-digit annual growth.

In 2005, China surpassed the U.S. to become the world's leading exporter of technology products according to data from the OECD. In 2004 alone, China exported $180 billion in computer equipment, mobile phones and other digital equipment, surging past America's $149 billion. Similar to all excesses, China's economy will eventually correct over the next few years. However, its oscillation through the global economic cycle is on an up-trend.

Today, virtually every major U.S. corporation has moved at least a portion of its operations to China. Some have moved entire facilities there. Even Mary K Cosmetics expects its largest source of future growth to be in China. As well, most high-end retailers predict China will soon be the world's largest market for the wealthy. Already, it commands the third largest market for luxury goods.

Commodity Bulls Live in China

The only limitations to its expansion are natural resources, such as oil, steel, and other construction and industrial use metals and materials. By serving as China's number one customer for consumer goods, Americans have helped drive the price of commodities to record levels. But high commodity prices are bad for most economies, including the U.S. Thus, Greenspan's credit bubble has ultimately fueled China's thirst for commodities. In part, this credit bubble has been transferred into the commodities bubble we see today.

China's oil demand accounts for nearly 40 percent of global increases in oil each year. As a result, China has aggressively pursued increased access to oil by forming alliances and striking deals with foreign governments. In 2005, investors thought to represent the Chinese government made offers to buy Exxon, bought land in the Canadian oil sands, began construction on a $12 billion pipeline from Canada, and struck key oil and gas deals with Iran and Saudi Arabia.

It's obvious that China has become an ally and supporter of Iran. And it has used its veto powers in the United Nations in exchange for access to lucrative oil deals. At some point, this could create difficulties for the United States, as Iran now has another ally (in addition to Russia) for use in diplomatic battle while it continues its uranium-enrichment program.

Make no mistake; the biggest threat to China's rapidly growing economy rests in its ability to secure larger quantities of commodities. There should be no doubt that *the current bull market in commodities is being led by China's growth demands for raw materials.* And when its economy corrects, the bottom will fall out of commodity prices worldwide, excluding oil. This will be good news (although short-term) for the U.S. economy, which is fueled by inexpensive commodities.

Holding America Hostage

All of this business from America has not only led to a huge trade surplus for China, but it's also resulted in a large ownership of U.S. government bonds. China is now America's number two creditor, behind the UK, with over $1.44 trillion in U.S. Treasury securities and other dollar-denominated assets. As a result, China now has significant influence in the U.S. economy.

Over 75 percent of China's reserves are in the dwindling dollar. As the dollar continues to weaken, it will diversify its foreign reserves into other currencies such as the Euro and Yen. Either way, the question is when China will begin to sell dollars rather than if. If this transition is poorly handled, the impact on the stock market could be devastating, causing interest rates to soar and the dollar to plunge further. Of course, China would not be unscathed by such a drastic move. Its interest rates would soar as well, causing a collapse in its stock market. And its central bank would take a big hit. Finally, lower spending by U.S. consumers and businesses would disrupt China's economy, causing further havoc.

Surely, China would not bite the hand that feeds it. But it's growing stronger each day, fueled by the effects of U.S. exportation of jobs and investment capital. *At some point, China will no longer depend upon U.S. consumers to the same extent it does today. When that time comes, it will hold the fate of the U.S. economy within its grasp.*

India

Not far behind China, India has averaged 7 percent GDP growth over the past several years. Much of this growth has come from service sector outsourcing, whereas China's growth has come primarily from manufacturing export revenues. India has benefited from U.S. outsourcing trends, as companies have been under pressure from Wall Street to increase profits. As you might recall, corporate America has responded remarkably well, accounting for recent gains in the stock market since 2003.

India is the world's outsourcing leader, with its IT industry having served as the main catalyst of its most recent growth. But it doesn't end with direct call-center outsourcing. Similar to China, U.S. companies have more recently established a large physical presence in India, from GE to Intel, spending billions on new production and research facilities.

Microsoft, Oracle and dozens of other software companies are hiring new Indian graduates for their multinational plants as a less expense alternative to U.S. workers. While U.S. companies are saving up to 80 percent in employee costs from outsourcing, Indians are also benefiting by earning salaries up to three times the average wage earner.

War on the Dollar

Not many will dispute that the United States is the world economic and military leader. Some might even call America an empire. Unlike a typical empire which taxes the nations it controls, America uses the dollar as its weapon of economic control, with Saudi Arabia as its partner.

Prior to the partial decoupling of gold from the dollar during the Great Depression, America was far from being an empire. Even during the post-war boom, while the U.S. was clearly the world economic powerhouse, it still lacked true empire status. But when President Nixon defaulted on payments of gold for dollars to France and other nations, this began the indirect taxation by America on all nations of the world. This stands as the key event that positioned America as the global empire.

Shortly after defaulting on its promise to redeem dollars for gold, Washington negotiated with Saudi Arabia in the early '70s to forever support the Saudi Royal Family's reign as long as it demanded dollar payments for oil sales. And soon after, the rest of OPEC followed suit. *After OPEC transitioned to dollar-denominated oil transactions, the dollar became backed by oil.* This is why Washington insists that America enjoys a long-standing healthy relationship with Saudi Arabia.

Washington knows well that Saudi Arabia is not a moral ally, but a financial one, having positioned the dollar as the world currency. Consequently, as more dollars are printed, *foreign nations are forced to accept dollar payments and therefore suffer the effects of diminished buying power.* Because all nations must use the dollar to buy oil, the inflation created by the currency printing frenzy of the Fed is spread is across the globe, minimizing the effects of diminished buying power in the U.S. *Think of it as an indirect tax on the rest of the world.*

Since all nations must have the dollar to buy oil, and because the dollar is only backed by the "full faith and credit of the United States government," all nations are forced to accept a currency of unknown value. Only by linking the dollar to oil payments does this currency retain any inherent value. That, my friend, is how the U.S. empire controls the world. And the dollar-oil link is the only thing that maintains this control. This is why Washington loves Saudi Arabia. And this is why Washington drags its feet when questioned about alternative energy initiatives. America needs the world to continue its oil-dependence in order to leverage the global dollar-oil link.

But much of the world has changed drastically over the past two decades. No longer does OPEC depend upon the U.S. economic engine for oil revenues. As well, *free trade is serving to indirectly sever the dollar's clout by forces that have caused America to lose much of its wealth, income and intellectual property.* Herein lays another Achilles' heel of America. If the dollar loses its strength as the universal standard—either by global abandonment or by OPEC allowing other currency alternatives—the United States will be headed for a catastrophe of historic proportions from which it may never recover.

Attacking the Dollar

In November of 2000, Saddam Hussein demanded Euro-denominated payments for oil. Without coincidence, the U.S. invaded Iraq and overthrew him three years later. In March 2006, Iran started an international oil exchange (the Iranian Oil Bourse) for buyers and sellers of crude oil to be paid only in Euros. If successful, this could be one of the catalysts that helps destroy the dollar as the universal currency standard.

Now that Iran is trying to decouple the dollar from oil, it appears as if a military conflict of some sort is inevitable unless Iran ends the Oil Bourse or it fails. *Perhaps you now realize why Iran is developing uranium-enrichment facilities.* In my opinion, the White House has already deployed a group of CIA agents to disrupt the momentum of this oil exchange. America's next president will most likely be more successful than Bush with diplomatic negotiations in Iran.

If this exchange persists, it could lead to an eventual replacement of the Euro for at least some of the OPEC nations. Payment in Euros for oil would be good for most of the world but disastrous to America. The Middle East and Russia do a significant amount of commerce with Europe. So a shift to the Euro would make exchange rate disparities much smaller. As well, China wants to diversify into other foreign currencies and add gold to its central banks.

Certainly, it would be no easy task to remove the dollar as the universal currency standard, especially since the two largest oil exchanges are owned by the U.S.—the New York Mercantile Exchange (NYMEX) and London's International Petroleum Exchange (IPE). But there is already an alliance between Iran, China, Russia, and India (the Shanghai Cooperative Group) that could present barriers for America in diplomatic negotiations requiring the oversight of the United Nations.

If in fact the dollar becomes viewed as a questionable standard of currency, this would create havoc in America. Interest rates would soar to double-digits, and inflation would skyrocket. Any significant sell-off in U.S. Treasuries could create a domino effect, as nations rush to exit, causing the price of the dollar to descend further. And the global credit market would most likely implode. Thus, *even if America fixes its socioeconomic problems, the risk of an international crisis is huge, and could be triggered by a global battle for oil or the attack on the petrodollar.*

One or more of any potential international episodes—terrorist attacks, continued problems in Iraq, Iran, or a fight for the world's last remaining oil reserves—could lead to future military actions and perhaps WWIII. Many wars have been fought over oil. Even when oil does not appear to be a primary cause, adequate supplies during war are absolutely critical for military power. The Middle East controls the world's largest and highest quality oil reserves. And given the new era of extreme Islamic activities and links to OPEC, there could be a worldwide disaster brewing over the next ten to twenty years, with China and Russia as key participants.

PART IV

WHAT TO DO

15

LOADED CANNONS

Despite recent reports of outstanding employment numbers and record earnings, the state of the U.S. economy and financial markets are not what they appear. As mentioned previously, much of this data has been due to the "smoke and mirrors" trickery of the government, record low corporate taxes, loose credit, and overseas expansions by corporations. These elements have combined to produce short-term gains that have surfaced at the expense of record consumer and national debt, a wave of job losses, underemployment, stagnant wages, and a healthcare crisis that remains unaddressed.

With credit tightening and home equity loans depleted, consumers will soon falter due to subdued real job and wage growth, declining job quality and benefits, and a negative savings rate. The full effect of these trends could surface sometime in 2008, as $4 trillion of outstanding residential mortgage debt is set to reprice upwards by the end of 2007. As well, rising interest payments on over $2 trillion of revolving consumer debt is sure to take its toll on consumers.

The effects of these trends may not be sufficient to cause a devastating depression. But at some point, America will pay the price for over two decades of excess consumer and government consumption that has resulted in a massive credit bubble, free trade policies that have sent millions of jobs abroad, pension, Social Security, and healthcare crises—all consequences of America's declining living standards. These problems will be further magnified when the boomers begin to retire in a few years. Finally, if in fact peak oil is reached over the next few years, a global meltdown is all but certain.

Contrary to popular belief, the U.S. economy is still in a correction phase as a result of the previous bull market period. This decade-plus period of economic "growth" was fueled by inexpensive oil, credit spending and massive foreign capital investment. Many feel the U.S. has recovered from the affects of the Internet bubble. But Greenspan's rate collapse caused a shift of assets from the stock market into real estate.

In the process of mitigating the stock market fallout, Greenspan expanded the credit bubble to very dangerous levels. Consequently, the indirect effects of this bubble and the indisputable weakness of the U.S. economy have caused the dollar to remain low. Just as low long-term rates have pressured the dollar, the weak dollar has also served to keep rates low. Now the weakness of the dollar has emerged as the leading force behind soaring oil and gold prices. The expansion of global trade and the weak dollar have combined with China's inexorable demand for raw materials to create a commodities bubble.

Throughout the duration of the current secular bear market, I am predicting low single-digit average annual returns for the Dow Jones and S&P 500 indices for 2001 through the 2012 period. Note this period is exclusive of any catastrophic episodes that might push America into a depression.

At a time when they are most needed, government benefits such as Social Security, Medicaid, and Medicare are not meeting the growing demands of millions. As well, most pension plans are underfunded and threaten to force many retirees back into the workforce. *At the crux of America's problems are its poorly designed free trade and healthcare policies, both serving as a unified force to assure the nation's continued decline.*

No one knows for certain to what extent current economic conditions will contribute to America's financial apocalypse. The economy might stage a gradual and superficial rebound in a few years as it has recently, or it could remain sluggish and sink deeper as the problems continue to unfold. Alternatively, a sudden event could unmask the inherent weakness of the economy. Indeed, this is usually how major crises occur. Just when you think things have gotten better, reality sets in and takes everyone by surprise. Regardless, the fact is that the economy has not shown any real improvements since its fallout early in President Bush's tenure. And it's not going to get any better for several years unless radical policy changes are made immediately.

What Recovery?

Hidden from the reports by Washington and the media is the fact that consumer spending has been fueled by home equity loans, other cash-out financings and record levels of consumer debt. It hasn't been job creation or wage growth that's supported this phantom recovery. As a matter of fact, net job and real wage growth have been virtually absent, while outsourcing continues to devastate workers, leaving millions without healthcare for themselves and their families. Finally, Bush's tax cuts have registered no improvements in disposable income. They've only provided benefit to wealthy Americans and large corporations, while expanding the nation's debt.

As has been occurring for many years, America continues to spend money it does not have. Adding insult to injury, Asia has benefited from unfair trade practices while helping expand America's credit bubble. Dozens of U.S. industries have closed their doors due to price fixing and currency manipulation by China. But many more companies have managed to grow profits through outsourcing and relocation. In contrast, laid-off workers have had few options.

Washington remains powerless to stop unfair pricing and currency manipulation due to the restrictions set in place by the World trade Organization. But our great leaders knew what they were doing when they entered free trade. The goal was to empower corporate America, with no regard for the working class. And industry lobbyists have rewarded them with large "donations." The recent scandals linking numerous politicians with bribes are just the tip of a huge iceberg that remains hidden from voters.

In fall 2005, the average household savings rate plunged to -2.8 percent for the first time ever. Meanwhile, consumer debt continued to make new highs. Yet, Washington allowed mortgage companies to provide credit to virtually anyone with a pulse. As interest rates continue to rise, we will see just how "good" the economy really is. If the economy is so "good" why has it been driven by credit spending? If the economy is so "good" why are consumers loaded with debt? And why have companies been sitting on over $2 trillion of cash, choosing not to invest in new projects other than those overseas?

During strong recoveries tax revenues are high, normally accounting for a large portion of the GDP. But during the current "recovery" we have seen the opposite. *Economic recoveries also lead to net job and real wage growth, as well as an increase in savings rates, none of which have occurred.* The inflation-adjusted income of the average U.S. household has declined every year President Bush has been in office. In contrast, credit-based consumption has mounted steady gains along with federal and consumer debt. Specifically, consumption growth outpaced GDP by 6 percent annually from 1994 through 2005. In other words, *America has been consuming 6 percent more than it has produced for over a decade.*

Bush's Records

President Bush has set many records during his tenure. I've already discussed his annual deficits, which have led to an increase in the national debt by 65 percent in less than two terms. As well, a record number of pension plans became underfunded during his first term. This trend has extended through his second term.

Due to America's consumption-income disparity, debt service payments reached their highs for median income families since 1995, and for all income classes since Bush took office. *During his first term, America registered a record number of personal bankruptcies at over 5 million.* After securing a second term, Bush passed the strict bankruptcy reform bill in late 2005, assuring no escape for millions. In fairness to the President, many of these problems were the result of Greenspan's monetary policies. But he has only worsened the outcome by facilitating the growth of this historic credit-spending spree.

Surely someone has benefited under Bush's watch. Indeed, corporate America has recorded its best four and one-half year period of profit growth since the post-WWII period; nearly six decades. Supporters of Bush's tenure might point to the record number of home owners as an impressive reflection of the economy. But you really don't own your home until the mortgage is paid off. Rather than record home ownership, I expect the housing bubble to be remembered for record foreclosures and possibly a blowup in the MBS market, sending the stock and bond markets plummeting.

The real source of GDP growth since its trough in 2001 has been from one source—credit spending by Washington and consumers. In 2005 alone, Washington spent nearly $1 trillion for the relief efforts due to Katrina, the wars in Iraq and Afghanistan, and for interest payments to the national debt—all considered a wash since no improvements were made in living standards. That amounts to 7.5 percent of the 2005 GDP of around $13.4 trillion, accounting for nearly 200 percent of 2005 GDP growth.

Over the next decade, the President has already committed nearly $1 trillion in annual spending for just a few programs. The GOA has estimated that an additional $8.0 to $8.5 trillion (an additional $2.4 trillion for Iraq, $300 billion for Katrina, and $5.5 to $6.0 trillion for Part D Medicare) will be needed to fund these programs. Other sources such as the CBO quote these future liabilities to be even higher. This ensures the continuation of America's "growth illusion" since GDP will grow from these expenditures alone. But these funds will have to be borrowed from foreign nations.

In exchange for this spending spree, Americans have seen declines in both the quality and number of jobs created, while living standards in Asia continue to improve. Since the end of the recession in 2001 (now removed from government data, Chapter Eleven), real average weekly and hourly wages have been in decline (as of summer 2006).

President Bush has led the weakest job recovery in the history of America, adding an average of only 34,000 jobs per month for a 0.3 percent annual growth rate. During all other post-war periods, job growth has averaged 2.2 percent. President Bush's job progress looks even worse considering job quality has also declined. Finally, the recent unemployment numbers that fell below 5 percent in the spring of 2006 were primarily a result of more underemployed and non-traditional positions that offer few if any benefits, as well as millions of discouraged workers who weren't counted in the data. President Bush continues to report real job growth by cherry-picking misleading statistics. With little surprise, most of the jobs added during Bush's tenure have been defense and government-related.

The President's tax cuts didn't provide any improvement to the economy. They only served to increase spending, while median incomes declined. Even the U.S. Census Bureau reports that real median household incomes have declined for every year President Bush has been in office (2001 to 2004), falling from $46,058 to $44,389 (adjusted for inflation).

But the effects of a weak economy on consumers have been shielded by record credit-spending that has led to record trade deficits with China. We see the first indicators of what the future holds, with household debt soaring by 11.1 percent in 2004 to 121.2 percent of disposable income by the third quarter of 2005. This growth in debt spending has even surpassed the high inflation period of 1986. Despite the low interest rate environment during the current period, the average U.S. household had a debt service payment of 13.8 percent of disposable income; another record for President Bush. As of late 2007, the debt service payment is approaching 15 percent.

But this massive consumer debt has registered positive effects for Washington. Estimates are that *in 2005, anywhere from 40 to 60 percent of the GDP growth was due to consumer spending fueled by home equity loans.* Similar results were recorded for 2004. Thus, when you combine consumer credit-spending with the $3 trillion-plus of non-productive government spending, clearly GDP growth since 2003 has been an illusion.

Finally, when one adds the $3 trillion spent from 2003 to 2005 for Social Security benefits Medicaid and Medicare, it's quite easy to appreciate the illusiveness of GDP data. This grand illusion will only magnify, as these expenses balloon when the boomers reach retirement age. It's now clear that Washington has only designed a recovery for corporate America at the expense of American jobs and record levels of debt.

Throughout 2005, Mr. Greenspan and Wall Street refused to acknowledge inflation as a major problem as oil prices surpassed historical highs. Meanwhile, America's largest oil companies reported record profits (as they have for the past four out of five consecutive years) at the expense of consumers. As a reward for their extortion, many oil industry CEOs were awarded 9-figure retirement packages.

Figure 15-1. Growth Rates of Major Economic Indicators (measured through business cycle trough)

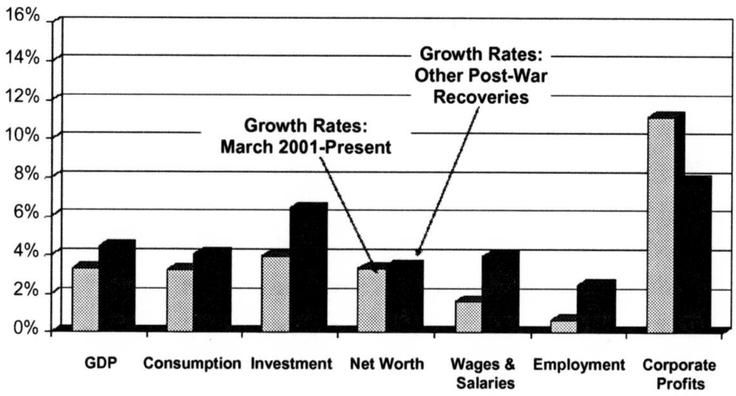

Source: CBPP calculations based on Commerce Department, Labor Department, and Federal Reserve Board data.

Even today, Bernanke only mentions inflation as a minor potential difficulty, when in fact it has become a major enemy of the economy. Finally, pension plans continue to struggle, in large part due to a healthcare crisis which Washington continues to deny. Thus, *with household savings rates at all-time lows, consumer debt at all-time highs, record Federal debt and trade deficits, no real job or wage growth, a prolonged military conflict in Iraq, a weak dollar, record energy prices, increasing inflation, a record number of underfunded pensions, increasing dependency on Social Security, a healthcare crisis that keeps getting worse, and the largest real estate bubble in history, how can anyone claim that the U.S. economy is improving? Are you kidding?*

Despite the risks, America continues its record-setting spending spree. Consumers have maxed out their credit cards while extracting over $2 trillion in equity from their homes in the past five years alone.

Total household debt is now over 100 percent of GDP and over 150 percent of disposable income. Meanwhile Washington watches, many fooled by their own deceit, while others are praying for a miracle.

Since 1989, the rate of foreclosures has increased five-fold to over 550,000 in 2001, reaching an all-time high in the summer of 2003. Between 2001 and 2002, before interest rates collapsed, the Federal Reserve estimated that up to 45 percent of all refinancing transactions resulted in extraction of equity from homes, causing higher monthly payments, while reducing total home equity. For 2007, the foreclosure rate is expected to shatter previous highs, heading north of 2 million.

Bankruptcies have soared since the Internet bubble deflation. In 2002 Americans reported 1.5 million personal bankruptcies versus 289,000 in 1980. Since then, bankruptcies peaked at 1.8 million in 2004. Remarkably, over 90 percent of recent bankruptcies have been from middle-class families, while at least half have been due to medical bills. But now and in the future, unfortunate consumers will have no way out due to bankruptcy reform.

Up until mid-2005, Americans enjoyed a two-year period of record low interest rates, providing them with inexpensive access to credit. Now that rates are approaching their historic mean, the Fed is running out of tricks to prevent the meltdown. Deflation of the real estate bubble alone could lead to a recession in 2008. This might serve as a prelude to a darker period over the next decade, when the world's oil reservoirs reach peak production, and after nearly half of America's 76 million boomers reach retirement age.

American Workers

Because employee benefits comprise about 42 percent of total payroll costs, the competitive effects of free trade have caused businesses to lower the benefits portion of total compensation rather than reduce wages. With no choice, workers have responded by contributing less to their retirement plans and savings, neglecting today what will surely present as a problem in the future.

As a way to mask declining living standards, Americans are

working longer hours. Many have more than one job or a side business, while two-income households have become the norm. As the average American struggles just to pay their bills, they enjoy less leisure time, have higher rates of stress, and spend much less time with their families than in the past.

Compared to most other developed nations, Americans have shorter life spans, fewer vacation days, and work longer hours. Finally, America remains the only developed nation that does not provide healthcare to its citizens. In the U.S., when you lose your job, you also lose your health insurance; not only for yourself, but also for your family; that is if your employer provided it in the first place. And the effects of free trade don't exactly improve the chances of healthcare coverage. More U.S. companies are hiring contractors, part-time employees, and coming up with other employee arrangements that allow them escape the costs of full employee benefits.

America has exhausted the surplus wealth generated during its post-war manufacturing dominance. It has entered the twenty-first century with declining competitiveness, excessive inflation for all basic necessities, and a federal government that relies on foreign capital to pay its bills. Meanwhile, the real value of minimum wage has been in decline for over four decades, while CEO compensation reaches new highs.

Figure 15-2. Real Value of Minimum Wage (1947-2006)*

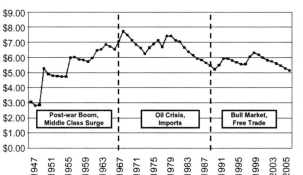

Notice how minimum wage soared during the post-war economic boom, leading to the dominance of America's middle-class.

Notice its decline during the oil crisis and entry of Asian goods during the 1970s and 1980s.

Finally, notice how the "booming economy" of the 1990s caused no increases in minimum wage.

*Through May 2006

Source: Economic Policy Institute; modifications and comments to the right made by the author.

Figure 15-3. Ratio of CEO to Average Worker Pay (1965-2005)

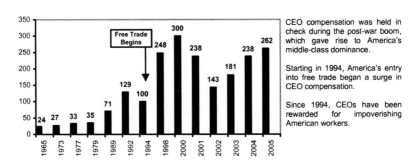

Source: Economic Policy Institute; comments to the right made by the author.

Government Benefits

In previous chapters, I've discussed the trend of increasing mandatory spending. I explained these expenses were due to social programs for low-income, retired and disabled Americans, as well the interest expense for U.S. Treasury bonds. The Congressional Budget Office has estimated that mandatory expenditures will rise to 14 percent of GDP by 2016.

But these projections do not incorporate estimates of pension bailout expenses, Homeland Security, Part D Medicare, or the money earmarked for Iraq. I argue these items should be treated as mandatory expenditures, thereby increasing the number to around 21 percent. But this is only the beginning, as these expenditures are expected to soar by 2030, as the boomer generation becomes fully immersed in the benefit stage of Social Security and Medicare.

Even without adding these expenditures, *the CBO estimates by 2050, about 27 percent of the nation's GDP will be used for mandatory expenditures.* In my opinion, the CBO has severely underestimated the severity of America's finances. Accordingly, without radical fiscal change or drastic benefit cuts, I would expect this level to be reached by 2025. The question arises; with mandatory spending expected to soar by 2016, and mushroom thereafter, where will the U.S. government obtain the funds needed to fuel the economy?

Figure 15-4. Federal Revenues, Outlays, Deficits % Surpluses (1950-2075) as a % of GDP

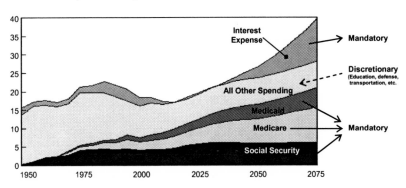

Source: Congressional Budget Office

Update

For 2007, the experts continued their long track record of predictions, helping guide consumers and investors down the road to ruins. In 2006, along with the EIA, many oil company CEOs continued to downplay the obvious uptrend in crude prices, stating that oil would average $40 to $50 per barrel, and stabilize at $30 per barrel over a longer period. In 2007, these same experts raised their forecasts to $60 per barrel, stabilizing to $50 per barrel over a longer period.

In January of 2007, the chief economist of the National Association of realtors insisted that steady improvements in home sales would support further price appreciation, "despite all the wild projections." And Federal Reserve Chairman Bernanke took over where Greenspan left off, stating in May 2007 that he "did not expect significant spillovers from the sub-prime market to the rest of the economy or the financial system." Even if these experts had read the first edition of this book, or the one I released in 2007, "Cashing in on the Real Estate Bubble," I doubt they would have changed their mind. They have their own agendas to serve.

Almost every analyst, economist, financial and nonfinancial talk show hosts continued to deny the presence of a real estate bubble throughout the fall of 2007. These are the same people who continue to deny America's healthcare crisis, while brainwashing viewers that the economy is strong. Clearly, they either have a political agenda or are simply ignorant. In some cases, they spew out their ignorance, while supporting their agendas, both political and financial. Unfortunately, these media figures continue to deceive Americans, who for some reason have come trust what they say.

Most television and radio talk show hosts need to stick with what they know best—entertainment and trivia. If you are a listener of radio talk show hosts such as Rush Limbaugh and many others, you need to realize they have no idea what is going in matters related to the economy, the healthcare crisis, or any other topic that requires expertise. For some reason, Americans have allowed these entertainers to influence their thoughts.

The same is true of most shows on the major television networks. The danger with some of these shows is that when they do feature "experts," most accept what they say because the host has identified them as an expert. This occurs daily on NBC, CBS, ABC, FOX, CNBC, CNN and all other networks. When Ophra Winfrey or any other mainstream talk show host features a financial "expert," you need to understand this person is usually a guest as a part of a publicity campaign sponsored by a large publisher to promote a book or service.

Unfortunately, most real experts won't be wasting their time marketing themselves on television. While there are a small handful of media figures that know what's going on, they can be difficult to spot because they're often discredited by the mainstream media or they have limited exposure. My advice is to listen to real experts who have no agendas, rather than the parade of lies broadcast by the popular press. And if the "expert" is a government official, a fund manager, economist or analyst on Wall Street, you can bet they are going to paint a rosier picture than reality.

16

CONSEQUENCES

In order to navigate through turbulent periods, the Federal Reserve exerts its monetary powers, while trying to maximize growth. Like all humans, the Fed is far from perfect. As a result, economic contractions are inevitable. When severe, economic contractions lead to recessions. This is the price paid for maximizing growth. But the pain of a recession is usually more intense than the heightened prosperity seen during expansions.

Quite simply, consumers and investors alike take losses much harder than gains. Fortunately, changes to U.S. economic and monetary policy over the past several decades have allowed the nation to dampen devastating swings in the economic cycle. As a result, recessions are now usually brief, while expansions are much longer. But still, busts follow all booms.

The primary manner by which the Fed influences the economy is by controlling the money supply. When the money supply increases beyond normal levels, this increases available credit relative to the amount of available goods and services. If this relationship continues over a sustained period, inflation will result. As consumers spend more on items, demand outstrips supply forcing producers to raise prices. Some of the consequences of inflation are rising commodity prices and changes in currency exchange rates; both huge macroeconomic forces.

Commodities represent the backbone of all economies. When commodity prices rise, the cost of all goods and services follows. For instance, when the price of crude oil rises, transportation costs increase resulting in higher costs for all goods and services. Ultimately, an increase in fuel prices shrinks disposable income. Soon, consumer sentiment declines. This is followed by a drop in consumer spending. As a result, fewer consumers venture to shopping malls and restaurants, and retail sales suffer. High oil prices also raise utility bills and airline prices, shrinking disposable income further.

High crude prices also increase the cost of basic materials—paint, building materials, fertilizers and plastic goods—since they're made from crude. New development projects become more expensive, while all consumer goods increase in price due to crude-based materials and/or due to increased shipping costs. Even food prices increase since crops and livestock feed requires fertilizer, as well as the higher cost of fuel used by farm equipment.

Modest inflation is characteristic of a healthy economy because it acts to balance the supply and demand tug-of-war for goods and services. However, when key economic indicators move out of balance, such as interest rates, inventories, etc., this can lead to above average levels of inflation. When high levels of inflation extend over a long period it results in a collapse of real wages, savings and investment returns.

While inflation has a delayed effect upon the economy, it's often under-reported due to the prevalent use of core inflation, which excludes food and energy costs. As well, Washington's use of hedonic pricing and Bush's record trade deficits have served well to mask the real inflation that exists today. Washington has only managed to lower the effects of inflation by borrowing money. In fact, Bush has transferred much of the current inflation into federal debt, financed by the foreign trade surpluses in Asia.

During inflation, bonds perform poorly, while the performance of common stocks is often a mixed bag. When inflation is high, bonds are a poor investment choice for two reasons. First, bondholders receive a fixed coupon rate which is eroded by the high cost of goods. In other words, the buying power is reduced.

As an attempt to lower inflation, the Fed tightens the money supply. This is often achieved by raising short-term rates. Thus, because inflation ushers in higher interest rates, those who bought bonds prior to rate hikes will see the market price of the bonds decline, resulting in diminished liquidity. Basically, you have to hold these bonds until rates decline or until maturity—that is, unless you're willing to sell them at a loss. In the meantime, those coupon payments won't amount to much. *Only when investors are able to time their purchase of bonds at the peak of interest rates and/or when such bonds are indexed to inflation will they come out ahead.* This emphasizes the critical need for bond investors to really understand the economy or else find a bond fund manager that does.

A gradual rise in inflation allows some companies to raise prices for goods and services. And this can actually result in earnings growth; good for stockholders. But only certain industries are able to do this, such as alcoholic beverage, tobacco, and gaming, for obvious reasons. In contrast, *a sharp increase in inflation is bad for nearly all industries because it produces a shock effect within the economy.* The longer inflation remains high, the greater the chance of further interest rate hikes. Therefore, a trend of rising inflation can destroy the investment returns from bonds unless they are indexed to inflation. With rare exception, common stocks get hammered too.

In general, *the best investments during an inflationary environment are commodities, REITS, and Treasury Inflation-Protected Securities (TIPS), or any other assets tied to floating interest rates.* Gold also tends to perform well during inflation. While commodities are not directly linked to rising interest rates, they tend to be relatively shielded from inflationary effects because consumers and businesses must pay whatever price is charged since these items comprise the basic building blocks of the economy. Of course, you aren't going to see a lot of economic growth during high inflation, so the demand for commodities is not stellar. Thus, while commodities won't significantly outperform the overall market, they also won't get hammered like other assets.

Like everything else, inflation occurs as a part of a cycle which alternates with compensatory periods of relative deflation. Deflation occurs due to a decrease in money supply causing less credit relative to the amount of goods and services available. This results in a lower demand for goods and services, triggering a reduction in prices by businesses. In contrast, whenever deflation is absent, at least a small amount of inflation will be present. Therefore, *inflation is the norm and deflation, while still a part of this cycle, is less common and therefore less familiar to most consumers.*

Because inflation is a normal phenomenon, deflation tends to only occur when excesses in inflation have resulted in credit bubbles, such as those seen during the late 1920s and 1990s. The U.S. recently experienced a modest deflationary period (2001 to 2004). But the last major deflationary period occurred some 70 years earlier in the midst of the Great Depression. During the 1930s, deflation appeared due to the inability of banks to lend money and the lack of credit worthiness of consumers. Those who had credit didn't want to borrow money because they felt prices would continue to decline, making the goods they might have purchased worthless. This deflationary period rebalanced the supply and demand for goods that was made lop-sided by the actions of the Fed.

Was the recent deflationary period sufficient to restore the economy back to normal? Not at all. In fact, Greenspan's response has created a strong inflationary trend. Now, America is faced with a real estate and credit bubble that have only begun to deflate.

Inflation or Deflation?

There appears to be a debate whether the meltdown will occur by inflation or deflation. As mentioned previously, the U.S. already faces an inflationary environment fueled by record oil prices. Considering I expect oil to remain high, I'm betting on inflation to be the cause and/or the consequence of the fallout. If conditions get really bad, deflation could be a later sequela.

As discussed in Chapter Ten, the MBS market could experience a severe blow-up. This would lead to defaults on trillions of dollars in loans, resulting in a deflationary environment. This would be one of the worst-case scenarios because it would lead to the loss of huge sums of money from banks and pension funds, affecting nearly every American. Needless to say, the stock and bond markets would get hammered. Compensatory alterations in monetary and fiscal policy might later cause extreme inflation. We have recently seen signs of this possibility, with the sub-prime fallout already having affected virtually every financial institution. I expect further losses through 2009.

Alternatively, even without a severe collapse of the MBS market, the real estate correction will lead to heavy losses throughout the financial industry. Under this more likely scenario, while avoiding deflation, America would continue current inflationary trends due to high oil prices and a weak dollar. Thus, regardless of the magnitude of the correction, the next decade or two more will most certainly be characterized by extreme inflation. A severe catastrophe might usher in a deflationary period as an after-shock, but only after inflation has caused significant damage.

Much of the deflationary pressure during the 2001 to 2004 period was due to an inventory buildup after the Internet meltdown. Severe loosening of credit was required to soften the blow of the economic correction. Bush's tax cuts were also initiated to combat deflation and stimulate consumer spending. However since 2001, the dollar has been in decline, which would appear to counteract any deflationary effects from these actions.

Thrown into the picture is the unhindered access of inexpensive goods from Asia, which has added to the post-deflationary period. As previously discussed, much of the effect of inexpensive imports has been due to currency manipulation. Keeping the Yuan pegged to the dollar has helped counter the affects of a weak dollar and furthered the expansion of the credit bubble. Together, these forces have added an additional inflationary component to the economy. But remember that Washington has transformed this inflation into debt due to China's massive purchase of U.S. Treasuries.

When China properly values its currency, the cost of Asian imports will rise. Prior to that time it is likely that China will more widely diversify into other foreign currencies and gold. That too will cause the price of Chinese imports to increase. By that time, it is likely that China will be generating a much larger portion of its growth internally, by encouraging its consumers to spend. With the average Chinese household stashing away 25 percent of disposable income, Chinese consumers have amassed a lot of buying power.

Similarities to the Great Depression

It seems like every nation is experiencing rapid growth at America's expense, from Brazil to South Korea, England to China. In America, the only benefactors of the post-Internet bubble period have been the wealthy elite and corporations, which continue to strengthen at the expense of the poor and middle-class.

America's working class continues to lose ground on every front. Job quality is declining, wage growth is absent, inflation in energy and utilities is crippling incomes, consumer credit and mortgage debt are at record highs (on a per-dollar and GDP basis), healthcare coverage is unavailable to millions, food prices are on the rise, and most boomers have insufficient retirement funds. Given the scale of the money-printing frenzy by the U.S. Treasury since 2001, *it is highly likely that a correction of Greenspan's credit bubble will adversely impact the global financial system. In fact, there is now heightened risk of a blow-up in the $29 trillion global credit derivatives market.*

Today's global economy depends on cheap U.S. dollar credit. When interest rates are forced higher, aftershocks from America's meltdown will hit Europe and Asia unlike anything seen since the 1930s. Debts that now appear manageable will suddenly become un-payable, resulting in record bankruptcies and foreclosures. This will lead to massive losses for financial institutions worldwide.

As consumer and business spending halts, Washington will rush to create an environment that will restore order and commerce. If not orchestrated carefully, this could lead to hyperinflation and further devastation. This prompts a review of the five main factors that contributed to the "Great Depression." All of these characteristics are already present in modern America, although some differences exist.

Consumer Credit

Contrary to popular belief, many Americans lived off of credit during the Roaring '20s. However, back then credit cards didn't exist. Instead, consumers bought items on layaway or installment plans. The Fed increased the money supply, catalyzing the boom during the '20s, as consumers continued to spend what they did not have. In place of credit cards, they used huge levels of margin debt to purchase stocks while spending wages on unnecessary items.

Washington supported big business, creating a huge wealth and savings gap. As a result, most Americans became reliant on credit. By the late '20s, 60 percent of all autos and 80 percent of all radios in the U.S. were purchased using some type of installment credit. During this "booming" decade, the total amount of outstanding installment credit more than doubled from $1.38 billion to nearly $3 billion. In today's dollars one might think in terms of trillions. This overuse of credit created a false demand for goods, which resulted in overproduction. And this tilted the supply-demand equilibrium.

When monetary tightening began, this triggered the typical sequence of events seen in an economic contraction—diminished spending, less demand for products, increased inventories and layoffs. Many consumers couldn't afford to pay for items bought on installment; those who could either didn't have any money left to buy new items or feared even more price declines, causing inventories to pile up further.

Today, stock margin debt has more strict controls but consumer credit doesn't, nor do mortgage loan approvals. Remarkably, stock margin debt has reached new highs. Consumers have borrowed money to the tune of 6 percent annually for over a decade. Sooner or later rising interest rates are going to crush their budgets.

When one compares the irresponsible lending practices within the current bubble to lending practices of banks and brokerage firms prior to the Crash of '29, we see many common themes. Similar to the '20s, much of the today's real estate bubble has swelled due to the lack of controls in the financial system. This has encouraged millions of consumers to pile up debt, while investors take huge gambles.

In both cases, the wealth effect led to financial irresponsibility and speculation. In the '20s, high loan-to-value margin debt encouraged millions to speculate in the first major stock market bubble in U.S. history. Likewise, the current real estate bubble has swelled due to the excessive use of interest-only, option-ARMs, high loan-to-value mortgages, home equity loans, and massive expansion of the sub-prime mortgage market. We saw a similar level of speculation prior to the Internet collapse. Most Americans still haven't learned their lesson.

Overproduction

During WWI, the government made a strong commitment to help farmers supply agricultural products to U.S. troops and foreign allies. Farm expenses were subsidized with outrageous prices for wheat and other grains. Still, farmers were unable to keep up with demand, which forced prices higher. In response, Washington encouraged farmers to buy more land and modernize their equipment so they could reach full production capacity.

After the war ended, Washington ended these supportive policies. This led to a huge excess of agricultural goods which ultimately depressed pricing. In order to counter these effects, farmers produced even more hoping to "make up the difference in volume." However, this led to major price declines when sales didn't materialize. A bushel of wheat that once sold for $2 fell to $0.67. Meanwhile, Washington did nothing to help stabilize agricultural pricing. While manufacturing industries such as steel, railroad, and textiles were profitable, agriculture suffered. Farmers became delinquent on loans, many leading to foreclosures. Soon, rural banks holding these loans failed. While the Agricultural Credits Act of 1923 was an attempt to rescue the agricultural fallout, it was too little too late.

Corporations recently experienced a build up of inventories in the early stages of the Internet bubble deflation. This build up has taken 4 years and record low interest rates to deplete. Soon there will be a huge housing inventory when the real estate bubble deflates. And this will expand to the credit market.

Income and Savings Disparity

As we know, history often repeats. And the booming economy of the '20s was no exception to other periods of economic growth, whereby the wealthy got richer at the expense of the middle class and the poor. While the unequal distribution of wealth during the '20s didn't actually cause the depression, it was certainly one of the leading factors that contributed to its severity.

President Coolidge favored big business and all who invested in them. The Revenue Act of 1926 reduced federal income and inheritance taxes lowering income taxes for the wealthy by as much as 65 percent relative to low-income Americans. In the '20s, the income of the wealthiest 1 percent of Americans rose by 75 percent, while that of the nation as a whole rose by only 9 percent. The top 0.1 percent of Americans had a total income equal to the bottom 42 percent of all Americans. This ultra-wealthy elite group accounted for 34 percent of all household savings, while 80 percent of Americans had no savings at all.

Much of the wealth held by the richest Americans was due to soaring stock prices. But it was also due to the control and exploitation by corporations and those who owned them. Of course, the lowest income Americans entered the stock market at the top, as is the usual case with asset bubbles.

In addition, the Supreme Court ruled minimum wage laws to be unconstitutional. Already, we have seen that only the wealthiest 10 percent of Americans have benefited over the past two decades, while the real income of the remaining 90 percent has barely moved. Household savings are near 0, debt (consumer and federal) continues to surpass record highs. Even the recent passage of minimum wage hikes will be inadequate to make much of a difference.

Dependence on A Few Industries

During the '20s, only those industries related to auto and construction thrived. The automobile was a revolutionary innovation that changed the social, economic and business infrastructure of America. It led to the growth of the rubber, glass, and steel industries, as well as motels, gas stations, and roadside restaurants. But when demand for these products fell, the entire economy was devastated.

Today, America is more dependent on a smaller number of industries than in the previous four decades due to the collapse of manufacturing. Oil and finance companies dominate the economy and exploit consumers while Washington turns its back. However, America's oil industry could easily collapse due to war with Iran, OPEC price manipulation, or the effects of peak oil.

Meanwhile, the financial system could collapse due to the continued weakness of the dollar and the increasing momentum of the Euro as the new global standard. As well, the financial system remains highly leveraged, specifically in the credit derivatives market. Finally, if the dollar loses its position as the global currency, America will most certainly encounter catastrophic consequences.

The "Crash of 1929"

Even during a period without widespread telephone use, no televisions, and no Internet, by the late '20s virtually everyone was invested in the stock market. Similar to the Internet bubble of the late 1990s, everyone was giving stock tips; a clear sign to get out of the market. Most Americans were speculating but didn't realize it. They felt that making money in the market was a sure thing; another warning sign of a swollen bubble. Greed took over, and many borrowed on ridiculous margin requirements that were as low as 10 to 25 percent.

After the first sell-off, investors panicked, causing many more to sell. This resulted in a further decline in stock prices. When margin calls triggered, most couldn't be filled and this caused a massive sell-off. The bottom fell out on October 29, 1929, known as "Black Tuesday" when a record number of shares were traded, sending the market tumbling.

Shortly after the crash, millions rushed to their banks in a panic to withdraw savings. But many banks had insufficient funds because they too had lost money in the market. By 1933, nearly 6000 banks in America, or about 25 percent of the nation's total banking system had failed. Because there was no FDIC at the time, over 9 million savings accounts were lost. Many had massive losses due to margin calls. Because they were unable to pay these loans they filed for bankruptcy. Since most consumers had no disposable income, demand for goods dropped off, causing lay-offs and corporate bankruptcies.

Today, stock exchanges halt trading if large sell-offs occur over a short period to minimize the chance of a massive sell-off. But as we saw after 9/11, the market can still suffer huge loses over a several-day period. The New Deal established the FDIC which provides banks with $100,000 of insurance per person. Several decades later, the SIPC was established to provide insurance against broker/dealer fraud or insolvency for each customer up to a maximum of $500,000. This figure includes a maximum of $100,000 on claims for cash. Recovered funds are used to pay investors whose claims exceed SIPC's protection limit of $500,000. But the SIPC has encountered numerous problems with asset recovery, resulting in long delays and other problems too long to mention. And investors are not covered for losses due to stock market performance, such as price declines, fraud, or bankruptcies.

The recent repel of the Glass-Steagall Act and the passage of the Gramm-Leach-Bliley Act has transformed commercial banks into Wall Street investment houses which now take on excessive risks. And any widespread bank failures could cause huge problems for the FDIC and SIPC.

Today, most U.S. banks hold astronomical liabilities on their books, while others have found ways to conceal these risks. If banks were forced to state their liabilities accurately, marked debt and assets to market, this alone could cause a panic. Finally, there's no real insurance for the $15 trillion in collateralized securities, nor is there any insurance for the $13.5 trillion invested in the stock market. These markets are also linked to the $29 trillion credit derivatives market.

It's only been a few years since the Internet bubble burst. Yet many investors act as if nothing happened, as evidenced by massive speculation in the stock market. The SEC allows infomercials from shady companies that claim to teach novices how to trade for a living by "watching red and green lights." In essence, the SEC is permitting the manipulation of millions of desperate Americans who are strapped for cash or worried about inadequate retirement funds.

Millions of novices have entered the world of high-risk investing. Anyone with a computer can short a stock with the click of a mouse, without truly realizing the risk of this maneuver. Unfortunately, most people ignore things that are difficult to understand, such as risk.

Instead, greed causes them to focus on rewards, which ultimately leads to their demise.

The stock market has never been more volatile and difficult to navigate due to the massive growth of hedge funds. As well, programmed trading now dominates market activity. This fact alone is reason for concern. Potentially, hundreds of trillions of dollars in derivatives are linked to the capital markets. And due to poor transparency, no one really knows for certain what the total risk exposure is.

The Next "New Deal"?

By the time the depression was in full swing, most Americans were financially and emotionally devastated. But this catastrophe wasn't created overnight. It was the product of two decades of neglect and abuse by Washington and corporate America. The solution was a series of drastic laws and government programs that offered financial stability to a battered nation.

Back then, the U.S. government didn't have the kind of debt and future liabilities it has today, so it will be limited in the ways it can restructure itself. As well, the credit markets were non-existent. Today, these markets comprise a large portion of the global financial system. Thus, it is likely that the effects of America's correction will be spread throughout the globe.

Radical changes in social and economic policy usually only occur after a crisis because no politician wants to risk re-election by raising taxes, cutting benefits, or decreasing the power and exploitation of large corporations. Washington prefers to hide the truth. But once the meltdown is evident, politicians will have no choice but to take action. And Americans will welcome these changes as the only way to regain hope for their future.

Similar to decades ago, the next new Deal will arrive only after the depression has taken full effect. If Washington decides to create a full solution, part of the package will include a national healthcare system, a truly reformed educational system, and a restructuring of free trade and Social Security.

17

INVESTMENT STRATEGIES

During the bull market of the '90s, Wall Street analysts abandoned economic cycle theory in favor of sector performance driven by technological innovation. Only as an afterthought were economics considered. As a result, most analysts latched onto *bottom-up* fundamental analysis, which stresses business and industry change as a way to spot investment opportunities. This methodology is in direct opposition to the *top-down* approach, which emphasizes the effects of the economy on productivity and therefore market and industry performance.

With the emergence of the Internet in the midst of what was already an amazing bull market, a paradigm shift was heralded all around Wall Street. This provided further support for the bottom-up investment approach. That was a period of unrealistic proportions. Now we're back to the realities of asset performance ruled by economics and the cycling of sectors.

Since 2001, we've witnessed a bull market in precious metals, REITs, and commodities. With the exception of mortgage REITs, I expect these trends to continue over most of the duration of the secular bear market. After the mortgage REITs bottom out, I expect the commodities bubble (excluding oil) to correct perhaps commencing in 2010. In contrast, the bull market in precious metals should last at least through 2014. In part, this bull market has been and will continue to be fueled by the weakness of the dollar. In contrast, *the commodities bull is both a consequence and catalyst of the dollar's weakness, as well as the strength of China's economy.*

For over a decade, China has been able to post double-digit growth despite high commodity prices, due to massive investment of foreign capital and trade surpluses—all effects of unfair trade dynamics. But even for China, continued high commodity prices will eventually cause a problem. I would expect the full effects of China's correction to be apparent by 2011; but no one really knows. In contrast, India might be better insulated from the fallout of the commodities bubble since it has not been as dependent on raw materials for its growth.

Declining commodities will be the first of many legs needed to reinvigorate the U.S. economy. In fact, I expect the dollar to gain some strength when commodity prices correct. *But do not mistake the future collapse in commodity prices as a sign of permanent recovery.* There are too many major issues to contend with before America can reverse its downward spiral.

Regardless, investors certainly cannot lie down and wait for the meltdown because they could miss many lucrative opportunities. After all, during the '90s, there were many respected investors who predicted the crash of the raging bull. However, most of them made these predictions several years before it actually occurred and therefore missed out on tremendous investment returns.

It's much easier to predict <u>what</u> will happen rather than <u>when</u>. It might be ten or twenty years before America's inescapable correction period. Therefore, the first thing investors need to do is remain cautious, despite any "great news" from Wall Street and other masters of propaganda. As well, they should remain pessimistic when the market rallies. Throughout this period, *strong rallies should generally be considered selling opportunities, while sell-offs should be approached with great care.*

Hedging Inflation and Volatility

The common consensus is that inflation is worse for bonds than equities. But this is not necessarily true. Inflation can be equally destructive for all asset classes except real estate, certain currencies, and securities indexed to inflation. In many cases gold can provide a good hedge as well. *Therefore, investors wishing to hedge against inflation should take positions in TIPS, (Treasury Inflation Protected Securities) REITs, gold and well-managed bond funds. However, they should avoid mortgage REITs.*

The stock market tends to decline with rising gold (current), rising inflation (current), a weak dollar (current), and high interest rates (coming in a few years). *Thus, investors looking to minimize portfolio volatility should hold a small portion of non-mortgage REITS and precious metal stocks or ETFs,* since they have the lowest correlation relative to other common stocks. In other words, REITS and precious metals typically cushion large and/or prolonged market declines. I feel that the bull market in rental unit-based REITS and precious metals will continue for several more years. Finally, investors should also consider some foreign currency exposure.

Hedging Against Deflation

If deflation becomes a problem, investors have little choice for investments. The *emphasis during a deflationary environment should be on capital preservation.* Always remember that minimizing losses is more important than extracting gains since cash is in limited quantities. Cash will be king in such an environment, if present.

Alternatively, certificates of deposit in stable banks and Treasury bills will also provide safety along with modest gains. Gold would do quite well. However, real estate would get crushed along with most stocks. If in fact a depression does occur, even cash and U.S. Treasuries won't bode well. Thus, investors should also consider foreign bond funds and foreign currency exposure.

Gold and Inflation

Gold has been shown to provide a great hedge against deflationary conditions. And in many cases, it has also performed well during inflation. But to say that gold will always provide a hedge during inflationary periods would probably be unfounded. The most recent evidence of gold's demand during a deflationary environment occurred during the last recession (recently removed from record books) when the gold bull market commenced. In 2001, since breaking out of a price beyond $275, gold has surged to over $800.

This leads us to the inverse correlation between gold and stock market performance. Statistical analysis shows that over the past thirty years, *the correlation between gold and the Dow Jones Industrial Average actually declined during the worst-performing 30 months of this index, thereby serving as a hedge against the most severe market declines.* The inverse relationship between gold prices and stock market performance might be explained by the investor-neglect of gold during strong bull market periods, causing severe undervaluation of this precious metal. Likewise, *the retreat of investors from an overvalued stock market during a post-bubble correction could cause a rush into gold as a safer, more attractively valued asset class.*

While gold is variable in its ability to hedge inflation, it has the added appeal of worldwide acceptance, and is not linked to currencies. On Friday, January 18, 1980, gold reached its all-time high of $877 per ounce. The price of gold today in 1980 inflation-adjusted dollars is equivalent to about $2400. Compare that with its current level of around $800. Clearly, gold has a long way to go before reaching an inflation-adjusted record high. Although I cannot say for certain whether this will occur over the next decade, I am fairly confident gold will reach the $1200 mark by 2010 (revised forecast) for many compelling reasons.

This Time it's Different

Rising gold prices usually result from deflationary conditions, not inflationary. While there have been many instances when rising gold has mirrored periods of increasing inflation, much of this behavior has been attributable to factors other than inflation itself. During a prolonged deflationary environment, GDP is reduced, leading to a decline in the purchase power parity of the currency. Therefore, buying gold during a deflationary environment provides a nice hedge against relative changes in foreign currencies.

It so happens that many investors also shift into a gold hedge during inflation, which only reduces the buying power domestically. However, since the dollar is the global unit of currency, inflation also acts to diminish its purchase power parity. And because gold is not linked to any currencies, this might explain why it's the investment choice for many who are worried about either deflation or inflation.

While the '70s and early '80s showed a correlation between inflation and gold prices, in my opinion there were many other factors that led to this phenomenon. Not only was the price of oil spiking, but there were numerous global issues causing investors to flock to gold as a secure investment. Whether gold, inflation, and high oil prices will demonstrate such a correlation again will be dependent upon the overall health of the global economy. If oil continues its surge (a likely possibility) gold will most likely mirror the inflation escalation we are seeing and will continue to see over the next several years. In other words, a price per ounce of $2000 for gold is not at all unreasonable within the next decade.

You may have noticed back in the 2001 to 2004 period when deflation was evident, gold made a major upward move. After a correction in price in early 2004, gold continued its bullish trend later that year. Since 2005, gold has continued its bullish trend, but not due to deflation or inflation per say. *The current rise in gold is due to the rise in commodity prices, the weak dollar, and the weakness of the U.S. monetary policy. Combined, these elements have an inflationary effect.*

While significant inflation is certainly present in the economy, it is neither due to nor a direct consequence of the price of gold. Rather, rising energy and healthcare costs, and a decline in total wage compensation are causing inflation. *Although many economic experts claim that rising oil prices cannot in itself create inflation, they are absolutely wrong.* It is the manner by which Washington is able to manipulate data that has led to this inaccurate conclusion.

Finally, consider the possibility that the Fed may eventually create even more inflation in order to pay off much of the federal debt. A period of sustained inflation would artificially increase the GDP and earnings growth of corporate America. There are some who contend that the government has caused high inflation in the past to pay down debt. As final support for this possibility, Bernanke is considered an expert in the economics of inflation. Perhaps Washington feels he'll be able to raise and lower inflation as needed. But they may be in for a rude awakening.

Gold ETFs

Gold exchange-traded funds (ETFs) make investing in gold more convenient, less expensive, and less risky for smaller investors. Unlike other ETFs, gold (and silver) ETFs are presumed to buy gold (and silver) bullion and store it in a central bank. Therefore, investors in precious metal ETFs theoretically own a stake in the metal as opposed to owning shares in mining companies. In fact, gold ETFs trade at $1/10^{th}$ the price of gold per ounce.

Whether you actually own the gold or not is up for debate. First, consider that the gold ETFs are not audited in detail. That is, they don't have to show auditors the actual vault the gold is held in. ETFs only have to show the certificates promising to pay each investor in gold. As well, because ETFs can be shorted, you could end up with a very confusing paper trail that is difficult to track.

The main advantage of precious metal ETFs is that they protect investors from company-specific and political risks. These risks can be very high, especially when companies are mining in unpredictable and politically volatile nations such as South America and Africa. As well, ETFs don't expose investors to company-specific risks, such as the derivatives exposure frequently used by precious metal mining firms. Because many of the smaller mining companies use leverage, they can multiply their earnings during a gold bull market. But this can also work against them when gold prices correct. Precious metal ETFs shield investors from these risks, exposing them only to the risks related to the trading prices of the metal (i.e. the macroeconomic risks).

In 2005, two gold ETFs were launched—iShares Comex Gold Trust (IAU) and StreetTracks Gold Shares (GLD). If the ETFs are purchasing and storing gold according to investor demand, this should help deplete reserves, causing an increase in price.

Compared to Gold Funds, ETFs:
- Are more tax-efficient
- Have lower costs
- Can be hedged with options
- Have no penalties for liquidation
- Can be shorted
- Not exposed to company-specific risk
- Not exposed to political risk

Since inception less than three years ago, over $15 billion has been invested in GLD, making it one of the fastest growing ETFs in history. With little doubt, it's going to get much larger.

Silver

Similar to gold, investment demand for silver has been minimal over the past several years, but has recently picked up due to the weak dollar. Unlike gold, silver is consumed for consumer goods, making it difficult to build high inventory levels. Silver demand arises from three main uses; industrial/decorative, photography and jewellery, and silverware. Together, these three categories represent more than 95 percent of annual silver consumption.

Silver's high demand for industrial applications is due to its unique physical, mechanical, and chemical properties—strength, malleability and ductility, electrical and thermal conductivity, sensitivity to and high reflectance of light, and its ability to endure extreme temperature ranges. In many cases, no substitute materials can mimic silver's physical and chemical characteristics.

For the most part, silver prices remained constant for more than 150 years, failing to keep up with inflation. By around 1980, the price of silver soared to over $22 per ounce. Currently, the price of silver is just over $14 per ounce. Over the next few years, I expect silver to cross the $30 mark (revised 2007) without a depression. A depression could cause silver to soar well above the $60 mark (revised 2007).

The mining of silver has unique dynamics that favor a low-risk, high appreciation potential. Specifically, about 65 percent of silver mine production is the by-product from copper, zinc, and lead mining. Only 35 percent of silver demand comes from pure silver mines and gold primary mines, where silver is also a by-product. Along with global macroeconomic trends, the unique relationship between silver, gold and the base metals supports my forecasts for enormous silver price appreciation.

Regardless of the future economic environment, silver is destined to continue its rise along with gold. *Under strong economic conditions, silver's use in industry will no doubt propel its price to new highs. In contrast, under a weak economic scenario, silver prices would soar even more due to decreases in base metal use and therefore silver mining output, reducing inventories further.* Therefore, silver demand should remain strong for several years.

Given my forecast for overall global economic weakness over the next twenty years, *I expect silver to have more upside than gold.* The first silver ETF was released by Barclays (SLV) in 2006 and already totals over $2 billion. However, its performance has lagged that of gold. Note that, unlike the gold ETFs, each share of SLV represents 10 ounces of silver.

Dollar

After a tailspin since the Internet meltdown, the dollar has recently experienced a minor rebound. However, the dollar's longer-term trend remains down. Do not mistake any short-term rebound in the dollar with a trend reversal. Throughout this book I have detailed the reasons for the weak dollar and I cannot see things improving in America anytime soon. Therefore, investors should consider exposure to other currencies such as the Euro and Yen as a hedge against U.S.-dollar denominated assets.

Asset Classes

Cash

In my opinion, over the next 6 to 8 years, cash will perform in line with the DJIA and S&P 500 on an annualized basis. This is based both upon my expectations for low average annual market returns as well as average to relatively high short-term interest rates.

Bonds

Investment in fixed income is a mixed bag. Overall, the best route for cautious investors is to raise cash and wait for long-term rates to take off. Thus far, long bond rates have been suppressed due to the weakness of the dollar. However, as America's overall credit risk continues to grow in combination with rising inflation, I am expecting rates to approach 8.00 by 2010. The best way to play this forecast is to buy TIPS (Treasury Inflation-Protected Securities). If you wait for rates to increase, you'll be best positioned to utilize the higher coupon rates plus a payout that's indexed to inflation. More passive investors might want to consider buying into a TIPS mutual fund now.

Because most consumer debt is repackaged into marketable securities, (i.e. the collateralized securities markets) investors should stay away from certain institutions that engage in these transactions. In addition, many finance companies have much larger exposure to credit derivatives. And they have many ways to hide their real exposures.

In contrast, some financial institutions might profit well from a credit meltdown. But it's too difficult to predict the winners, so I would stay clear altogether, unless you want to take short positions. No doubt the *high-yield bond markets will heat up, creating potentially lucrative investment opportunities.* But once again, you should stay clear of this unless you know how to perform a credit risk analysis of distressed securities, and only if you're willing to monitor changes diligently.

As recommended in "Cashing in on the Real Estate Bubble," experienced traders with high risk tolerance may want to wait for an initial sell signal when mortgage-related companies get into trouble and short these stocks. But always buy protective calls or enter buy-limit orders to limit loses. Very experienced investors with a high risk tolerance and short-term objectives might look for entry points in some of the larger beaten-down banks, such as Citigroup. This can be a very dangerous territory to get involved with so you'll need to be careful, using options to limit downside losses. Be patient and very careful.

Example of Inflation on Investments

As an illustration of the potential damaging effects of inflation, I'll provide a simple example. To calculate the real annual return on a bond, multiply the amount (principle) of the bond by the interest rate. For example, a $10,000 U.S. Treasury Bill with a coupon of 5 percent would be worth $10,500 after one year. Therefore, the gross return would be $500.

In order to obtain the net return from this investment, you must factor in taxes and inflation. To calculate the effect of taxes, subtract the percentage of income tax from the interest, (let's assume a 30 percent tax bracket, or $150) leaving you with $350. Finally, the average annual inflation rate in the U.S. over the past few decades has been around 2.5 percent. So, in order to calculate the net return of the T-bill, multiply the after-tax total of $10,350 by 0.975 and subtract this from $10,350. This would give you a real annual return of $91.25, which comes out to less than 1 percent of your original investment amount.

The Case for TIPS

As you can appreciate from the previous example, when inflation rises above its mean, you'll lose money if you own bonds unless you have some type of hedge. Therefore, *investors concerned about high inflation should consider purchasing TIPS since coupon payments are indexed to inflation.* As well, there are some funds that take short positions in U.S. Treasuries. These funds are designed to perform well with rising inflation [ProFund Advisors (RRPIX) or Rydex Juno Fund (RYJUX)]. Once again, I expect both inflation and long-term interest rates to surge over the next several years.

Note that if you purchase shares of a TIPS mutual fund, the fund manager is expected to manage increases in interest rates. In other words, if the right calls are made on future rate increases, you can buy the fund now and expect to do well. If the fund leverages its bets successfully you'll do even better. As the fund manager anticipates rate increases, a portion of the bonds will be sold in advance of rate hikes to prevent a drop in the value of the bonds, and to raise cash for the purchase bonds with the new, higher rate.

In 2001, the U.S. Treasury Department announced it would stop holding auctions for new 30-year U.S. Treasury bonds beginning in early 2002. In less than two years after these auctions stopped, short and long-term rates sunk to 40-year lows. Looking ahead, one could reasonably assume that, with interest rates at these levels, the demand for the 30-year would surely be low. Therefore, if you think the timing of this announcement and the subsequent lowing of rates was unrelated, then you missed the message sent by the U.S. Treasury.

In my opinion, Washington realized the economy was in such bad shape that Greenspan would have to collapse short-term rates to stimulate consumer spending. If the U.S. Treasury continued to auction off new bonds while rates dropped, this could have created a problem with the yield curve due to decreased demand in the secondary markets. This would have jeopardized the reckless deficit spending by President Bush. However, as I had anticipated, in 2005 *the Treasury Department announced it would bring back auctions for the 30-year bonds by early 2007. What does that imply about the future direction of long-term rates?*

Equities

As mentioned, investors should not pull completely out of the market and wait for a catastrophe to strike because they could miss several years of gains. Rather, a defensive stance emphasizing risk management is advised. As a general rule, equities should constitute no more than 50 percent of the total investment portfolio prior to any clear signs of the meltdown. Conservative investors might wish to allocate no more than 30 percent in equities (depending upon the specific securities).

Cash will be king, and those who have it during the crisis will be positioned to take advantage of large sell-offs. However, every investor has a different financial profile so it's impossible to provide definitive guidelines without knowing specific information. Therefore, *investors should discuss their concerns with a knowledgeable financial advisor and let him or her determine the appropriate allocation based upon your financial profile.*

Mutual Funds

In general, most mutual funds perform poorly during prolonged bear markets due to their mandatory exposure to market risk (since they must remain invested) and high fees (even no-load funds can have excessive fees). However, investors should consider funds when seeking diversified exposure in foreign bonds, emerging markets such as Southeast Asia, foreign currency exposure, and funds that use various investment tools that benefit from bearish conditions, such as shorting strategies and alternative assets. I would recommend a diversified exposure to these less familiar asset classes—meaning you should invest in funds rather than invest in individual securities.

Make sure that the company has many different fund types so you can shift from say a gold sector fund into an oil fund within the family without exit fees. Also note that there are several closed-end funds that offer diversified exposure in foreign assets with lower fees. However, *you need to understand how closed-end funds work, paying particular attention to the amount of leverage used.* Here is where your financial advisor has a chance to show some added value.

ETFs

Ever since their introduction just a few years ago, ETFs have grown to represent an enormous percentage of assets invested in the stock market. Virtually every type of sector, industry, and index can be found within the ETF universe. Rather than paying the high fees charged by mutual funds, investors can get the industry and sector exposure of their choice. And they have the added flexibility of being able to rotate sectors without the exit penalties charged by some funds. The only transaction costs are those charged by your broker, which are typically around $10 per trade for online brokers.

The main drawback of this strategy is that *it requires significant time and expertise to manage your investments.* A more conservative approach is to buy more broad-based ETFs that mimic the DJIA, S&P 500, and bond indices. However, such ETFs would require active management since I do not expect the broad indices to perform well over the next several years.

Finally, it is important to note that ETFs can be sold short. This means that even if the ETF mimics an index, it could fall more (via shorting) or rise higher (via covering short positions) than the index. Thus, ETFs have an element of potential built-in leverage, so be careful.

Foreign Currencies

There's little doubt that even without a depression-type period, the dollar will continue to remain weak until at least 2011. As China begins to properly revalue its currency, other Asian nations will follow resulting in higher-priced imports from these regions. Fortunately, most goods needed by Americans can be purchased internally or via its NAFTA and CAFTA trading partners, so there's little need to spend the weak dollar against stronger foreign currencies. I would expect the Euro to continue to provide healthy returns for many years. But investors would be cautioned against investing in foreign bonds or currencies on their own. They should assign this task to a mutual fund or money manager.

One indirect way to partially hedge against dollar-depreciated assets due to inflation is to invest in American Depository Receipts (ADRs). Although this is a rather conservative hedging strategy, it could provide a much higher level of protection if inflation becomes very high. As well, investors should look to U.S. companies that have a significant multinational presence such as Microsoft. Although General Electric also has significant international exposure, I would be very cautious since much of its business is financial.

Industry Groups

Precious Metals

When dealing with precious metals, it's important to keep in mind that this asset class tends to have periods of extreme volatility. Therefore, it can result in drawdowns of 30 percent or more in just a couple of months. Investors must monitor the longer-term trend, which I expect to remain up for several years. But I could be wrong. To manage risk, in general you should only add to positions after large sell-offs and trim positions after long rallies. This will help reduce portfolio volatility and lower the overall cost basis of these positions.

Whatever you do, *don't become too heavily exposed in this asset class* since too much of a good thing can quickly turn into a very bad investment that remains down for a long time. Imagine investors who happened to load up on gold during its peak nearly three decades ago. Since then, they've either sold for large losses or waited all these years and still haven't broken even (when adjusted for inflation). And *if your cash gets tied up in the market, you may not have sufficient funds to take advantage of market opportunities.* You certainly don't want to use margin under any circumstances.

Gaining exposure in precious metals is possible by investing in futures, (which I highly advise against unless you have extensive experience) individual stocks, mutual funds, ETFs and of course through buying them directly. Due to the unique company and political risks already mentioned, many investors may prefer to invest in precious metal ETFs. While mutual funds provide diversification, they may not be the best way to play the metals because the fees are not only high, but you're exposing yourself to company, fund manager and other risks. However, gold mutual funds offer the potential of higher returns. Alternatively, some impulsive investors may wish to directly purchase gold and silver and have it stored in a bank vault. There are some companies that will store it for you in large banks overseas. This approach would combat the impulsivity to trade frequently.

Energy and Utilities

As inflation mounts, energy and utility prices will continue to soar. In addition, further weakness in the dollar will continue to increase energy prices since most fossil fuels are paid for with dollars.

Similar to the precious metals, energy stocks can be quite volatile. *Therefore, a lower risk method to gain exposure in energy is through the purchase of oil and gas trusts.* These securities represent investment management companies that fund several oil exploration projects. Investors receive the majority of earnings as cash dividends. In general, they tend to have a relatively high dividend yield. As a group, the Canadian oil trusts are paying the highest dividend yields due in part to their tax-exempt status (which will change in a couple of years).

Keep in mind that energy is very cyclical. Thus, investors with these securities should expect periods of large declines, similar to the precious metals. Due to their high dividends, oil and gas trusts would be expected to exhibit lower volatility than other oil and gas stocks. However, *don't invest blindly based on dividends because they aren't guaranteed since they're from common stocks. They can be cut or eliminated at anytime.* If dividends were cut, this could cause the stock price to decline which might lock you in for a long time. You need to do some research to understand how these trusts are managed so you are aware of the risks.

Finally, note that when dealing with stocks that have a high dividend payout, the price per share tends to move towards the direction that makes the dividend yield close to the historical mean over the long term. This assumes no adverse material events have occurred. If so, this could lead to a cut in the dividend which would most likely push the share price down.

Alternative Energy

This might be a place to rest a <u>small</u> amount of assets for investors who have an aggressive investment stance. But it could be a while before these companies see much market activity. If and when they do, they could soar. Still, this might only provide short-term trading opportunities.

This sector can be extremely volatile, so the best way to manage risk is to buy low and sell after surges, rather than buying more. Investors with high risk tolerance and skilled trading abilities may look for short-term trading opportunities based on event-related activity, such as funding from Washington.

Ethanol companies experienced a surge in 2006, in part due to Bush's increased financial incentives for development of this fuel source. Already a major component of the petroleum industry, ethanol is used as an alternative additive to substitute for toxic chemicals, thereby creating less pollution. There has been a recent push for ethanol-powered vehicles using an 85 percent blend of ethanol and gasoline (known s E-85). U.S. auto manufacturers are already rolling out new models.

The demand for ethanol combined with limited supplies resulted in the previous surge in these stocks. But as I predicted in the previous version of this book, the ethanol surge was short-term, as even the E-85 solution is temporary. More important, higher corn prices have squeezed profit margins of all ethanol producers. Finally, since ethanol is water-soluble, pipelines dedicated to ethanol transport are needed in order to increase distribution. As it stands today, ethanol is transported by truck and train, which requires fossil fuels. So you can imagine how this has squeezed profit margins of producers. Companies are still unwilling to spend the needed $2 million per mile of new pipeline because they know ethanol's future is very uncertain.

At the time of the release of this book, all ethanol stocks are at historic lows. Some of these companies might represent attractive values for a short-intermediate holding period. Even more attractive might be consideration of call contracts. But this investment strategy should be considered speculative and must be treated accordingly.

It is entirely possible that the forthcoming surge in gasoline prices could offset high corn prices, causing ethanol stocks to surge. Therefore, aggressive investors should pay close attention to trends in this sector, as well as new developments in the overall energy industry (economic and political) in order to maximize gains and minimize risk.

The cellulose ethanol companies might provide a more long-term solution to peak oil since cellulose is the primary structural component of green plants. If it becomes feasible to produce cellulose-based ethanol on a large scale, these companies could do quite well. Aggressive investors might also consider a small investment in the fuel cell industry, which should receive continued funding. *Finally, long-term or conservative investors should avoid ethanol and fuel cell stocks altogether due to their questionable long-term viability.* As a final word, investors should be careful with valuations of all alternative energy stocks since most of these companies are new, have limited revenues and no earnings.

Regardless of your enthusiasm for alternative energy stocks, understand that the constraints are less related to gaps in technology and more dependent upon politics. Therefore, only when Washington finally decides to make a strong and sustained commitment to alternative energy will these companies be viewed as more serious investments. I have previously discussed the forces serving to keep the dollar-oil link firmly in place.

Healthcare

While I do not expect the pharmaceutical industry to deliver the blockbuster earnings growth of the previous decade, big names like Merck and Pfizer provide more safety and therefore less risk. As well, the blue-chip biotechs like Amgen should do well for investors with longer horizons. If purchased at relatively low valuations, the biopharmas might deliver excellent returns if timely exits are made.

A few years ago in my investment newsletter, I made very strong recommendations backed with compelling reasons for an investment in Merck at the $25 to $32 price range. Since that period, the price has doubled and no longer is there a much upside relative to some of its peers. I have since shifted my emphasis to Pfizer due to its undervaluation and strong dividend yield. Overall, Part D Medicare promises to catapult the drug makers back to the top position over the next several years. So this should be a good place for patient investors.

Companies involved in the nutritional market, telemedicine and healthcare IT are certain to make a huge impact on healthcare over the next two decades. But it's very difficult to determine the future winners right now. You might be on the lookout for my book on telemedicine, co-authored with one of the early pioneers of healthcare informatics and telemetry. We expect the book to be released by late 2008.

Global Economies

China & India

Simply on sheer volume alone, several Chinese funds (there are some nice closed-end funds paying high dividends) and stocks should continue to perform well for at least the next 2 years. However, China cannot maintain its double-digit growth forever. At some point, its rapidly expanding bubble will burst. Therefore, I would be more of a short-term investor in select Chinese funds and at least trim positions down thereafter. Investors should limit their exposure in foreign securities to a very small portion of total assets since transparency is limited and accounting rules are often quite different.

When China showcases its vibrant economy to the world during the 2008 Summer Olympics, this could result in a further surge in asset prices. Most likely within one to two years after this, the smart money will begin making its exit.

Asset Allocation

Below, I've listed a generic investment strategy based upon the type of position investors may have. In order to determine whether one is conservative, moderate or aggressive they should speak with a registered financial professional. As well, they should allow these professionals to determine their proportionate share of suitable securities. These are very important steps to take.

Conservative Position	Moderate Position	Aggressive Position
Cash	Cash, Dollar Hedge	Cash, Dollar Hedge
	Chinese Funds	Chinese & German Funds
Precious Metals	Precious Metals	Precious Metals
Oil Trusts	Oil Trusts	Energy/Alt. & Traditional
Healthcare	Healthcare/Alt Healthcare	Healthcare/Alt Healthcare
TIPS	TIPS	TIPS

Market Predictions

The stock market will most likely provide maximum annualized returns of 3 percent during the current secular bear market period (from 2001 to 2012-2014). Thus, *even though the DJIA might reach 15,000 by 2012, this will still only represent about 3 percent annualized returns since the beginning of the bear market period in 2001.*

We have recently seen the DJIA surpass the 14,000 mark, despite problems in the housing bubble. Because most investors still fail to recognize the risks to the economy, it would not be surprising to see the DJIA reach 16,500 by or before 2012. However, what matters most is whether the DJIA is trending up, down, or flat. Investors need to focus on mid- to longer-term trends in order to see where the market is headed because once the economy corrects, the DJIA could easily fall to 10,500.

Beyond the 2014 time period, there may be a short bull market lasting a couple of years, sending the DJIA to the 18,000 range. The economic and market disaster might occur during the 2016 to 2020 period. If this scenario occurs, I expect losses ranging from 30 to 40 percent from previous highs. Assuming modest gains in the market during this period, these corrections might send the DJIA to the 10,000 to 12,500 range.

These ranges will depend upon both the timing and reaction of the economic fallout. The later it occurs, the higher the market will be after the correction. What's important to consider are the annualized returns over the appropriate time frame. Finally, note that if Social Security is privatized, the market will have much more stability. Other government interventions could also lesson the blow.

Risk Management

Managing Risk

Throughout this book, I've discussed the risks to the U.S. economy with potential effects on the stock and bond markets. Investors also need to consider the risk characteristics of the asset classes and industries I've highlighted. Because many of these industry groups are considered non-traditional, they have many risks that are independent of traditional securities. To reiterate, investment risk should always be considered with all securities, no matter how promising they appear.

First, investors should consider *company risk*, or the risk of company underperformance or even business failure due to adverse economic conditions. As an obvious example, we can look to the mortgage and financial industries as having very high levels of risk due to the real estate correction that is currently in its early stages. At some point, as stock prices head to multi-year lows, some of these companies may represent investment opportunities. Next, we look at company risk due to competitive forces. This analysis can become quite complex if investors are not already familiar with the competitive landscape of the industry and sector for which the company is categorized.

When assessing risk in less traditional industry groups such as the metals, energy, and foreign equities, the same variables discussed above apply. But we must also consider risks unique to each group. For instance, metals, mining and energy companies can have variable levels of political risk depending upon the type of company and source of production. Companies like U.S. Steel and Nucor don't have much political risk (other than that in the U.S.) because these industries have their primary production facilities in North America. But they face unique competitive risks due to unfair trade practices imposed by China, as well as restrictions against industry protection by the WTO.

When considering precious metal mining companies, investors should note the locations of the primary exploration sites and develop a feel for the stability of the government in those regions. For instance, Apex Silver (SIL) has its primary exploration facilities in Bolivia, a South American nation that has been known to have a considerable amount of political instability. If the Bolivian government decides to nationalize mining regions, this could deliver a severe blow to foreign mining firms in that nation.

Investors must also understand that *many of the smaller mining companies make extensive use of leverage in the form of derivatives.* While effective use of derivatives can lead to tremendous gains if the price of precious metals goes up, it can also lead to large losses if the price remains steady or declines. Finally, investors can also lose if management makes the wrong bets with derivatives. This is one of the reasons why the larger mining companies such as Newmont Mining don't benefit as much as the smaller companies from a rise in gold prices. But this smaller potential upside is traded in for lower risk.

Large mining companies like Newmont typically use derivatives more conservatively to stabilize earnings (by locking in metal prices), so they are considered lower-risk. As discussed, the use of gold and silver ETFs can eliminate political and company-specific risks, while providing lower volatility relative to investment in individual precious metal stocks or funds.

When considering investment in energy, investors should understand the business structure, political and regulatory landscape. Some of the things to consider are the primary sources of exploration and the types of business they engage in (exploration, refinement, distribution, retail). Larger companies such as Exxon and Chevron have various sources of exploration so political risk is relatively small. Regardless how high energy prices may go, I do not feel the risk-reward is worth the price of market risk (the risk that the market will decline) because there is not much upside in the large cap oil stocks until prices come down. That's another reason I prefer the oil trusts.

Managing Economic and Market Risks

Overall, investors should consider maintaining at least a 50 percent cash position, regardless whether they choose to implement the strategies discussed in this chapter. The higher short-term interest rates rise, the more attractive money market returns will be. Only after clear signs of increasing long-term interest rates and higher inflation should investors substitute some of their cash holdings for TIPS. Alternatively, if you feel confident in a fund manager's ability to manage interest rate changes, you should consider buying now.

Ultimately, each investor will have a unique financial profile and investment horizon, leading to a different level of risk tolerance. Therefore, you should consult your financial advisor prior to making any investment decisions. It's important to make certain that the advisor remains open to consider the possibilities mentioned in this book. If they're biased or lack adequate sophistication, they may recommend the standard portfolios that perform well only during bull markets.

Overall, cash will be king during this period because much uncertainty remains. In addition to other asset protection strategies previously mentioned, some may chose derivatives and short positions. But these strategies should only be used conservatively, and only by very experienced investors. Alternatively, investors may wish to gain exposure in funds that specialize in various hedging strategies.

Final Thoughts

Looking back in history, one can argue that present-day America shares many similarities with the early part of the twentieth century. Both periods share global unrest, wide swings in monetary policy, excessive power and influence by corporations, wide disparities in income and wealth, and a heavy reliance on debt. These characteristics helped shape the booming period that ushered in the Roaring '20s, similar to the economic boom encountered in the 1990s.

Unlike the correction that occurred in the 1930s, Greenspan mitigated the fallout of the Internet bubble, facilitating the shift of investment assets into a real estate bubble. This served to swell the massive credit bubble further. As such, America still has not witnessed a correction of sufficient magnitude to restore a long period of excessive consumption and misaligned wealth and income distribution.

It is unlikely that the next Great Depression will create an unemployment rate of over 25 percent, similar to that seen in 1933. Rather than a very high unemployment rate, the depression will be characterized by massive underemployment, fewer employee benefits, combined with a very high living expense. Since Washington has created new ways to manipulate data, specific figures don't really matter in a comparative sense. *At the end of the day, the only things that will matter to the American people will be their life, liberty, freedom, and hope for their future.*

Does history repeat itself? The clear answer is yes, it most certainly does. What stand out as variables in this cycle are the manner and timing in which the process will unravel. The question is <u>not whether</u> America will encounter economic devastation <u>but when</u>, in what sequence, and over what duration. Regardless whether inflation or deflation will be the culprit, it is clear that America is headed for a major economic meltdown that will lead to a severe depression. The effects of this correction are likely to be felt around the globe due to America's position in the world economy.

This time the depression may not be caused by a stock market crash. The meltdown might be caused by the real estate bubble, credit bubble, the effects of peak oil or even a major terrorist attack. Alternatively, America might simply continue its gradual downward trajectory. In fact, this might be the worst of all fates since many would be unaware of further economic decline until several years later. Such a scenario might fail to inspire Washington to enact drastic reforms needed to restore unity and financial equity in a timely manner. And this could lead to a more permanent decline for America.

There is no way for America to avoid a painful correction period. There are simply too many problems and no painless solutions. It's too late for tax cuts; the debt is too high and future liabilities are too great. Most likely, America will keep running on empty until its economic engine stalls and a crisis occurs. Devastation of this magnitude will force Washington to enact needed changes.

The future of America includes a long period of economic, political and social realignment. If handled in a timely and responsible manner, this period will not represent an end to its reign as an empire, but merely an adjustment needed to restore its greatness. And those who are alert to these realities will stand to profit.

At some point, politicians will be forced to act on behalf of the American people. With no choice, corporate America will relinquish control back to Washington. And politicians will begin to serve the people rather than special interests. Entrepreneurs will arise from the dust, helping to position the United States firmly within the New Economy. If all goes well, future generations will reclaim the lifestyles their grandparents enjoyed. Amidst the difficult period, a New America will emerge, perhaps even greater than before. If these reforms are not provided in a timely manner, America's rebirth might only come after the next world war, or perhaps not for a very long time.

216

References

The Great Depression

Gene Smiley. Rethinking the Great Depression. Ivan R. Dee, 2003.

David Kyvig. Daily Life in the United States, 1920-1940: How Americans Lived During the Roaring 20s and the Great Depression. Ivan R. Dee, 2004.

Robert Mcelvaine. The Great Depression: America 1929-1941. Three Rivers Press, 1993.

Poverty & Wealth

U.S. Bureau of Census

U.S. Department of Labor and Statistics

Barbara Hagenbaugh. Nation's Wealth Disparity. USA Today, January 22, 2003.

Bernard Wasow. The New American Economy: A Rising Tide that Lifts Only Yachts. The Century Foundation. 2004.

Edward Wolff. The Wealth Divide: The Growing Gap in the United States Between the Rich and the Rest. Multinational Monitor, May 2003.

Friedman and Richards. Capital Gains and Dividend Tax Cuts: Data Make Clear that High-Income Households Benefit the Most. Center on Budget and Policy Priorities, January 30, 2006.

Greenstein and Shapiro. Poverty Up, Incomes Down for Second Straight Year in 2002. Center on Budget and Policy Priorities, September 23, 2003.

Income Inequality Grew Across the Country Over the Past Two Decades: Early Signs Suggest Inequality Now Growing Again After Brief Interruption. Center on Budget and Policy Priorities, January 26, 2006.

Income Inequality Grew Across the Country Over the Past Two Decades: Early Signs Suggest Inequality Now Growing Again After Brief Interruption. Center on Budget Policy and Priorities, January 26, 2006.

Low-Income Children in the United States (2004). National Center for Children in Poverty. http://nccp.org/pub_cpf04.html

Ohlemacher. Calculating Poverty in U.S. Fuels Debate. Associated Press, Feb 21, 2006.

Robert Frank. The US Led a Resurgence Last Year Among Millionaires World-Wide. Wall Street Journal, June 15, 2004.

Valdas Anelauskas. Discovering America as It Is. Clarity Press, 1999.
How Poor is Poor? Associated Press, February 21, 2006.

Does Inequality Matter? The Economist, June 14, 2001.

Federal Deficit

Dean Baker and David Rosnick. The Forty-Four Trillion Dollar Deficit Scare. Center for Economic and Policy Research, September 10, 2003.

Lawrence Kotlikoff. Deficit Delusion. The Public Interest (Summer 1986): 53-65.

Lawrence Kotlikoff. From Deficit Delusion to the Fiscal Balance Rule—Looking for a Meaningful Way to Describe Fiscal Policy. National Bureau of Economic Research working paper no. 2841, February 1989.

Lawrence Kotlikoff. Generational Accounts—A Meaningful Alternative to Deficit Accounting. In Tax Policy and the Economy, vol. 5, edited by David Bradford. 1991.

Martin Crutsinger. U.S. Aims to Address China Trade Deficit. Associated Press, February 20, 2006.

Martin Crutsinger. U.S. Trade Deficit Hits High on Storms. Associated Press, November 10, 2005.

Peter G. Peterson. Riding for a Fall. Foreign Affairs, September/October 2004.

Pedro Nicolaci da Costa. Big Deficit Looms Behind Revival of 30-yr Bond. Reuters, Feb 8, 2006.

Federal Debt

Interest on the Federal Debt http://www.publicdebt.treas.gov/opd/opdint.htm

Debt to the Penny. http://www.publicdebt.treas.gov/opd/opdpenny.htm

Dean Baker. Dangerous Trends: The Growth of Debt in the U.S. Economy. Center for Economic Policy Research, September 7, 2004.

Liqun Liu, Andrew Rettenmaier and Thomas Saving. A Debt is a Debt. Texas A&M University, Private Enterprise Research Center. Perspective on Policy, Sept 2002.

Peter G. Peterson. Riding for a Fall. Foreign Affairs, September/October 2004.

Consumer Debt

Bernard Wasow. Rages to Riches? The American Dream is Less Common in the United States than Elsewhere. The Century Foundation, 2004.

Carly Zander. Federal Reserve Releases New Statistics About Credit Cards, reports LowCards.com. Send2Press Newswire, March 2, 2006.

Chris Faulkner-MacDonagh and Martin Muhleisen. Are U.S. Households Living Beyond Their Means? Finance & Development, March 2004.

Consumer Credit. Federal Reserve Statistical Release, February 7, 2006.

Deanne Loonin. The Life and Debt Cycle. Part One: The Implications of Rising Credit Card Debt Among Other Consumers. National Consumer Law Center, July 2006.

Dean Baker. Dangerous Trends: The Growth of Debt in the U.S. Economy. Center for Economic Policy Research, September 7, 2004.

Dennis Cauchon and John Waggoner. The Looming National Benefit Crisis. USA Today, Oct 3, 2004.

Facts About Consumer Credit Card Debt and Bankruptcy. Consumer Federation of America, Aug. 7, 2006.

Jason Zweig. The Oracle Speaks. CNN Money, May 2, 2005.

Mauricio Soto. Will Baby Boomers Drown in Debt? Center for Retirement Research at Boston College. An Issue in Brief. Just the Facts on Retirement Issues, March 2005, Number 15.

Tamara Draut and Javier Silva. Borrowing to Make Ends Meet: The Growth of Credit Card Debt in the '90s. Demos, 2003.

John Gist and Carlos Figueiredo. Deeper in Debt: Trends Among Midlife and Older Americans. AARP Public Policy Institute, April 2002.

Laura Bruce. Low Rates: A Temptation for Deeper Debt. Bankrate.com, April 13, 2005.

Life and Debt: Why American Families Are Borrowing to the Hilt. A Century Foundation Guide to the Issues. The Century Foundation, 2004.

Martin Bosworth. Congress Passes Bankruptcy Bill. ConsumerAffairs.com, Apr 14, 2005.

Melody Warwick. Your Credit Card Payment Just Doubled. Bankrate.com

Patricia Sabatini. Study: Credit Card Issuers Ensnare Many Debt Traps. Pittsburg Post-Gazette, July 28, 2006.

Susan Walker. U.S. Consumer Credit Card Debt May Crash Economy. FoxNews.com, Dec 31, 2004.

The Plastic Safety Net: The Reality Behind Debt in America. Center for Responsible Credit Lending. Demos, Oct. 2005.

Thomas Garrett. Up, Up, and Away: Personal Bankruptcies Soar! Federal Reserve Bank of St. Louis, October 2005.

William Mapother. Taming Consumer Debt. Credit Union National Association, Apr 2004.

Economic Recovery

Board of Governors of the Federal Reserve System www.federalreserve.gov

Federal Reserve Bank of New York www.ny.frb.org

Federal Reserve Bank of St. Louis www.stlouisfed.org

Federal Reserve Bank of San Francisco www.frbsf.org
United States Bureau of Census www.census.gov

U.S. Department of Commerce: Bureau of Economic Analysis www.bea.gov

National Bureau of Economic Research www.nber.org

Bureau of Labor and Statistics www.bls.gov

National Association of Manufacturers

K. Shapiro and A. Aron-Dine. How Does this Recovery Measure Up? Center on Budget and Policy Priorities, Jan. 9, 2006.

Jason Zweig. The Oracle Speaks. CNN Money, May 2, 2005.

Frank Shosak. Making Sense of Money Supply Data. Mises Institute, Dec. 17, 2003.

John Carlson and Benjamin Keen. MZM: A Monetary Aggregate for the 1990s? Federal Reserve Bank of Cleveland Economic Review, 1996.

No Consensus on Stock Market Valuation. CBS News, July 27, 2005.

Jeffery Wenger. Share of Workers in 'Nonstandard' Jobs Declines: Latest Survey Shows a Narrowing—Yet Still Wide—Gap in Pay and Benefits. Economic Policy Institute, 2006.

Rex Nutting. Profits Surge to 40-year High. MarketWatch, March 30, 2006.

Asha Bangalore. The FOMC, Federal Funds Rate, and Unemployment Rate. Northern Trust Daily Global Commentary, April 24, 2006.

Paul Craig Roberts. Where Are the Jobs? Business Week, March 22, 2004.

Let the Dollar Drop. The Economist, May 8, 2005.

Flow of Funds Accounts of the United States. Flows and Outstandings, First Quarter 2006. Federal Reserve Statistical Release, Z1. Board of Governors of the Federal Reserve System, June 8, 2006.

David Walker. The Long-Term Fiscal Challenge and How the Public Perceives It. Government Accounting Office.

Yolanda K. Kodrzycki. Discouraged and Other Marginally Attached Workers: Evidence on Their Role in the Labor Market. New England Economic Review, May/June 2000.

OECD Factbook 2005: Economic, Environmental and Social Statistics. 2006.

Joel Friedman and Robert Greenstein. Administration Proposals to Hide Tax-Cut Costs. Center on Budget Policy and Priorities, February 14, 2006.

Robert Greenstein and Isaac Shapiro. Poverty Up, Incomes Down for Second Straight Year in 2002. Center on Budget Policy and Priorities, September 23, 2003.

Robert Parker. Will the Real Economy Please Stand Up? The National Association of Business Economists, 2003.

220

Paul A. Volcker. An Economy on Thin Ice. MoneyNews (adapted from a speech in Feb 2005 at an economic summit sponsored by Stanford Institute for Economic Policy Research, Apr 10, 2005.

Paul A. Volcker. The Most Dangerous Economy Ever. MoneyNews, April 14, 2005.

Jeanne Sahadi. House Passes Bankruptcy Bill. CNNMoney.com, April 14, 2005.

U.S. Senate Committee on Banking, Housing, and Urban Affairs; Hearing on "Risks of a Growing Balance of Payments Deficit." Prepared Testimony of Paul Volcker, Federal Reserve System, July 25, 2001.

Q&A About Bush's $2.77 Trillion Budget. Reuters, February 6, 2006.

Mark Felsenthal. Treasury Says Extending Tax Cuts Would Cost Blns. Reuters, February 6, 2006.

Mary Dalrymple. Bush's Budget Seeks to Preserve Tax Cuts. Associated Press, February 6, 2006.

25-year Record U.S. Inflation Surge Sparks Debate. Agence France Presse, October 15, 2005.

United States Senate Budget Committee. FY06 Budget Resolution: Challenges and Opportunities.

Isaac Shapiro and Joel Friedman. Tax Returns: A Comprehensive Assessment of the Bush Administration's Record on Cutting Taxes. Center on Budget and Policy Priorities, Apr 23, 2004.

Richard Freeman and William Rogers III. The Weak Jobs Recovery: Whatever Happened to the Great American Jobs Machine? January 2005.

The American Jobs Creation Act of 2003. Summary of H.R. 2896 as Passed by Committee. Committee on Ways and Means, October 28, 2003.

www.bankruptcydata.com

U.S. Budget

United States Bureau of Census www.census.gov

U.S. Department of Commerce: Bureau of Economic Analysis www.bea.gov

National Bureau of Economic Research www.nber.org

Bureau of Labor and Statistics www.bls.gov

Office of Management and Budget, Congressional Budget Office www.whitehouse.gov

Friedman and Greenstein. Administration Proposes to Hide Tax-Cut Costs. Center on Budget and Policy Priorities, February 14, 2006.

J. Gruber. The Cost and Coverage Impact of the President's Health Insurance Budget Proposals. Center on Budget and Policy Priorities, February 15, 2006.

J. Horney, A. Sherman and S. Parrott. Program Cuts in the President's Budget: Cuts Grow Deeper Over Time and Will Hit States Hard. Center on Budget and Policy Priorities, February 23, 2006.

Friedman and Aron-Dine. Extending Expiring Tax Cuts and AMT Relief Would Cost $3.3 Trillion Through 2016. Center on Budget and Policy Priorities, February 6, 2006.

Park and Greenstein. Administration Defense of Health Savings Accounts Rests on Misleading Use of Statistics. Center on Budget and Policy Priorities, February 16, 2006.

Dave Koitz, Melissa Bobb and Ben Page. A 125-Year Picture of the Federal Government's Share of the Economy, 1950 to 2075. A series of issue summaries from the Congressional Budget Office, No. 1, July 3, 2002.

Basics of the Budget Process: A Briefing Paper. U.S. House of Representatives Committee on the Budget, Majority Caucus, 107th Congress, Washington, DC, February 2001.

Committee on the Budget, U.S. House of Representatives, 107th Congress, Washington D.C. Basics of the Budget Process, A Briefing Paper. February 2001.

Jagadeesh Gokhale and Kent Smetters. Fiscal and Generational Imbalances: New Budget Measures for New Budget Priorities. 2003.

http://www.aaas.org/spp/rd/nih05h.pdf   (2005 NIH budget)

http://www.aaas.org/spp/rd/nih06h.pdf (2006 NIH Budget)

http://www.whitehouse.gov/omb/budget/fy2006/nasa.html   (NASA 2006 budget)

http://www.whitehouse.gov/omb/budget/fy2005/nasa.html   (NASA 2005 budget)

Education, Technology & Research

Frank Bass, Nicole Dizon and Ben Feller. AP: States Omit Minorities' School Scores. Associated Press, April 17, 2006.

CIA World Factbook. www.cia.gov/cia/publications/factbook

National Science Foundation www.nsf.gov

National Institutes of Health www.nih.gov

National Science Board

www.economyincrisis.com

Emily Heffter and Nick Perry. Student Takes on College and Wins. The Seattle Times, Feb 26, 2006.

Michael Louie, Laila Weir, and Lisa White. State Oversight Lax for Vocational Schools. Sacramento Bee, Aug. 18, 2004.

Ronald Bovich. Lessons from a Scandal. American School Board, May 2006.

Bernard Wysocki. Once Collegial Research Schools Now Mean Business. Wall Street Journal, May 4, 2006.

Juliet Williams. Suit Filed Against High Schools' Exit Exam. Associated Press, Feb 9, 2006.

A Shortage of Scientists? Science in the News. www.vonews.com May 18, 2004.

William Symonds. America the Uneducated. BusinessWeek Online, November 21, 2005.

Peter Duesberg. Inventing the AIDS Virus. Regnery Publishing: Washington, D.C. 1996.

Baby Boomers

Walter Updegrave. Will Killing Social Security Kill the Markets as Well? CNN/Money, April 1, 2005.

Dean Baker. Dangerous Trends: The Growth of Debt in the U.S. Economy. Center for Economic Policy Research, September 7, 2004.

Jeff Sanford. Dying to Get Out: Will Baby Boomers Cashing Out Crash the Stock Market? Canadian Business Magazine, July 18-August 14, 2005.

Kyung-Mook Lim and David Weil. The Baby Boom and the Stock Market Boom. Mar 10, 2003.

Population and Migration: Demographic Trends OECD 2005 Factbook.

Alicia Munnell, Robert Hatch, and James Lee. Why is Life Expectancy So Low in the United States? Center for Retirement Research at Boston College, August 2004.

Household and Retirement Savings

Peter G. Peterson. Riding for a Fall. Foreign Affairs, September/October 2004.

The personal saving rate is available from the Bureau of Economic Analysis website. (3-14-2002). http://www.bea.doc.gov/bea/dn1.htm

Personal Financial Education, FederalReserveEducation.org, 2003.

Milt Marquis. What's Behind the Low U.S. Personal Saving Rate? Federal Reserve Bank of San Francisco, Economic Letter, 2002-09; March 29, 2002.

Bureau of Economic Analysis, data on personal saving as a percentage of disposable personal income. http://www.bea.doc.gov/bea/dn1.htm

Karen Dynan and Dean Maki. Does Stock Market Wealth Matter for Consumption? Finance and Economics Discussion Series, Board of Governors of the Federal Reserve System, 2001-23.

Milt Marquis. What's Behind the Low U.S. Personal Saving Rate? Federal Reserve Bank of San Francisco, Economic Letter, 2002-09; March 29, 2002.

James Poterba. Stock Market Wealth and Consumption. Journal of Economic Perspectives 14, no. 2 (Spring), pp. 99-118, 2000.

OECD Factbook 2005. Economic, Environmental and Social Statistics

Maki and Palumbo. Disentangling the Wealth Effect: A Cohort Analysis of Household Saving in the 1990s. Federal Reserve, April 2001.

Michael Ash. Who Got All of the 1990s Boom? Center for Popular Economics, July 2, 2002.

Gist and Figueiredo. Deeper in Debt: Trends Among Midlife and Older Americans. AARP Public Policy Institute, April 2002.

Golub-Sass, Francesca. Varani, Andrew. How Much is the Working-Age Population Saving? Center for Retirement Research at Boston College.

Center for Retirement Research at Boston College, October 2005, Number 34.

Barry Bosworth and Lisa Bell. The Decline in Household Savings: What Can We Learn From Survey Data? Center for Retirement Research at Boston College, December 2005.

James Poterba. Population Aging and Financial Markets. MIT and NBER, August 27, 2004.

Marco Terrones and Roberto Cardarelli. Global Imbalances: A Saving and Investment Perspective.

Beverly Goldberg. Inequality, Work, and Retirement: A Downward Spiral. The Century Foundation, August 1, 2006.

Beverly Goldberg. Working Retired: An Idea Whose Time May Never Come. The Century Foundation, April 19, 2006.

Chris Isodore. The Zero-savings Problem. CNNMoney, August 3, 2005.

Outsourcing, Free Trade, and American Workers

World Trade Organization http://www.wto.org/index.htm,

http://www.wto.org/English/docs_e/legal_e/legal_e.htm,

http://www.wto.org/English/docs_e/legal_e/itadec_e.doc

WTO Rules Cotton Subsidies Unfair. Rural News, April 28, 2004.

EU Scores a Steel Victory Over the US. BBC News, November 10, 2003.

General Agreement on Tariffs and Trade http://www.ciesin.org/TG/PI/TRADE/gatt.html, http://www.wto.org/English/docs_e/legal_e/gatt47_01_e.htm, http://gatt.stanford.edu/page/home

North American Free Trade Agreement http://www.fas.usda.gov/itp/Policy/NAFTA/nafta.html, http://www.mac.doc.gov/nafta, http://www-tech.mit.edu/Bulletins/nafta.html

Timothy Aeppel. An Inflation Debate Brews Over Intangibles at the Mall. Wall Street Journal, May 9, 2005.

Aitken and Harrison. Do Domestic Firms Benefit from Direct Foreign Investment? Evidence from Venezuela. American Economic Review, 1999.

John Aldrich. The Discovery of Comparative Advantage. Journal of the History of Economic Thought, Volume 26, Number 3, September 2004.

Craig Barrett. America Should Open Its Doors Wide to Foreign Talent. The Financial Times, Feb. 1, 2006.

Coe and Helpman. International R&D Spillovers. European Economic Review, Vol. 39, 1995, 859-887.

R. Dornbusch, S. Fischer and P. Samuelson. Comparative Advantage, Trade, and Payments in a Ricardian Model with a Continuum of Goods. AER, 1977.

Eaton and Kortum. International Technology Diffusion: Theory and Measurement. International Economic Review, August 1999, Vol. 40, No. 3, 537-569.

J. Haskel, S. Pereira and M. Slaughter. Does Inward Foreign Direct Investment Boost the Productivity of Domestic Firms? NBER Working Papers, 8724, 2002.

B. Javorcik. Does Foreign Direct Investment Increase the Productivity of Domestic Firms? In search of spillovers through backward linkages. American Economic Review, 2004.

W. Keller. Geographic Localization of International Technology Diffusion. American Economic Review, March 2002, Vol. 92, No. 1, 120-142.

W. Keller and S. Yeaple. Multinational Enterprises, International Trade and Productivity Growth: firm-level evidence from the US. NBER Working Paper No. 9504, 2003.

P. Krugman. Increasing Returns, Monopolistic Competition, and International Trade. JIE, 1979.

Bob McTeer and Robert L. Formaini. David Ricardo: Theory of Free International Trade. Economic Insights. Volume 9, Number 2. Federal Reserve Bank of Dallas.

Robert Morley. The Death of American Manufacturing. TheTrumpet.com, Feb 2006.

Bob Powell. A Systems Thinking Perspective on Manufacturing and Trade Policy. Continuous Improvement Associates, December 24, 2003.

Kate Randall. US Minimum Wage Remains at $5.15 an Hour: Failed Republican Bill Tied Increase to Inheritance Tax Cuts. World Socialist Website, August 2006 www.wsws.org.

Job Openings and Labor Turnover: November 2005. Bureau of Labor Statistics. United States Department of Labor, January 10, 2006.

Rising Above the Gathering Storm: Energizing and Employing America for a Brighter Future. A Disturbing Mosaic. February 2006.

Paul Craig Roberts. The Harsh Truth About Outsourcing. BusinessWeek, March 22, 2004.

Vivek Wadhwa. About That Engineering Gap. BusinessWeek Online, Dec 13, 2005.

John Williams. Analysis Behind and Beyond Government Statistics. GRA Archives, Oct 6, 2004.

Private Healthcare

Health System Tweaks Proposed. USA Today, November 19, 2002.

Doctors Find Broken System on Both Sides of the Bed. USA Today, Dec 25, 2002.

More Patients Get Stuck With the Bills. USA Today, April 30, 2002.

Medical Bills Play Big Role in Bankruptcies. USA Today, April 25, 2000.

Medical Costs Can Add Up To Some Healthy Deduction. USA Today, Feb 11, 2002.

States Reduce Services, Drop Many From Medicaid Rolls. USA Today, Mar 12, 2003.

Help Both Uninsured And Seniors. USA Today, February 5, 2003.

Why People File for Bankruptcy Study. USA Today, July 10, 1997.

Medical Bills Are A Large Factor in Bankruptcy Filings. The Washington Post, April 25, 2000.

224

The U.S. Spends More Money On Healthcare Than Any Other Country. Consumer Reports, Sept. 2000.

Half of HMOs Lost Money in 1999. USA Today, September 8, 2000.

U.S. Healthcare System Gets a Critical Diagnosis. USA Today, October 16, 2000.

Medical Costs Are Rising and Insurance Premiums Could Jump As High as 20%. USA Today, Dec. 8, 2000.

Report: Health System Broken. USA Today, March 2, 2001.

Insurers' Ability to Manage, Deny Medical Care Will Be Clipped. The Kiplinger Letter, Aug 3, 2001.

Health Benefits for Retirees Continue Decline. USA Today, August 13, 2001.

Prescriptions Up as Drug Makers Spend More on Ads. USA Today, August 13, 2001.

Insurance Caps Leave Some Struggling To Pay. USA Today, August 13, 2001.

Healthy Individuals Often Turned Down for Coverage. USA Today, August 13, 2001.

Retiree Health Benefits Not Like the Good Old Days. Dallas Morning News, August 19, 2001.

Health Insurance Premiums, Economic Slowdown Listed as Factors in Declining Coverage. Dallas Morning News, August 19, 2000.

Health Insurance Prices To Soar. USA Today, August 27, 2001.

Millions of Americans Lack Health Insurance. USA Today, October 11, 2001.

More HMOs to Drop Patients. USA Today, October 25, 2001.

Prescription Drug Costs Rise by $21 Billion. USA Today, October 25, 2001.

U.S. Study, Medical Bills Main Culprit in Bankruptcies. Common Dreams News Center, Nov. 15, 2001.

Health Care Spending Rose 6.9% In 2000. USA Today, January 7, 2002.

Healthcare Crisis in America. United Service Association For Health Care, 2003.

Why Congress Should Subsidize Health Insurance Coverage for Laid Off Workers. Consumers Union Press Release, October 22, 2001.

Number of Americans Without Health Insurance Reaches Highest Level on Record. Center on Budget and Policy Priorities, August 26 2004.

The Henry J. Kaiser Family Foundation. The Uninsured: A Primer, Key Facts About Americans without Health Insurance, November 10, 2004.

U.S. Department of Labor, Bureau of Labor Statistics. December 22, 2005. www.bls.gov/oco/cg/cgs035.htm

The Urban Institute. Key Findings from the 2002 National Health Interview Survey, Aug 9, 2004.
The Henry J. Kaiser Family Foundation. Access to Care for the Uninsured: An Update, Sept 29, 2003.

The Henry J. Kaiser Family Foundation. Employee Health Benefits: 2004 Annual Survey, September 9, 2004. http://www.kff.org/insurance/7148/index.cfm

The Henry J. Kaiser Family Foundation. The Uninsured: A Primer, Key Facts About Americans Without Health Insurance. November 10, 2004.

The Henry J. Kaiser Family Foundation. Health Care Worries in Context with Other Worries. Oct 4, 2004.

Health Care Expectations: Future Strategy and Direction 2005. Hewitt Associates LLC, Nov 17, 2004.

Institute of Medicine. Insuring America's Health - Principles and Recommendations. The National Academies Press, 2004.

Institute of Medicine. Care Without Coverage - Too Little, Too Late. The National Academies Press, 2002.

How Many People Lack Health Insurance and For How Long? Congressional Budget Office, May 12, 2003.

Employee Benefit Research Institute, "Sources of Health Insurance and Characteristics of the Uninsured: Analysis of the March 2004 Current Population Survey." Issue Brief No. 276, December 2004.

Institute of Medicine. Hidden Costs, Values Lost: Uninsurance in America. The National Academies Press, June 17, 2003.

The Commonwealth Fund. Wages, Health Benefits, and Workers' Health. Issue Brief, Oct 2004.

Committee on the Consequences of Uninsurance. Health Insurance is a Family Matter. Washington, D.C.: The National Academies Press, 2002.

Prescription Drug Trends 2004. The Henry J. Kaiser Family Foundation, October 25, 2004.

Cost Sharing Cuts Employers' Drug Spending but Employees Don't Get the Savings. RAND, 2002.

Trends in the Health of Americans. National Center for Health Statistics. Hyattsville, Maryland. 2004.

Uninsurance Facts and Figures. The Institute of Medicine, drawn from Coverage Matters, 2001; Insuring America's Health, 2004.

Trends in U.S. Health Coverage, 2001-2003. Center for Studying Health System Change, Aug 2004.

Families USA, One in Three: Non-Elderly Americans Without Health Insurance. 2002-2003.

Health Insurance Coverage in America, 2003 Data Update. The Henry J. Kaiser Family Foundation. November 2004.

The Effects of Congressional Proposals on Prescription Drug Costs for Medicare Beneficiaries. Department of Health and Human Services, Office of the Assistant Secretary for Public Affairs. June 19, 2002.

Assessment of Approaches to Evaluating Telemedicine. Prepared by the Lewin Group for the office of the Assistant Secretary for Planning and Evaluation, Department of Health and Human Services, December 2000.

Rising Healthcare Costs Making Employers and Employees Sick. PricewaterCoopers, Trendsetter Barometer, Apr 1, 2004.

Employer Health Benefits 2003 Annual Survey. The Henry J. Kaiser Family Foundation.

U.S. Census Bureau.

Medical Cost Reference Guide. BlueCross BlueShield, 2002.

Largest Health Care Fraud Case in U.S. History Settled HCA Investigation Nets Record Total pf $1.7 Billion. U.S. Department of Justice. June 26, 2003.

U.S. Intervenes in $175 Million Drug Fraud Suit Against Abbott Labs. Thompson West. Find Law, May 2006.

Rx for Fraud. Forbes, June 20, 2005.

Health Care Compliance Association. http://www.hcca-info.org

Dangerous Prescription. Frontline, PBS.

226

The U.S. Health Care System: Best in the World, or Just the Most Expensive? Bureau of Education, U. of Maine, 2001.

Doctors Are the Third Leading Cause of Death in the US, Causing 250,000 Deaths Every Year. Journal of the American Medical Association, July 26, 2000; 284(4) 483-5.

Insuring America's Health: Principles and Recommendations. The National Academy of Sciences, 2004.

Western Europe, Not the US, Ranks as World's Healthiest Region. Reuters London, Mar 25, 2002.

Theresa Agovino. Young Adults Lacking Health Insurance. Associated Press, May 24, 2005. Joanne Laurier. 82 Million Americans Lacked Health Insurance in 2002-2003. World Socialist Website, June 23, 2004.

Ahman and Gold. Average Out-of-Pocket Health Care Costs for Medicare and Choice Enrollees Increase 10 Percent in 2003. The Commonwealth Fund, August 2003.

Marcia Angell. The Truth About Drug Companies: How They Deceive Us and What to Do About It. Random House: New York. 2004.

J. Appleby. More Insured Workers Unable to Pay Medical Bills. USA Today, April 29, 2005.

Cathi Callahan and James Mays. Working Paper: Estimating the Number of Individuals in the United States Without Health Insurance. Prepared for the Office of the Assistant Secretary for Planning and Evaluation, Department of Health and Human Services, March 31, 2005.

Michael Chernew. Rising Health Care Costs and the Decline in Insurance Coverage. Economic Research Initiative on the Uninsured, ERIU Working Paper, September 8, 2002.

J. Cohen. Design and methods of the Medical Expenditure Panel Survey Household Component. Rockville (MD): Agency for Health Care Policy and Research; 1997. MEPS Methodology Report No. 1. AHCPR Pub. No. 97-0026.

S. Cohen. Sample design of the 1996 Medical Expenditure Panel Survey Household Component. Rockville (MD): Agency for Health Care Policy and Research; 1997. MEPS Methodology Report No. 2 AHCPR Pub. No. 97-0027.

Mark Coleman. A Report on the Institute of Medicine Committee on Uninsurance. Keynote Address to the "Voices of Detroit Initiative" Annual Meeting, May 19, 2003.

M. Dalrymple. Senators Seek Tax Credit for Unemployed. Associated Press, October 9, 2003.

C. DeNavas-Walt, B. Proctor, and R. J. Mills. Income, Poverty, and Health Insurance Coverage in the United States: 2003. U.S. Census Bureau, August 2004.

Jessica Fraser. Statistics Prove Prescription Drugs Are 16,400% More Deadly Than Terrorists. News Target, July 5, 2005.

Gary. Growing Health Care Concerns Fuel Cautious Support for Change. ABC News, Oct 20, 2004.

Leif Wellington Haase. A New Deal For Health: How to Cover Everyone and Get Medical Costs Under Control. The Century Foundation. June 1, 2005.

Matthew Harper and Peter Kang. The World's Ten Best-Selling Drugs. Forbes, March 22, 2006.

John Iglehart. The Challenges Facing Private Health Insurance. Health Affairs, November/December 2004. http://content.healthaffairs.org/cgi/content/extract/23/6/9

Marilyn Moon. Growth in Medical Spending: What Will Beneficiaries Pay? The Commonwealth Fund, May 1999.

R. Pear. U.S. Health Care Spending Reaches All-Time High: 15% of GDP. The New York Times, January 3, 2004.

Melody Peterson. Bayer Agrees to Pay U.S. $257 Million in Drug Fraud. New York Times, April 2003.

Tiffany Ray. Law Changes Health-Care Bankruptcies. Birmingham Business Journal, Nov. 11, 2005.

Malcolm Sparrow. License to Steal: Why Fraud Plagues America's Health Care System. Westview Press, 1996.

Sarah Reber and Laura Tyson. Rising Health Insurance Costs Slow Job Growth and Reduce Wages and Job Quality. Unpublished paper, quoted in http://www.csls.ca/events/nylabor/freeman_rodgers.pdf Aug 19, 2004.

Steve Sellery. The Uninsured Healthcare Crisis in America. Econ-Atrocity Bulletin, July 6, 2005.

J. Smith. Healthy Bodies and Thick Wallets: The Dual Relation Between Health And Economic Status. Journal of Economic Perspectives 13(2): 145-166.

Smith, Cowan, Sensenig and Catlin. Health Spending Growth Slows in 2003. Health Affairs 24:1 (2005): 185-194.

Christopher Snowbeck. Medical Bills Figure in Personal Bankruptcy. Pittsburg Post-Gazette, Aug. 06 2004.

Christopher Snowbeck. Unisured Waiting in Line. Pittsburg Post-Gazette, July 16, 2004.

Christopher Snowbeck. Foregoing Health Insurance Can Be a Costly Gamble. Pittsburg Post-Gazette, February 22, 2004.

Christopher Snowbeck. How Those With the Least are Charged the Most. Pittsburg Post-Gazette, March 24, 2004.

Susan Starr Sered and Rushika Fernandopulle. Uninsured in America: Life and Death in the Land of Opportunity. The University of California Press, 2005.

Bernadette Tansey. Huge penalty in drug fraud Pfizer settles felony case in Neurontin off-label promotion. SF Gate, May 14, 2004.

Medicaid

Centers for Medicare and Medicaid Services (CMS).

Kaiser Commission on Medicaid and the Uninsured

National Coalition on Health Care.

Leighton Ku and Bethany Kessler. The Number and Cost of Immigration on Medicaid: National and State Estimates. The Urban Institute, December 16, 1997.

Carolyn Lochhead. Speeches Ignore Impending U.S. Debt Disaster. SF Chronicle, Sep 12, 2004.

Medicare

Centers for Medicare and Medicaid Services (CMS). Medicare.org

U.S. Department of Health and Human Services.

Centers for Medicare and Medicaid Services, Office of the Actuary, National Health Statistics Group; and U.S. Department of Commerce, Bureau of Economic Analysis and Bureau of the Census. 2003. http://www.cms.hhs.gov/statistics/nhe/projections-2003/t2.asp

Dennis Cauchon and John Waggoner. The Looming National Benefit Crisis. USA Today, Oct 3, 2004.

Andrew Rettenmaier and Thomas Saving. With an Eye to the Future. Texas A&M University, Private Enterprise Research Center. Perspective on Policy, May 2004.

Liqun Liu, Andrew Rettenmaier, and Thomas Saving. A Debt is a Debt. Texas A&M University, Private Enterprise Research Center. Perspective on Policy, September 2002.

228

Andrew Rettenmaier and Thomas Saving. Just What the Doctor Ordered? Texas A&M University, Private Enterprise Research Center. Perspective on Policy, August 2002.

Cathi Callahan and James Mays. Estimating the Number of Individuals in the United States Without Health Insurance. Working Paper. Prepared for the Office of the Assistant Secretary for Planning and Evaluation, Department of Health and Human Services, March 31, 2005.

The Effects of Congressional Proposals on Prescription Drug Costs for Medicare Beneficiaries. Department of Health and Human Services. Office of the Assistant Secretary for Public Affairs, June 19, 2002.

Medicare Premiums Hike. LA Times, September 7, 2004.

D.R. Francis. Medicare Reform Carries Huge Fiscal Toll. Christian Science Monitor, Oct 17, 2003.

Medicare HMOs Cutting Coverage, Increasing Rates. USA Today, Nov 23, 2001.

Paul Van de Water and Joni Lavery. Medicare Finances: Findings of the 2006 Trustees Report. National Academy of Social Insurance, No.13, May 2006.

Medicare Sourcebook. National Academy of Social Insurance. www.nasi.org

Statistical data on Poverty, Medicare and Social Security. National Committee to Preserve Social Security and Medicare (NCPSSM). www.ncpssm.org

The Privatization of Medicare. National Committee to Preserve Social Security and Medicare (NCPSSM), June 2006.

The Future of Social Security and Medicare: Demographics vs the Cost of Health Care. National Committee to Preserve Social Security and Medicare (NCPSSM), May 2006.

Martin Crutsinger. Social Security Financial Health Declining. Associated Press, May 2, 2006.

Leif Wellington Haase. Taking Stock in the Medicare Drug Benefit. The Century Foundation, May 18, 2006.

Leif Wellington Haase. The Senate's Medicare Drug Bill: Where It Works, Where It Falls Short. The Century Foundation, June 19, 2003.

Shannon Jones and Barry Grey. Medicare Bill Marks Major Step in Destruction of Government Health Plan for U.S. Seniors. World Socialist Website, November 26, 2003.

Ricardo Alonzo-Zaldivar and Joanna Neuman. Give and Take in New Rules for New Year. LA Times, January 1, 2006.

Medicare Premiums Jumps 13.5%. CBS/Associated Press, October 16, 2003.

Scott Burns. Costs of Medicare Snowball. Dallas Morning News, April 9, 2005.

Increase in Medicare Payments to Doctors This Year Will Raise Beneficiaries' Part B Premiums More Than Expected Next Year, Officials Say. Medilexicon.com, April 2, 2005.

Food Industry Additives and Morbidity

Russell L. Blaylock, MD. Excitotoxins: The Taste that Kills. Health Press, 1995.

B. Yastag. Obesity is Now on Everyone's Plate. *JAMA*. 291 (10): 1186-1188, March 10, 2004.

S.G Bouret, S.J. Draper, and R.B. Simley. Trophic Action of Leptin on Hypothalamus Neurons that Regulate Feeding. Science. 2; 304 (5667), 108-110, April, 2, 2004.

B. Frieder and V. E. Grimm. Prenatal Monosodium Glutamate (MSG) Treatment Given Through the Mother's Diet Causes Behavioral Deficits in Rat Offspring. Intern J Neurosci. 23: 117-126, 1984.

Centers for Disease Control, National Center for Chronic Disease Prevention and Health Promotion. Physical Activity and Good Nutrition: Essential Elements to Prevent Chronic Diseases and Obesity 2003. Nutr Clin Care. 6(3):135-8. Review.,Oct - Dec, 2003.

J.W. Olney. Brain Lesions, Obesity, and Other Disturbances in Mice Treated with Monosodium Glutamate. Science. 164(880):719-21, May 9, 1969.

J.W. Olney and O.L Ho. Brain Damage in Infant Mice Following Oral Intake of Glutamate, Aspartate, or Cysteine. Nature (Lond). 227: 609-611, 1970.

Edwin Park and Robert Greenstein. Administration Defense of Health Savings Accounts Rests on Misleading Use of Statistics. Center on Budget Policy and Priorities, February 16, 2006.

FDA and Big Pharma and Healthcare Fraud

PBS Frontline Feature: Dangerous Prescription, 2005.

Marcia Angell. Research for Sale. The New England Journal of Medicine, May 18, 2000; 342.

Thomas Bodenheimer. Uneasy Alliance—Clinical Investigators and the Pharmaceutical Industry. The New England Journal of Medicine, May 18, 2000; 342, No. 20.

Brian Vaszily. Spin and the Pharmaceutical Industry: Proudly Protecting Profits by Scaring You. www.mercola.com July 26, 2003.

Bernadette Tansey. Huge Penalty in Drug Fraud Pfizer Settles Felony Case in Neurotonin Off-label Promotion. SFGate.com May 14, 2004.

Most Media Coverage of Drugs Highly Biased. June 10, 2000. www.mercola.com

U.S. Intervenes in $175M Drug Fraud Suit Against Abbott Labs. FindLaw, June 14, 2006.

Melody Peterson. "Bayer Agrees to Pay U.S. $257 Million In Drug Fraud." The New York Times, April 17, 2003.

Waging War on Prescription Drug Abuse: New Medco Analysis Reveals Prescription Drug Abusers Engage in Doctor Shopping and Script. PRNewswire-FirstCall, September 29, 2005.

MyRxForLess Owners Guilty of Importing Phony Pharmaceuticals from Mexico. January 28, 2005. http://mathiasconsulting.com/cases/prescriptions

James Hood. Pharmacy Benefit Managers Scrutinized. Consumer Affairs. Oct 28, 2004.

Former Hospital Secretary Sentenced. Press Release, February 9, 2006.

Pensions and Retirement

Marcy Gordon. Pension Agency Reports $22.3 B Shortfall. Associated Press, Nov 15, 2005.

Andrew Bridges. Nearly One in 10 Pension Plans Said Frozen. Associated Press, Dec 21, 2005.

Nanette Byrnes. Rising Tensions Over Pensions. BusinessWeek, May 16, 2005.

Susan Cornwell. Delphi Senn Moving Pensions to US Agency. Reuters, October 10, 2005.

Matt Krantz. Stocks Rebound, But Pensions Haven't. USA Today. July 17, 2005.

Corporate America's Legacy Costs: Now for the Reckoning. The Economist, Oct. 13, 2005.

Pension Plan Funding Under Social Security. Forbes, June 10, 2005.

Jonathan Elsberg. Underfunded Pensions and Perverse Incentives. Center for Popular Economics, August 17, 2005.

PBGC Releases Fiscal Year 2004 Financial Results. PBGC No. 05-10. PBGC Public Affairs, Nov. 15, 2004.

Pension Benefit Guaranty Corporation Performance and Accountability Report. Fiscal Year 2004, Nov. 15, 2004.

Yvonne Sin. Minimum Pension Guarantees. The World Bank, Washington. Presented at the Russian Federation, Moscow, 3-5 July 2003.

Jim Abrams. Pensions Moving Slowly in Congress. The Associated Press, Oct 23, 2005.

230

Albert Crenshaw. Panel Votes for Higher Pension Insurance Fees. The Washington Post, Oct. 27, 2005.

David John. America's Pensions: The Next Saving and Loan Crisis? Testimony Before the Select Committee on Aging, United States Senate. The Heritage Foundation, October 14, 2003.

Stephen McCourt. Defined Benefit and Defined Contribution Plans: A History, Market Overview, and Comparative Analysis. Benefits Compensation Digest. Vol. 43, No.2 February 2006.

U.S. Chamber of Commerce

David John. Treasury Department Proposal for Defined Benefits Includes Important Reforms. The Heritage Foundation, August 7, 2003.

Lawrence Bader. Pension Deficits: An Unnecessary Evil. Financial Analysts Journal, 2004.

Roger Lowenstein. The End of Pensions. New York Times, 2006.

Craig Smith. Retired Seniors Find Little Security. Pittsburg Tribune-Review, June 5, 2006.

David Francis. Tension Over Pensions: Can They Be Saved? Christian Science Monitor, Jan. 23, 2006.

Richard Johnson, Gordon Mermin, and Cori Uccello. How Secure are Retirement Nest Eggs. Center for Retirement Research, Boston College. Number 45. April 2006.

Alicia Munnell, Francesca Golub-Sass, Mauricio Soto and Francis Vitagliano. Why are Healthy Employers Freezing Their Pensions? Center for Retirement Research, Boston College. Number 44. Mar. 2006.

Alicia Munnell, Anthony Webb and Luke Delorme. A New National Retirement Risk Index. Center for Retirement Research, Boston College. Number 48. June 2006.

Alicia Munnell and Annika Sunden. 401(k) Plans Are Still Coming Up Short. Center for Retirement Research, Boston College. Number 43. March 2006.

Alicia Munnell. A Bird's Eye View of the Social Security Debate. Center for Retirement Research at Boston College. Issue in Brief Number 25 December 2004.

Alicia Munnell, Robert Hatch, and James Lee. Why is the Life Expectancy So Low in the United States? Center for Retirement Research at Boston College. Number 21. August 2004.

Alicia Munnell. Population Aging: It's Not Just the Baby Boom. Center for Retirement Research at Boston College. An Issue in Brief. Number 16. April 2004.

Alicia Munnell, Annika Sunden and Elizabeth Lidstone. How Important Are Private Pensions? Center for Retirement Research at Boston College. An Issue in Brief. Number 8, February 2002.

Gary Burless and Joseph Quinn. Is Working Longer the Answer for an Aging Workforce? Center for Retirement Research at Boston College. An Issue in Brief. Number 11, Dec 2002.

Courtney Coile and Kevin Milligan. How Portfolios Evolve After Retirement: The Effect of Health Shocks. Center for Retirement Research at Boston College, December 2005.

Barbara Butrica, Joshua Goldwyn, and Richard Johnson. Understanding Expenditure Patterns in Retirement. Center for Retirement Research at Boston College, January 2005.

Mauricio Soto. Will Baby Boomers Drown in Debt? Center for Retirement Research at Boston College. Number 15. March 2005.

Francesca Golub-Sass and Andrew Varani. How Much Are Workers Saving? Center for Retirement Research at Boston College. Issue in Brief Number 34 October 2005.

Richard Johnson, Gordon Mermin and Cori Uccello. How Secure Are Our Nest Eggs? Center for Retirement Research at Boston College, Number 45. April 2006.

Courtney Coile. Milligan, Kevin. How Portfolios Evolve After Retirement: The Effect of Health Shocks. Center for Retirement Research at Boston College, October 2005.

Barry Bosworth and Lisa Bell. The Decline in Household Saving: What Can We Learn From Survey Data. Center for Retirement Research at Boston College, October 2005.

Richard Johnson, Gordon Mermin and Cori Uccello. When the Nest Egg Cracks: Financial Consequences of Health Problems, Marital Status Changes and Job Layoffs at Older Ages. Center for Retirement Research at Boston College, October 2005.

James Lee. Changing 401(k) Defaults on Cashing Out: Another Step in the Right Direction. Center for Retirement Research at Boston College. Just the Facts Number 12, September 2004.

Robert Triest and Natalia Jivan. How Do Pensions Affect Actual and Expected Retirement Ages? Center for Retirement Research at Boston College. Working Paper. November 2004.

Cori Uccello. Are Americans Saving Enough for Retirement? Center for Retirement Research at Boston College, Number 7, July 2001.

Mike Orszag, The Shortcomings of 401(k) Plans. European Pensions and Investment News.

Report of the Working Group on Defined Benefit Plan Funding And Discount Rate Issues. U.S. Department of Labor, Employee Benefits Security Administration, February 14, 2006.

Mark Glickman and Charles Jeszeck. PBGC and the Current Challenges Facing the U.S. Defined Benefit Pension System. U.S. Government Accountability Office, April 4, 2005.

An Analysis of Frozen Defined Benefit Plans. Pension Benefit Guaranty Corporation, Dec 21, 2005.

August Cole. U.S. Pension Peril Grows with Bankruptcies. MarketWatch, June 20, 2006.

August Cole. Rising Rates Ease Pressure on Pension Plans. MarketWatch, June 22, 2006.

William Watts. Legislation Won't Save Defined Benefit Pensions. MarketWatch, June 22, 2006.

Andrea Coombes. Dis-United in Outlook for Retirement. MarketWatch, June 20, 2006.

Andrea Coombes. Retirement Outlook? Poor. MarketWatch, June 6, 2006.

Milliman 2006 Pension Study

Bush Signs Massive Pension Overhaul. Associated Press, August 17, 2006.

Sue Kirchhoff. Pension Act: Does It Add to Instability? USA Today, August 9, 2006.

Ellen Hoffman. Is Your Pension Plan Retiring Before You? BusinessWeek Online, April 21, 2006.

Pension Publications Fact Sheets. Pension Rights Center. www.pensionrights.org

Tom Shean. Even Healthy Companies Are Killing Pension Plans. The Virginian-Piloy, June 18, 2006.

Daniel Gross. The Big Freeze. American Association of Retired Persons, March 2006.

Mary Williams Walsh. I.B.M. to Freeze Pension Plans to Trim Costs. New York Times, Jan. 6, 2006.

Geoffrey Colvin. The End of a Dream. Fortune, June 22, 2006.

Ellen Schultz, Charles Forelle and Theo Francis. Forecast: More Pension Freezes on the Way. WSJ.com.

Mary Williams Walsh. More Companies Ending Promises for Retirement. New York Times, Jan 9, 2006.

Adam Geller. Even Healthy Companies Are Freezing Pensions. Associated Press, December 10, 2005.

Interview with Alicia Munnell. Retirement's Risky for Many Americans. Boston Globe, July 2, 2006.

The Shortcomings of 401(k) Plans. European Pensions and Investment News, June 21, 2004.

David Francis. Tension Over Pensions: Can They Be Saved? The Christian Science Monitor, Jan 23, 2006.

Lawrence Thompson. The Predictability of Retirement Income. National Academy of Social Insurance. Social Security Brief No.5.

Clifford Asness. Fight the Fed Model: The Relationship Between Stock Market Yields, Bond Market Yields, and Future Returns. AQR Capital Management, LCC, Dec 2002.

Pension Benefit Guarantee Corporation www.pbgc.gov

Charles R. Morris. Apart at the Seams: The Collapse of Private Pension and Health Care Protections. A Century Foundation Report, 2006.

Mark Glickman and Charles Jeszeck. PBGC and the Current Challenges Facing the U.S. Defined Benefit Pension System. U.S. Government Accountability Office, April 4, 2005.

An Analysis of Frozen Defined Benefit Plans. PBGC, December 21, 2005.

Report of the Working Group on Defined Benefit Plan Funding And Discount Rate Issues. Employee Benefits Security Administration. U.S. Department of Labor, February 14, 2006.

Susan Cornwell. Airlines Could Get More Relief from Pension Bill. Reuters, November 10, 2005.

Joanna Lahey. Do Older Workers Face Discrimination? Center for Retirement Research at Boston College. An Issue in Brief. Number 33, July 2005.

Eileen Powell. Workers Have Retirement Overconfidence. Associated Press, April 4, 2006.

Brandt Urban. GM Earnings Announcements Knocks $2.9 Billion from Market Cap. The Monroe Street Journal, March 21, 2005.

Can You Afford to Retire? PBS Frontline Feature, 2006.

Steven Kandarian, Executive Director, Pension Benefit Guaranty Corporation. Government Affairs Subcommittee on Financial Management, The Budget, and International Security. September 15, 2003.

David John. Treasury Department Proposal for Defined Benefits Includes Important Reforms. The Heritage Foundation, August 7, 2003.

Caroline Daniel and Stephanie Kirchgaessner. US Pension Body Reform Key to Savings. Financial Times. Feb 6, 2006.

Real Estate Bubble

Board of Governors of the Federal Reserve System www.federalreserve.gov

Federal Reserve Bank of New York www.ny.frb.org

Federal Reserve Bank of St. Louis www.stlouisfed.org

Federal Reserve Bank of San Francisco www.frbsf.org

United States Bureau of Census www.census.gov

U.S. Department of Commerce: Bureau of Economic Analysis www.bea.gov

National Bureau of Economic Research www.nber.org

Bureau of Labor and Statistics www.bls.gov

Office of Management and Budget, Congressional Budget Office www.whitehouse.gov

National Home Equity Mortgage Association www.nhema.org

National Mortgage Association of America (Fannie Mae) www.fanniemae.com

Mortgage Bankers Association of America www.mbaa.org

National Association of Realtors www.realtor.org

Office of Federal Housing Oversight www.ofheo.gov

Office of Federal Housing Enterprise Oversight www.ofheo.gov

National Reverse Mortgage Lenders Association www.reversemortgage.org

Federal Depository Insurance Corporation www.fdic.gov

Federal Home Loan Mortgage Corporation (Freddie Mac) www.freddiemac.com

Sallie Mae www.salliemae.org

Government National Mortgage Association (Ginnie Mae) www.ginniemae.gov
Department of Housing and Urban Development (HUD) www.hud.gov

Federal Housing Finance Board www.fhfb.gov

Bond Market Association www.bondmarkets.com

U.S. Social Security Administration

Dean Baker. Dangerous Trends: The Growth of Debt in the U.S. Economy. Center for Economic Policy Research, September 7, 2004.

Dean Baker. The Run-Up in Home Prices: Is It real or is It Another Bubble? Center for Economic Policy Research, August, 5, 2002.

Dean Baker. Too Much Bubbly at the Fed?: The New York Federal Reserve's Analysis of the Run-Up in Home Prices. Center for Economic Policy Research, June 12, 2004.

Maya MacGuineas. Homeowner Tax Breaks are Breaking the Budget. Fiscal Policy Program at the New America Foundation, October 30, 2005.

Peter Coy. The Home Vexing Greenspan. News Analysis, June 10, 2005.

Dana Dratch. Bubble Fear? Rethink Your Mortgage. Bankrate.com, March 10, 2006.

Noelle Know. Some Homeowners Struggle to Keep Up With Adjustable Rates. USA Today, April 3, 2006.

Jason Zweig. The Oracle Speaks. CNN Money, May 2, 2005.

Gary Shilling. The Housing Bubble Will Probably Burst. January 2006.

Scott Wright. Real Estate Bubble 3. May 27, 2005.

Peter Miller. Will There Be a Real Estate Bubble? April 23, 2002.

Michael House. Oversight on Government Sponsored Enterprises: The Risks and Benefits to Consumers. Testimony to Senate Government Affairs Committee, July 21, 2003.

Lew Sichelman. Is Household Wealth Rising or Falling? Realtytimes.com.
Les Christie. Take This House and Shove It. CNNMoney.com, December 8, 2005.

Fred Foldvary. Real Estate Cycles. The Progress Report, 2004.

Nicholas von Hoffman. Pop Goes the real Estate Bubble. October 5, 2005.

Forrest Pafenberg. Single-Family Mortgages Originated and Outstanding: 1990-2004. Office of Federal Housing Enterprise Oversight, July 2005.

Richard Freeman. Fannie and Freddie Were Lenders': U.S. Real Estate Bubble Nears Its End. Executive Intelligence Review, June 21, 2002.

Dider Sornette. Is the Real Estate Bubble ready to Burst? UCLA Today, 2004.

Frank Nothaft. The Next Decade for Mortgage Finance. Special Commentary from the Office of the Chief Economist, Freddie Mac, June 23, 2004

A Supervisor's Perspective on Mortgage Markets and Mortgage Lending Practices. Remarks by Governor Susan Schmidt Bies at the Mortgage Bankers Association Presidents Conference, Half Moon Bay, California. June 14, 2006.

Federal National Mortgage Association Form 8-K, The United States Securities and Exchange Commission, Mar. 21, 2006.

New Home Sales Drop in the West. East Bay Business Times, March 24, 2006.

Michael Corkery. Hot Homes Get Cold in Once-Booming Markets. The Wall Street Journal, Apr. 22, 2006.

Predatory Appraisal Stealing the American Dream. The National Community Reinvestment Coalition.

John Bellamy Foster. The Household Debt Bubble. May 2006.

Mike Wells. Local Mortgage Firms Searched by Federal Agents. Columbia Daily Tribune, April 2, 2005.

Peter Coy. Buyer (And Seller) Beware. BusinessWeek Online, April 4, 2006.

Noelle Knox. Some Homeowners Struggle to Keep Up With Adjustable Rates. USA Today, Apr. 3, 2006.

Larry S. Levy. The Fraud of Appraisal Regulation. Financial Sense, July 2004.

Bob Burnitt. Appraisal Fraud: So What Else is New, Pal? Financial Sense, Mar 2005.

Richard Freeman. Fannie and Freddie Were Lenders': U.S. Real Estate Bubble Nears Its End. Executive Intelligence Review, June 21, 2002.

Greenspan Calls for Curbs on Fannie Mae, Freddie Mac Growth. Bloomberg, April 6, 2005.

Oversight on Government Sponsored Enterprises: The Risks and Benefits to Consumers. Testimony of W. Michael House, July 21, 2003.

Robert Tanner. Property Taxes Questioned As Prices Zoom. Associated Press, May 22, 2006.

Social Security

Social Security Administration

Seniorjournal.com

Craig Smith. Retired Seniors Find Little Security. Pittsburg Tribune-Review, June 5, 2006.

Gar Alperovitz. Time for Moral Outrage About Social Security. CommonDreams.org, January 31, 2005.

Social Security Primer. National Committee to Preserve Social Security and Medicare, Feb 2006.

The Truth About Social Security. National Committee to Preserve Social Security and Medicare.

National Committee to Preserve Social Security and Medicare. Myths and Realities About Social Security and Privatization. March 2005.

Personal Retirement Accounts are a Recipe for Benefit Cuts. National Committee to Preserve Social Security and Medicare, February 2006.

An Op-ed on Social Security: Risks Far Outweigh Benefits of Privatized Social Security. National Committee to Preserve Social Security and Medicare, September 30, 2004.

Sylvester Schieber. Social Security: Past, Present and Future. National Academy of Social Insurance. Social Security Brief No 5. March 1999.

Marie Smith. The Future of Social Security. Social Security Conference, Menendez Pelayo Conference, Santander, Spain. July 18, 2005.

2004 Report of the OASDI Board of Trustees and Social Security Office of the Chief Actuary.

E. J. Dionne. Why Social Insurance? National Academy of Social Insurance. Social Security Brief No 6. January 1999.

What is Social Security Disability Insurance? National Academy of Social Insurance.

Social Security Finances: A Primer. National Academy of Social Insurance, April 2005.

Virginia Reno and Anita Cardwell. Social Security Finances: Findings of the 2006 Trustees Report. National Academy of Social Insurance. Social Security Brief No 21. May 2006.

Virginia Reno and Joni Lavery. Can We Afford Social Security When Baby Boomers Retire? National Academy of Social Insurance. Social Security Brief No 22. May 2006.

Virginia Reno and Joni Lavery. Options to Balance Social Security Funds Over the Next 75 Years. National Academy of Social Insurance. Social Security Brief No 18. February 2005.

Virginia Reno and Joni Lavery. Social Security: What Role for Life Annuities in Individual Accounts? Issues, Options, and Tradeoffs. National Academy of Social Insurance. Social Security Brief No.5.

Lockhart versus the United States, Supreme Court of the United States. http://www.law.cornell.edu/supct/html/04-881.ZO.html

Evaluating Issues in Privatizing Social Security. The Report of the Panel on the Privitization of Social Security. National Academy of Social Insurance.

Richard Kogan and Robert Greenstein. President Portrays Social Security Shortfall as Enormous But His Tax Cuts and Drug Benefit Will Cost at Least Five Times as Much. Center on Budget and Policy Priorities, 2005.

Board of Trustees. 2005. The 2005 Annual Report of the Board of Trustees of the Federal Old-Age and Survivors Insurance and Disability Insurance Trust Funds. Washington, D.C.: U.S. Government Printing Office.

U.S. Social Security Administration (SSA). 2005. Income of the Population 55 or Older, 2002. Washington, D.C.: Social Security Administration.

Alicia Munnell. A Bird's Eye View of the Social Security Debate. Center for Retirement Research at Boston College, An Issue in Brief 25.

U.S. Social Security Administration (SSA). 2004. *Effect* of COLA on Social Security Benefits. Washington, D.C.: Social Security Administration. www.ssa.gov/OACT/COLA/colaeffect.html.

Robert Clark and Joseph Quinn. The Economic Status of the Elderly. National Academy of Social Insurance. Medicare Brief No 4. May 1999.

Leonesio and Vaughan. Increasing the Early Retirement Age Under Social Security: Health, Work, and Financial Resources. National Academy of Social Insurance. Health and Income Security for an Aging Workforce. No. 7. December 2003.

Robert Clark and Joseph Quinn. The Economic Status of the Elderly. National Academy of Social Insurance. Medicare Brief No.4 May 1999.

Jason Furman and Robert Greenstein. What the New Trustees' Report Shows about Social Security. Center on Budget and Policy Priorities, June 15, 2006.

Jason Furman. Does Social Security Face a Crisis in 2018? Center on Budget and Policy Priorities, January 11, 2004.

Greg Anrig. Ten Myths About Social Security. The Century Foundation, January 25, 2006.

Max Sawicky. Collision Course: The Bush Budget and Social Security. Economic Policy Institute, March 2005.

Jagadeesh Gokhale. Why America Needs Social Security Reform. CATO Institute, November 30, 2004.

Jagadeesh Gokhale. The Future of Retirement in the United States. CATO Institute, Jan 22, 2004.

Peter G. Peterson. Riding for a Fall. Foreign Affairs, September/October 2004.

236

Thomas Saving. The 2004 Report of the Social Security Trustees: Social Security Shortfalls and the Prospect for Reform. Texas A&M University, Private Enterprise Research Center. Perspective on Policy, September 2004.

Social Security and Medicare from a Trust Fund and Budget Perspective. ASPE issue Brief. April 2005.

Liqun Liu, Andrew Rettenmaier and Thomas Saving. A Debt is a Debt. Texas A&M University, Private Enterprise Research Center. Perspective on Policy, September 2002.

Andrew Rettenmaier and Thomas Saving. With an Eye to the Future. Texas A&M University, Private Enterprise Research Center. Perspective on Policy, May 2004.

James Horney and Richard Kogan. Private Accounts Would Substantially Increase Federal Debt and Interest Payments. Center on Budget and Policy Priorities, August 2, 2005.

The Outlook for Social Security: Potential Range of Social Security Outlays and Revenues Under Current Law. Congressional Budget Office, June 2004.

Greg Anrig and Bernard Wasow. Twelve Reasons Why Privatizing Social Security is a Bad Idea. The Century Foundation, February 14, 2005.

Greg Anrig and Bernard Wasow. What Would Really Happen Under Social Security Privitization? Part III: IRAs and 401(k)s You Can Not Control or Leave to Heirs. The Social Security Network, The Century Foundation.

Greg Anrig and Bernard Wasow. What Would Really Happen Under Social Security Privatization? The Social Security Network, December 10, 2001.

DeWitt, Larry. The Social Security Trust Funds and the Federal Budget. Research Note #20. Social Security Administration Historian's Office, March 4, 2005.

Social Security Sourcebook. National Academy of Social Insurance. www.nasi.org

Social Security Reform. A Century Foundation Guide to the Issues, Revised 2005 edition. The Century Foundation, 2005.

Public Policy in an Older America. A Century Foundation Guide to the Issues. The Century Foundation, 2006.

Austan Goolsbee. The Fees of Private Accounts and the Impact of Social Security Privatization on Financial Managers. University of Chicago, September 2004.

Alicia Munnell. Social Security's Financial Outlook: The 2006 Update in Perspective. Center for Retirement Research at Boston College, Number 46. April 2006.

Alicia Munnell. Social Security's Financial Outlook: The 2005 Update and a Look Back. Center for Retirement Research at Boston College, Number 16. March 2005.

Douglas Holtz-Eakin. The Outlook for Social Security. Congressional Budget Office, June 2004.

Statement of Hal Daub, Chairman, Social Security Advisory Board at the Nationwide Public Policy Forum on Retirement Security. June 28, 2004.

Michael Leonesio, Denton Vanghan, and Bernard Wixon. Increasing the Early Retirement Age Under Social Security: Health, Work, and Financial Resources. National Academy of Social Insurance. Health and Income Security, No. 7. December 2003.

Max Sawicky. Collision Course: The Bush Budget and Social Security. Economic Policy Institute, March 2005.

Richard Johnson and Rudolph Penner. Will Health Care Costs Erode Retirement Security? Center for Retirement Research at Boston College. An Issue in Brief. Number 23. October 2004.

Charles Hurt. Illegals Granted Social Security. The Washington Times, May 19, 2006.

Thomas Saving. The 2004 Report of the Social Security Trustees: Social Security Shortfalls and the Prospect for Reform. Texas A&M University, Private Enterprise Research Center, Sept 2004.

The World's Dependence on Oil

U.S. Energy Information Administration www.eia.gov

CIA World Factbook www.cia.gov

Society of Petroleum Engineers. www.spe.org

Association for the Study of Peak Oil and Gas. www.peakoil.net

American Petroleum Institute www.api.org

Chevron Inc. www.cheveron.com

Exxon-Mobil Inc. www.exxon.com

U.S Department of Energy. http://www.fe.doe.gov/programs/reserves/spr/spr-facts.html

Jean Leherrere. Estimates of Oil Reserves. Paper presented at the EMF/IEA/IEW Meeting IIASA, Laxenburg, Austria, June 10, 2001.

Wood, Long and Morehouse. Long-Term World Oil Supply Scenarios: The Future is Neither as Bleak or Rosy as Some Assert. EIA, August 18, 2004.

R. W. Bentley. Global Oil & Gas Depletion: An Overview. Energy Policy 30 (2002) 189-205.

Alfred Cavallo. Oil: The Illusion of Plenty. Bulletin of the Atomic Scientists, January/February 2004, Vol. 60, no 01.

William Engdahl. Iraq and the Problem of Peak Oil. Current Concerns, No 1, 2004.

Bamberger, Robert. Strategic Petroleum Reserve. CRS: Issue Brief for Congress: Resources, Aug. 2, 2001.

Matthew Simmons and King Hubbert. The World's Giant Oilfields. Center for Petroleum Supply Studies, Colorado School of Mines, January 2002.

Samsam Bakhtiari. 2002 to see birth of New World Energy Order. Oil and Gas Journal, Jan 7, 2002.

Kenneth Deffeyes. Peak of World Oil Production. paper No. 83-0, Geological Society of America Annual Meeting, November 2001.

King Hubbert. Nuclear Energy and the Fossil Fuels. Publication No. 95, Shell Development Company Exploration and Production Research Division. Presented before the Spring Meeting of the Southern District, Division of Production, American Petroleum Institute. Plaza Hotel, San Antonio, Texas, March 7-9, 1956.

Kjell Aleklett. International Energy Agency Accepts Peak Oil: An Analysis of Chapter 3 of the World Energy Outlook 2004. Association for the Study of Peak Oil and Gas (ASPO).

www.peakoil.net/uhdsg/weo2004/TheUppsalaCode.html

Rudolf Rechsteiner. Adding Fuel to Fire? The Role of Petroleum and Violent Conflicts. Presented at the swisspeace annual conference, October 30, 2003.

Bengt Soderbergh. Canada's Oil Sands Resources and Its Future Impact on Global Oil Supply. Masters of Science Degree Project, Systems Engineering, Uppsala University, 2005.

T. Ahlbrandt. The USGS World Petroleum Assessment 2000.

T. Quinn. Turning Tar Sands into Oil. Cleveland Plain Dealer, July 22, 2005.

David Greene, Janet Hopson and Jia Li. Running Out of and Into Oil: Analyzing Global Oil Depletion and Transition Through 2050. Prepared by the Oak Ridge national Laboratory for the U.S. Dept of Energy, October 2003.

Robert Hirsch, Roger Bezdek and Robert Wendling. Peaking of World Oil Production: Impacts, Mitigation, and Risk Management. February 8, 2005.

238

James A. Paul. The Iraq Oil Bonanza: Estimating Future Profits. Global Policy Forum, Jan 28, 2004.

James A. Paul. Oil Companies in Iraq: A Century of Rivalry and War. Global Policy Forum, Nov. 2003.

James A. Paul. Oil in Iraq: the heart of the Crisis. Global Policy Forum, Dec 2002.

US Dept of Energy Office Supports Peak Oil Theory. U.S. Department of Justice, Dec. 17, 2004.

T. Appenzeller, T. End of Cheap Oil. National Geographic, June 2004.

A. Cavello. Oil: Caveat Empty. Bulletin of the Atomic Scientists, May 25, 2005.

W. Youngquist. Survey of Energy Resources: Oil Shale. World Energy Council, Apr 24, 2005.

US: Caution Warranted on Oil Shale. Denver Post Editorial, April 18, 2005.

T. Sykes. Staring Down a Barrel of a Crisis. Australian Financial Review, Jan 15, 2005.

D. Ross. Plan War and the Hubbert Curve, An Interview with Richard Heinberg. ZNet Venezuela, April 17, 2004.

E.J. Schultz. Billionaire Microsoft Corp. Chairman Bill Gates is Investing in a Fresno Ethanol Company. Environmental News Network, November 17, 2005.

J. R. Healey. Alternate energy not in cards at ExxonMobil. USA Today, Oct 28, 2005.

National Democratic Committee. Americans' Pain at the Pump a Boom for Oil Companies. U.S. Newswire, Oct. 27, 2005.

Stocks Slump Despite Exxon's Staggering Profit. CNBC Market Dispatches, October 27, 2005.

Dean Baker. Taxing Exxon's Windfall From Hurricane Katrina. Center for Economic Policy and Research, Sept. 2005.

B. Hamilton. Automotive Gasoline. Open Press, January 18, 1995.

Small Business Association

Mystery Chinese Outfit Eyes Exxon. BBC News, October 31, 2005.

Ben Berkowitz. Exxon Dismisses Chinese Buyout Bid. Reuters, October 31, 2005.

Timothy Gardner. Green Energy Sales Seen Quadrupling in Decade. Reuters, March 6, 2006.

Grace Wong. Sorting Through the Ethanol Hype. CNNMoney.com, June 12, 2006.

Shell to Invest $17B in Canadian Oil Production. International Market Insight Report, Dec 2005.

Wealth of Major Projects for Alberta's OILSANDS. International Market Insight Report, December 2005.

Husky's $10B Sunrise Oil Sands Project Approved. International Market Insight Report, December 2005.

CO2 Oil Injections Boost Oil Recovery Efficiency. International Market Insight Report, Dec 2005.

Garance Burke. Groups Set to Profit From Ethanol Shipping. Associated Press, February 22, 2006.

International Energy Outlook 2006. Chapter 3: World Oil Markets. Energy Information Administration. June 2006.

Power and Fraud in Corporate America

Corporate Share of US National Income Increases at Faster Rate than at Any Time Since 1945. Finfacts Team, Jun 5, 2006.

The American Jobs Creation Act of 2003. Summary of H.R. 2896 as passed by Committee. Committee on Means and Ways. October 28, 2003.
http://waysandmeans.house.gov/media/pdf/fsc/fscsummary.pdf

Kim Clark. A Parade of Profitability. U.S. News and World Report, July 9, 2006.

Christopher Swann. US Groups Boost Share of Economic Pie. June 4, 2006.

Chris Fishman. The Wal-Mart You Don't Know. Fast Company, December 2003.

Tim Hamilton. Study Finds Low Gasoline Inventories Unreasonably Driving Up Pump Prices. May 24, 2006.

Rx for Fraud. Forbes, June 20, 2005.

United States Senate Committee on the Judiciary. Consolidation in the Energy Industry: Raising Prices at the Pump? Testimony of Tim Hamilton, February 1, 2006.

Tim Hamilton. Running on Empty in the West: Low Gasoline Inventories Set the Stage for $4 at the Pump in 2006. The Foundation for Taxpayer and Consumer Rights, May 23, 2006.

S&P 500 Constituents Spent $100.2 Billion on Stock Buybacks During the First Quarter, Up 22.1% on Q1 2005. Finfacts.com, June 12, 2006.

Kathleen Pender. Write-offs Remove Excess Inventory from Books—Not Shelves: Accounting Move Can Often Distort Firms' Financial Data. San Francisco Chronicle, May 8, 2001.

Ed Wolff and Jared Bernstein. Inequality and Corporate Power. Global Policy Forum, June 2003.

Marcy Gordon. SEC Requires More Executive Pay Disclosure. Associated Press. July 26, 2006.

Declan McCullagh. Behind the Stock Options Uproar. News.com, July 26, 2006.

Randall Heron and Erik Lee. What Fraction of Stock Option Grants to Top Executives Have Been Backdated or Manipulated? July 14, 2006.

Adam Lashinsky. Options Gone Wild! Fortune, June 30, 2006.

Adam Lashinsky. Why Options Backdating is a Big Deal. Fortune, July 26, 2006.

Geoffrey Colvin. A Study in CEO Greed. Fortune, March 30, 2006.

Troy Wolverton. Options' Deluding Effect. TheStreet.com, June 7, 2006.

Jonathan Stempel. Halliburton Accused of Accounting Fraud. Reuters, August 6, 2004.

Carl Osgood. Cheney's Halliburton Paradigm for Fraud. Executive Intelligence Review, July 6, 2006.

Willie Green. Bayh Wants Study of Dangers Posed by Foreign Ownership of U.S. Debt. Chesterton Tribune.

Elisabeth Bumiller. Make Industries' Tax Cuts Permanent, President Urges. New York Times, Feb. 3, 2006.

Lynnley Browning. Richest & Largest U.S. Corporations Paying Less and Less Taxes. New York Times, Sept. 23, 2004.

Iman Anabtawi. Secret Compensation. UCLA School of Law & Economics Research Paper Series. Research Paper No.04-9.

Government Waste and Deception

Tamar Gabelnick and Anna Rich. In Focus: Globalized Weaponry. Federation of American Scientists. Volume 5, Number 16. May 2000.

International Action Network on Small Arms. Undermining Global Security: the European Union's Arms Exports, 2003.

Rosario-Malonzo, Jennifer del. US Military-Industrial Complex: Profiting from War. IBON Features. Special Report, 2002.

Senator John McCain's Floor Statement on Defense Authorization Bill. May 23, 2003.

Jack Triplett. Some Objections to Hedonic Indexes. Brookings Institution, July 3, 2004.

Paul R. Liegey. Developing an Hedonic Regression Model For DVD Players In the U.S. CPI. U.S. Department of Labor Statistics, October 16, 2001.

Antal E. Fekete. The Supply of Oxen at the Federal Reserve. Financial Sense, January 20, 2005.

Measurement Issues in the Consumer Price Index. BLS, U.S. Dept of Labor, June 1997.

Paul Liegey and Nicole Shepler. Adjusting VCR Prices for Quality Change: A Study Using Hedonic Methods. Bureau of Labor Statistics, Monthly Labor Review, September 1999.

Lee Russ. How the U.S. Measures Employment and Unemployment. Section News, Jan 8, 2006. Jennifer del Rosario-Malonzo. US Military-Industrial Complex: Profiting from War. IBON Features.

Mary Kokoski, Keith Waehrer, and Patricia Rozaklis. Using Hedonic Methods for Quality Adjustment in the CPI: The Consumer Audio Products Component. Bureau of Labor Statistics, U.S. Department of Labor, October 16, 2001.

Steven Landefeld and Bruce Grimm. A Note on the Impact of Hedonics and Computers on Real GDP. Survey of Current Business, December 2000.

How the Government Measures Unemployment. U.S. Department of Labor, Bureau of Labor Statistics, Labor Force Statistics from the Current Population Survey, July 2001.

Undermining Global Security: the European Union's Arms. Amnesty International, 2003.

Earl Baxter. Overseas Markets Upturn on the Near Term Horizon. Military Training Technology. Volume: 9, Issue 2. April 22, 2004.

Analysis of the 2002-03 Budget Bill, Health & Social Services, State of California, Legislative Analyst's Office. Tobacco Settlement Fund.

China

Special Feature-China. The Economic Review, November 2003.

Jen Lin-Liu. Catering to China's Fashionistas. Wall Street Journal, Sept 30, 2005.

Busy Signals. Economist.com, September 8, 2005.

Randeep Ramesh. Silk Road to Riches for China and India. Taipei Times, Oct 5, 2005.

Bian Yi. Nation Needs Renewable Energy Sources. China Daily, Oct 6, 2005 www.chinadaily.com

Paul Roberts. Our Post-Oil Future Needs a Push. Washingtonpost.com, July 14, 2005.

Doug Tsuruoka. China's Ever-Growing Oil Needs May Result in a Global Shortage. Globalsecurity.org, Jan. 26, 2005.

Dream Machines. The Economist, June 2, 2005.

Charolette Windle. Luxury Cars Inspire China's Dreamers. BBC News, April 27, 2005.

China's Oil Imports Rise to Hit Record High. Shenzhen Daily, November 23, 2004.

Stephanie Hoo. China Cuts Currency Link to U.S. Dollar. Associated Press, July 21, 2005.

David Berman. Base Metal Prices in 'Unchartered Territory:' Huge Chinese Demand. Financial Post, February 1, 2006.

OECD Finds That China is Biggest Exporter of Information Technology Goods in 2004, Surpassing US and EU. OECD, December 12, 2005.

David Lague. China Sees Foreign Cash Pile as Possible Peril. International Herald Tribune, Jan. 16, 2006.

China's Currency Manipulation and U.S. Trade. Economic Policy Institute, Economic Snapshots. October 30, 2003.

Eswar Prasad. Next Steps for China. International Monetary Fund, September 2005, Vol 42, No 3.

India
India's Tata Group Buying Tyco Network at Bargain Price. TechWeb.com InformationWeek, Nov. 1, 2004.

Zubair Ahmed. India's Car Market is Revving Up. BBC News, July 19, 2005.

Engardio, Hamm, and Kripalani. The Rise of India. BusinessWeek Online, Dec 8, 2003.